WORDS FOR TODAY 1996

Notes on Bible Readings

Cover photograph – Sonia Halliday
Jerusalem ancient path in the grounds of St. Peter in
Gallicantu. It is probable Jesus took this route from the
Garden of Gethsemane after he was arrested.

Editor – Maureen Edwards

Published by:
The International Bible Reading Association
1020 Bristol Road
Selly Oak
Birmingham
Great Britain
B29 6LB

ISBN 0-7197-0858-3
ISSN 0140-8275

Typeset by Avonset, Midsomer Norton, Bath, Avon
Printed and bound in Great Britain by
BPC Paperbacks Ltd, Aylesbury, Bucks

CONTENTS

EDITORIAL

Introducing the Gospel of John

Most of this year's themes come from the Fourth Gospel (until September, when the Lectionary takes us into the Gospel of Matthew). So we shall explore some of the great Johannine themes. Yet, although we may call John the 'spiritual' Gospel, it contains many down to earth features like the child who gave his packed lunch to feed the crowd, the woman at the well, and Thomas the proverbial doubter.

Most striking is Jesus' overt claim to be Messiah and Son of God. In the Synoptic Gospels, he did not reveal his identity even to the disciples until, at Caesarea Philippi, he drew from Peter a declaration of faith. Yet in John, from the beginning of his ministry, he says with great assurance, 'I am ...' and his miracles are 'signs' of his divine origin, leading people to faith in him. His persistent and seemingly outrageous claims become the focus of debates and discussions with both the establishment and his disciples.

The writer of this Gospel records no parables, but his story comes alive through images that reveal the essence of Jesus' ministry: he is the good shepherd, the bread of life, the vine, the light of the world ... Enshrined here are profound insights into the nature of the Godhead, and God's vision of 'the world' restored to oneness with the Father through the death of the Son.

The writer has a creative mind, deeply sensitive and open to both Greek and Jewish cultures, bringing together the diversity of first century thought into this unique book. There is the Platonic concept that beyond this world of space and time lies the real, spiritual, eternal, changeless world. So, for example, Jesus is the 'real bread'. But the Jewish world of thought (which has links with the Essene community at Qumran) is mirrored too: a battle between good and evil, light and darkness, pointing to a day when God will intervene and overthrow evil. Hence the relevance of Jesus' words, 'NOW is the judgment of this world

...' Here and now, evil, hypocrisy and injustice are shown up by the light of God in Jesus and by a new quality of life he infuses into those who come to him in faith and openness.

One of the lessons we need to learn from John is how to communicate with the contemporary world. This involves a willingness to listen to people whose traditions are different from ours, to be enriched by insights that come from their culture and experience – which is often one of suffering – that we may grow to express the gospel in ways that are meaningful to others. That is why it is important that the notes in this book come from many parts of the world.

Different approaches to Bible study

We welcome both Jews and Christians to our pages and, having edited their contributions, I am aware of the variety of insights through which you will be enriched. Some are biblical scholars who open up the text and explain its intricate meanings. Others come from different professions, or are involved in particular experiences and write from very practical standpoints. Jane Wallman as a visually-impaired person, or Rosemary Wass on a farm caring for sheep, speak to us with a directness that may not come across from a Bible Commentary. Harry Hagopian brings together the insights of the biblical historians and those who seek peace for Jerusalem today, while Brian Brown looks at the experiences of Jonah through the eyes of all who rejoiced at the turn of events in South Africa in 1994. Over the years, I have discovered that there is much to learn from both academic and experiential approaches to Bible study. Each is valid, and they are complementary.

Thank you

Many of you have written with views, questions and difficulties, or just words of appreciation. It is good to hear from you. Thank you for your suggestions, all of which will be taken seriously and influence our thinking as we plan for the future. Please pray for our International Consultation in 1996 which will determine the way IBRA develops in the next decade. And may God's peace be with you all.

Maureen Edwards

MORNING PRAYERS

Father-Creator, Provider-from of-old, Ancient-of-days – fresh-born from the womb of night are we. In the first dawning of the new day draw we nigh unto Thee. Forlorn are the eyes till they have seen the Chief.

Bushman's prayer, South Africa
From Another Day, edit. John Carden (SPCK)

Jesus, is this what you say to us today?
How blest are those who abhor easy pieties;
   the kingdom of heaven is theirs.
How blest are those who train in non-violence;
   they shall have the earth for their possession.
How blest are those who fast for justice;
   they shall be satisfied.
How blest are those who see enemies as human;
   mercy shall be shown to them.
How blest are those who live what they profess;
   they shall see God.
How blest are those who build bridges of reconciliation;
   God shall call them his friends.
How blest are those who show the outcast
    that someone understands;
   the kingdom of heaven is theirs.

Peter Matheson, Aotearoa New Zealand
From Your Will be Done (Christian Conference of Asia)

Eternal God ...
Early in the morning, before we begin our work,
we praise your glory.
Renew our bodies as fresh as the morning flowers.
Open our inner eyes, as the sun casts new light
upon the darkness which prevailed over the night.
Deliver us from all captivity.
Give us wings of freedom,
as a mighty stream running continuously from day to day.
We thank you for the gift of this morning,
and a new day to work with you. Amen

Masao Takenaka, Japan
From the Methodist Prayer Handbook 1992/3

EVENING PRAYERS

Lord, I thank Thee for night,
the time of cool and quiet,
the time of sweet enchantment
when a deep mystery pervades everything.
The time when soul speaks to soul in common desire
to partake of the hush of the ineffable.
The time when the moon and stars
speak to us of our high calling and destiny.
The time of repose and calm
when the fever of the mind subsides
and uncertainty gives place
to the sense of eternal purpose.
O Lord, I thank Thee for night.

Chandran Devenesan, India
From Another Day (SPCK)

As the earth keeps turning, hurtling through space, and
    night falls and day breaks from land to land,
Let us remember people – waking, sleeping, being born, and
    dying – one world, one humanity ...

From Jesus Christ, the Life of the World. A Worship Book 1983.
WCC Publications, World Council of Churches,
Geneva, Switzerland

A blessing

May wisdom herself take root in you,
grow strong and tall within you;
May she touch what is old and dead
and make you beautiful and fragrant
like cedars and olive-trees;
May she spread out her branches and shelter you;
And as the tree of life sustains and heals you,
so may your fruits and leaves be a source of life
for the world.

Alison Geary, United Kingdom
From Oceans of Prayer (NCEC)

7

How to use 'a quiet time'?

Have a visual focus – a cross, a plant, interesting stones ... Create a prayer table on which to display them with other symbols of your life and faith. Change them from time to time. In India, many Christians set aside a special room for prayer.

Use books of prayers (see page 49). The prayers of past Christians and from other parts of the world often articulate something we are trying to express, and remind us that we are part of a worldwide fellowship.

Read the Bible passage for the day and then the notes. Read the verses again, allowing the words to penetrate your whole being. Try to discover their message for you and the world around you. God's Word is alive and relevant, even if it does not always offer the comfort you expect. If necessary, refer back to other readings in the series, so that you see the links.

Don't shut out the world. Hold the news of each day in your mind as you read the Bible and pray. Imagine yourself as a person living in an area of the world that you are concerned about, and ask yourself, 'What is God saying through these words in this situation?

Use silence. Empty your mind of trivia and concentrate on God's presence and peace, God's light and love filling you and the world, cleansing us of all that is unworthy. Try this for longer periods.

The above suggestions are a response to a request from one of our readers. Not all of them will help everyone. Select what you find helpful, and do try something new! The woodcut is by Boy Dominguez of the Philippines (used with permission).

8

GOD OF GLORY – come to us

Notes based on the Good News Bible by

Peter Millar

Peter Millar, a minister of the Church of Scotland and a member of the Iona Community, worked for many years with his wife Dorothy in the Church of South India. Together they have written on a variety of subjects.

In the Western world, much of our Christianity is domesticated and privatized, to our cost, and the wider horizons of a suffering and beautiful world are neglected. Each day we do need passages of Scripture to 'comfort' us on our journey, but as we seek the Spirit's guidance, we soon realize that these same passages are challenging and 'uncomfortable'. Can we really sit passively reading Scripture in a world where injustice is a daily reality for millions of our sisters and brothers? Let us be 'restless' after reading the Word, and discover a new awareness of others, a deeper concern for the issues of our time, for God's incredibly beautiful, but plundered, earth. Christ is calling us to new levels of obedience. The late Father Jock Balrymple wrote: 'We can only go so far in taming God's Word. If we persist in removing its disturbing elements, we shall wake up one day to find that we have lost the Christian vision altogether.' So let us come to our daily readings prepared to be challenged and re-directed in our inner lives by the power of the living Word.

✳ *Lord Jesus, come to our world*
  and overturn our tired ideas of power and glory:
  cry over our cities, our refugee camps,
  our greed and superficial values
  until your wisdom invades our understanding
  and transforms our discipleship.

Monday January 1   *Isaiah 40.25-31* ✳
A renewing vision
A new year begins. We do not know what lies ahead. Yet this uncertainty enables us to understand the exiles. They were a pilgrim people. Stranded in Babylon – tired, weary and crushed

9

– the people of Judah wondered if God had forgotten them altogether. Why should they have to endure such hardship? Would it never end? And these same cries can be heard in many places today where our sisters and brothers continue to experience myriad forms of exploitation and injustice. In Babylon, the prophet walked alongside them in their agony and despair; he understood their powerlessness. He never made light of their predicament but in poetic language told them of the God of history, the sustainer of life. God would bring them new hope in the midst of their struggles.

As we start another year, these amazing words – 'Those who trust in the Lord for help will find their strength renewed' – remind us powerfully of God's renewing vision in the midst of the most basic realities of everyday living. We shall 'run and not get weary' if we place ourselves, and our world, in the hands of the living Lord.

✳ *Lord, I place myself in Your hands as another year*
begins:
may Your soft winds freshen my spirit;
may Your sunshine brighten my heart;
may the burdens of the day rest lightly upon me
and may I be enfolded in the mantle of Your love.

Adapted from an old Irish prayer

Tuesday January 2   Isaiah 42.1-9 *
A challenging role
These familiar words, of comfort and challenge, describe Israel, as a truly 'Servant nation' who is to be the great spiritual teacher and guide for all peoples: a liberating and life-giving community whose strength comes from obedience to God's holy will and purpose. Behind this conviction lies the knowledge that God, our creator, is at work in every aspect of human activity. Worship and work, prayer and compassionate involvement are held together – a truth we tend to lose sight of in our churches.

That connection between personal faith and an active concern for the world around us is never an easy one. Each morning in our worship at the Iona Community, we recall that connection in the words, 'The world belongs to God, the earth and all its people.' Isaiah knew that Israel could never fulfil such a role if the nation ceased to be attentive to the Lord. The God-given task and obedience to the divine will were a single entity. As we struggle to make these connections in our own time, we can take comfort from Isaiah's belief that God is always working 'new things' in our communities. There are signs of the Holy Spirit at work and our task is to discern them.

✳ *Lord God most high, we are happy to be called Christians, so make us all real ones. Cleanse our hearts and make them clear as crystals, so we may see you and the Holy Spirit may dwell in us.* Thailand (From Oceans of Prayer)

Wednesday January 3   Isaiah 49.8-13 *

A comforting promise

I remember reading these words in a small village church in South India. In that part of the Madras diocese the rains had failed that year, and there was great suffering among the villagers. Yet, as so often in India, the congregation was full of vitality, joy and laughter. They listened intently: these were words of power. It was as if they had been specially written for them. And so they had! Isaiah spoke directly to their daily experiences of poverty and lack of water. God would bring healing and a new day. Can those of you who live in areas where water is plentiful feel the power of these words? Do they strike you with the same immediacy and force? or are we perhaps so secure in our personal lives for them to be liberating and transforming as well as words of comfort?

The prophet knew that one day there would be restoration for God's people. The promise was sure. God would hear their cries and have pity on their suffering. Julian of Norwich expressed that in these words: 'We have been loved by God from before the beginning.'

In rural India, suffering is often caused by material deprivation. In better-off communities suffering is less obvious because it is rooted in a spiritual emptiness – the inner pain of the affluent. From many places our hands are outstretched to God as we seek his healing touch.

✳ *Jesus, being humble and gentle of spirit is not easy when outward success is what matters most.*
   Help me to understand that your way
   is often contrary to accepted values,
   and invites me to look at the world through new eyes.

A life-giving truth

Read again verse 14. Take time to read slowly these familiar words – and then spend a few moments in silence. No matter how well we know these words, can we allow this extraordinary truth to permeate our heart and mind? William Barclay *(The Daily Study Bible)* gives a free translation of verse 14: 'This word which created the world, this reason which controls the order of the world, has become a person and with our own eyes we saw him.' God is actually in our midst – in Jesus. In John's day, it was a staggeringly new conception: the eternal Word visible to human sight, full of grace and truth.

Until the end of time, women and men will discover new spiritual riches in these verses. Yet with our limited and partial knowledge, we can say with clarity that Jesus shows us how God would live this life we have to live.

Every year, many thousands make their way to the tiny island of Iona which lies off the west coast of Scotland. Many come to the ancient Abbey Church, because they are trying to discover the meaning of this 'Word made flesh'. And that journey in search of Christ often brings pain, especially in societies where prevailing values contradict the message of the gospel. Yet, is it not in our vulnerability and uncertainty that we often come closest to Christ's presence? The Word does truly dwell among us. Christ, the Lord, *is* present. Our searching for him may be long and hard with many interruptions on the road, but he waits for our coming – with an outstretched arm.

✱ *O Christ, the master carpenter, who at the last,*
through wood and nails, purchased our whole salvation,
wield well Your tools in the workshop of Your world,
so that we who come rough-hewn to Your bench
may be fashioned to a truer beauty of Your hand,
We ask it for Your own name's sake. Amen

Source Unknown

A prophetic insight

'... The Lamb of God who takes away the sin of the world.' These are words of power, but also of gentleness, that we need to hear again and again in our own time. The Gospel reminds us that Jesus confronts sin in all its depth and ugliness, not just the sin that permeates our own lives but structural sin which brings poverty, starvation and death to so many in the world.

For almost 1,500 years, the island of Iona has been a place of Christian pilgrimage. All kinds of people have discovered Christ's forgiveness in that holy place. They have found healing, renewal and a new direction for life, and returned home more open to the guiding light of the Holy Spirit. On Iona, our worship challenges us to repent of ways in which our affluent western lifestyle is linked to the poverty of others. And we bring our prayers before God, asking that we may have renewed compassion for our plundered earth. In a world of so much human need, we can never be content with any form of privatized Christianity. Christ continually calls his Church to be an out-reaching community of love.

The Spirit came upon Jesus like a dove. John recognized his Saviour. It was the beginning of a completely new chapter in human experience. And we are part and parcel of that extraordinary event. Mother Teresa put it succinctly: 'We are not called, as Christians to be extraordinary people, but rather we are called to be ordinary people with an extraordinary love in our hearts.'

✳ *O Thou*
who hast given me eyes
to see the light
that fills my room,
give me the inward vision
to behold Thee in this place.   Chandran Devanesan, India
From Morning Noon and Night, edit. John Carden (CMS)

Epiphany, Saturday January 6   *Revelation 21.22-27* ✳

A visionary word

Here is a glorious and rich vision that lifts us beyond our narrow, cluttered lives into the heart of God's purpose and life. They are poetic words which fire our imagination and remind us of ultimate truth. They contain a mystery and a promise. The Kingdom of God is both in our midst and also, as the theologians say, 'an unrealised hope'. For most of us, it is all too easy to get clogged down in the minutiae of everyday living, yet the gospel is constantly placing us back on a pilgrim path. We are 'sojourners', on a journey to a much fuller life in God's presence.

At the funeral service of my friend David, the pastor said that he had gone from our midst, but that he would only have a short distance to travel to enter the Kingdom. It was a beautiful way of expressing an amazing truth – and it was true for David because he had given himself to Christ so fully on the first part of the journey.

Travelling towards a new Jerusalem – taking the longer view – being still before God so that we may discover the wider horizons of his Kingdom – all these thoughts come to me as I read this beautiful passage. And in my own personal journey, I have glimpsed the coming Kingdom most clearly among those whom we classify as 'marginalized'. That may seem a paradox, but is it? Perhaps it is one of the greatest truths of our time – that among the exploited and weak and poor, we see most clearly the Christ of earth and heaven.

✳ *O God, you have set before us a great hope that your Kingdom will come on earth, and have taught us to pray for its coming: make us ever ready to thank you for the signs of its dawning, and to pray for the perfect day when Your will shall be done on earth as it is in heaven.*
Iona Community Worship Book
© 1991 Iona Community

For personal reflection or group discussion

From your own experience, how do you connect the challenges posed by these passages with the issues of poverty and injustice? Can we discover new ways to listen to the voices of marginalized people in our world?

ACTION

Make contact with a group or organization, locally or nationally, which is working in the area of global justice.

GOD OF GLORY – Change us

Notes based on the New Jerusalem Bible by

Maureen Edwards

*Maureen Edwards was a teacher of Religious Education f
many years, including seven in Kenya, where she also wrot
programmes for schools' broadcasts. She then worked for ten
years with the Methodist Church Overseas Division (UK) before
becoming editor of Words for Today.*

Deep within us is an attitude that fears and resents change. Yet
we are part of a universe that is always changing. From being a
protected foetus, we emerge to experience a new existence,
growing and changing, and we live in a world of changing
political and social structures.

We may become 'set in our ways' but God, who moves
ahead of us, challenges us to develop new attitudes and ways.
When we do, God's glory shines through us.

1st Sunday after Epiphany, January 7   2 Corinthians 3.7-18

Open to change

Paul often shows how faith in Christ is reflected in past
traditions. The Law, the heart of the Jewish faith, engraved on
two tablets of stone, had been brought by Moses from the
presence of God. Moses, emerging from that intensely powerful
experience, shone with God's glory. According to Hebrew
tradition, no one could look at God and live, so Moses covered
his face.

Paul then points us to the glory that shines from Christ, 'the
image of God' (4.4). Christ has opened up another way to God.
Instead of the burden of condemnation – because we fail to be
the perfect people the Law challenges us to be – we are
acquitted! A new beginning is possible. Through the power of
the Spirit we can see the full reflection of God in Christ and be
transformed into his likeness, so that we can reflect something
of God's glory in the world.

But can we look into God's eyes, or is there something in our
nature that makes us respond to goodness by covering it up?

Do we fear the changes this would make to the way we live? Think of times when you felt diffident and hid from God, like those who made Moses cover his face.

✴ *Holy Spirit, increase our courage*
   to turn from self-satisfied religious attitudes
   that we may see
   and be challenged by Christ's goodness.
   Go on disturbing us to repent and be forgiven
   so that each day becomes a new beginning.

Monday January 8   *Colossians 1.1-14 ✴*

Power to change

Paul begins this letter in his customary style, giving thanks for the faith of his readers. In words which must have reminded them of their baptism, he says God has rescued them 'from the ruling force of darkness' and brought them into Christ's Kingdom of light. But he also reminds the Colossians that they are members of a worldwide ecumenical community (verse 6). He prays that they may reach 'the fullest knowledge' of God's will, so that they can live 'a life worthy of the Lord' (verses 9-10), empowered by 'his glorious strength'.

The change God wants us to make in our lives is so radical – from darkness to light – that nothing less than God's power will help us to make it.

✴ *Glorious God, you have redeemed us*
   and brought us back into your family,
   and now you challenge us to work together
   to change the world.
   Deepen our understanding of your will –
   and make us more receptive to your power to change.

Tuesday January 9   *Ephesians 2.1-10 ✴*

'God's work of art'

This new beginning we have been given is nothing less than a resurrection. We have been raised with Christ, from death to life. Our lives were obsessed with 'the demands of self-indulgence and our own whim' and God in his great love 'brought us to life with Christ'. No one can claim credit for this; it is a gift from God, a sign of 'how extraordinarily rich he is in grace'. It is a demonstration 'for all ages to come'. And so we are 'God's work of art', a new creation in Christ to serve others and make God's grace available to them.

This is a marvellous letter, full of vision. Read on, if you have time, and see how we are all drawn together into the perfect body of Christ (4.7-16).

Think back to the creation story in Genesis 1. At each stage of creation, 'God saw that it was good'. God had conceived the design and delighted in making it become a reality. God saw everything in pristine condition, fresh, full of potential and lasting beauty, a vision of what might be. Despite all that has happened in human history, God has never lost that vision of a perfect world. Think of yourself, remade by God's hands, a work of art. Think of your family and community recreated. And finally think of the world, the rich variety God has put into it and what it could be like when resurrected as God's Kingdom.

✳ *God of glory, take the veil from our eyes*
that we may share your vision for the world
and work with you to transform it.

Wednesday January 10   *Hebrews 13.1-6*

New encounters

The change that Christ brings opens up a world of new relationships. We are to welcome strangers, a tradition deeply rooted in many cultures (Genesis 18.1-8; Deuteronomy 10.16-19). Make a list of occasions, from both Old and New Testaments, where people cross cultures to welcome and greet one another. There are many.

Today, ease of travel enables us to meet and offer hospitality to one another, whether we take a journey or stay where we are, for it is a ministry of receiving to which we are called. This has been the most exciting and life-changing experience of my life for over twenty years. Through my work I have met people from many parts of the world – Christians and people of other Faiths. I have been welcomed with loving hospitality into many homes in Kenya, the Caribbean, Sri Lanka, India and Myanmar, and with my husband have welcomed people of even more cultures into our home. It has been a joy and a deeply enriching experience, and we thank God for allowing us to live at such a time. This is why I hope we can develop an inter-cultural exchange of insights in *Words for Today*. To open our lives and our homes to others broadens our horizons and builds bridges of trust and understanding.

* **Christic, the stranger,**
  you stand alone in the market-place,
  needing our friendship.
  Unjustly detained, you appeal to us from many prisons
  asking for our letters and prayers.
  Keep on knocking at our doors until we answer.

Thursday January 11   *1 Corinthians 15.35-50*

New bodies

Paul talks about one change none of us can avoid. Death to the old life must take place before the new emerges. It happens all around us in the natural world. Look at a seed. Paul echoes the words of Jesus (John 12.23-28). Unless it dies it will stay as 'a bare grain'. The natural world reveals a purpose for each of the bodies God has created. Each is equipped for its particular environment. In the same way, the bodies we now have, and all our handicaps, will be transformed into something glorious, so that we can live in God's presence: 'what is sown is weak, but what is raised is powerful' (verse 43). Our lives now – body, mind and spirit integrated into whole beings – only resemble Adam. But our resurrection bodies will be like Christ.

* **God of glory,**
  who strengthens us to live life to the full,
  give us wisdom so that we may discern
  when the time comes to let go of familiar experiences
  and enter fully and joyfully into your presence.

Friday January 12   *Corinthians 15.51-58*

'We shall be changed'

This most radical of all changes we undergo is both a mystery and the work of Christ. The transformation that comes through death is hidden from us, but Christ is fully involved in it. Just as his death and resurrection are reflected in every new beginning in our lives now, so we shall be raised with him, wholly forgiven, reborn with all the purity of a new child. Death and the power of sin are defeated, because God has overcome death, and in this we rejoice.

Read again these magnificent words from Paul and reflect. Give thanks for those you have known and loved who have died in faith, and give thanks that the same hope is ours.

✳ *Finish then thy new creation,*
  Pure and spotless let us be;
Let us see thy great salvation,
  Perfectly restored in thee:
Changed from glory into glory,
  Till in heaven we take our place,
Till we cast our crowns before thee,
  Lost in wonder, love, and praise!   *Charles Wesley*

Saturday January 13   *Psalm 86*

God is unchanging

This psalm, which is an anthology of quotations from other psalms, reflects on how life swings between periods of suffering and depression, when we cry out for help, and times of well-being when we are filled with praise. In all these experiences, good or bad, God is the same, utterly reliable, kind and forgiving, 'rich in faithful love'. For Jews there are reminders here of the Covenant. Yahweh has made them his people and will never forsake them. And for all of us there is a vision of one universal Lord (verse 9).

Read the psalm again and make a list of characteristics ascribed to God. Reflect on their significance for you. When has God rescued you from distress? When have you been aware in world news of God rescuing peoples and nations? Are there other words and phrases you would use to describe God through today's experiences?

✳ *God of incomparable love and faithfulness,*
  uncover our eyes
  that we may rejoice in your universal sovereignty
  and see our darkness transformed
  into your glorious light.

For personal reflection or group discussion

Think of changes you have had to accept in your family, community, church and nation. How can we distinguish between our misgivings and the movement of God? How can we be more open to God at work in and through us?

ACTION

Identify and welcome the stranger through whom Christ comes to you.

GOD OF GLORY – use us

Notes based on the Revised English Bible by

Rosemary Wakelin

Rosemary Wakelin, a Methodist minister in a new village in the Norwich circuit (UK), served with her husband, Dr Paul Wakelin, as a missionary in East Africa. For twenty-five years she has contributed regularly as a religious broadcaster on radio and television.

One of the most amazing ideas, which emerges early in the Old Testament, is that the God of glory not only knows and communicates with us, but wishes us to help him – to be involved in working out his righteous purposes for his creation. It did not take long for people to decide who was and who was not a suitable person for God to use. After all such an office carried status! But they soon found that God kept breaking out of imposed boundaries, to work through those who were open to receive him, regardless of what the majority thought. He is the God of surprises – and we still have not caught up!

2nd Sunday after Epiphany, January 14   *1 Samuel 3.1-21 **

Out of the mouths of babes

Perhaps Blake was right when he wrote that children come 'trailing clouds of glory'. This is a strange, poignant story of a little boy's life which was made a thank-offering to God for taking away from his mother what, according to her culture, was the terrible reproach of childlessness.

What would social workers today make of a mother abandoning her little son to the care of an old priest? We can only guess at how Samuel must have felt, but however lonely and, by our standards, unsuitable his environment was, Samuel appears serene. From birth he must have been soaked in the knowledge that he was special, so he was receptive to God's voice, even though at first he did not recognize it. He was given, by our understanding of child care, a most unsuitable message for a child to bear. But God's activity is central to the story, not our feelings and reactions. Eli had to coax the unwelcome news from Samuel, but he accepted it. For the Hebrews, responsibility for children – even grown-up – belonged to parents. We cushion children from sin's consequences – and maybe also from awareness of God's judgment.

✳ *O give me Samuel's mind,*
   A sweet unmurmuring faith,
Obedient and resigned
   To Thee in life and death,
That I may read with childlike eyes
Truths that are hidden from the wise.   James D Burns

Martin Luther King Day, January 15   *Galatians 1.11-24 ✳*

Chosen before birth

I remember a sermon I heard as a child in the grim days of the war. It was Christmas, and everything seemed bleak and hopeless. The minister recounted periods in world history when things looked equally bad. In each he pointed to a date: 'On that day, so and so was born,' – and each baby had grown up to be a person who changed the way things were. 'When things look hopeless – God sends a baby!' he said.

Paul said he was chosen even before he was born. He could have said No, but he allowed himself to be used – like Martin Luther King, whose father believed his son was to be someone special, and gave him a name to reflect that belief. He too was open to God's call and – although he knew it would probably end in an early, violent death – his mind was clear. What mattered was not what he felt, but that God's will should be done. We get anxious about the way things are – but somewhere, there's a baby ...!

✳ *You it was who fashioned my inward parts;*
   you knitted me together in my mother's womb ...
You know me through and through:
   my body was no mystery to you,
when I was formed in secret,
   woven in the depths of the earth ...
my life was fashioned
before it had come into being.   Psalm 139.13-16

   Gracious God, give me courage to say Yes
   to the way you want to use me.

21

Come and see

This is the most intimate of 'call' stories. We can only imagine the day they spent together – young men sharing dreams, fired by the vision of the very special young man who had invited them. Ideas must have flowed – the longing for freedom – for sovereignty, for the Messiah. Into this dry tinder, Jesus dropped his spark – his concept, not of a national kingdom, but the Kingdom of God, a community based on a vision that love would work. His Kingdom was not about love of power but the power of love.

Andrew's instant response was to fetch his brother. Jesus took one look at Simon and recognized the tough qualities essential for building his new community. Records show that the most successful method of recruitment to church membership is one to one invitation – by those who make the effort to 'come and see' for themselves, and then go and fetch someone else.

✳ *We pray for the wisdom, grace and power of the Holy Spirit, so that the Church may venture forth in faith with the gospel of love and be driven out to fill the country with peace and justice.*

Harold Fernando, Sri Lanka
From Oceans of Prayer (NCEC)

Covenant God

Small town prejudice was alive and well in the first century! The cryptic conversation between Jesus and Nathanael only makes sense when you remember that these are two Jews talking in language steeped in Jewish history and messianic expectation. Jesus' first statement about Nathanael (verse 46) recalls the false Jacob who changed when he 'saw' God, so becoming the first 'Israelite'. Nathanael's question is answered by Jesus with another reference (Micah 4.4) to the Messianic Age – the new community Jesus had come to initiate. They would be able to sit peacefully under their own fig trees. Nathanael, the true Israelite, sees the point and responds with an affirmation of faith. Jesus, excited by Nathanael's quick thinking and acceptance, pushes the vision on and draws again on Jacob – his vision of the ceaseless traffic between earth and heaven – the true commerce for human community.

* We do not seek independence
  But to be dependent on you
  And then on one another.
  Fashion us one people
  For your work
  Of reconciling, renewing, creating love.   *Côte d'Ivoire*
                                    From Oceans of Prayer (NCEC)

Thursday January 18   *1 Corinthians 1.10-18*

Week of Prayer for Christian Unity January 18-25
Nothing has changed!

Christians in Corinth struggle with a problem that bedevils the Church today. Paul begs them to hold together their fragile unity, sabotaged then as now by different ways of understanding the gospel and competition between those presenting it. He says Christ alone is unique and the preaching of the unadorned gospel his top priority.

What lay behind these factions? The history of the Church suggests that the root cause is what lies behind most of the world's problems – the desire for power. In his temptations (Luke 4.1-12), Jesus rejected three ways of acquiring power. The last – recruiting God's power and manipulating people in the name of God – is the one to which most Christians are prone. Verse 18 is Paul's reply to a Church that still prefers the love of power to the power of love. He unfolds the heart of the gospel – Jesus' completely reverses the world's priorities.

* My Lord, you wore no royal crown;
  you did not wield the powers of state,
  nor did you need a scholar's gown
  or priestly robe, to make you great.

  You never used a killer's sword
  to end an unjust tyranny;
  your only weapon was your word,
  for truth alone could set us free.

  You did not live a world away
  in hermit's cell or desert cave,
  but felt our pain and shared each day
  with those you came to seek and save.

  You made no mean or cunning move,
  chose no unworthy compromise,

23

but carved a track of burning love
through tangles of deceit and lies.

You came unequalled, undeserved,
to be what we were meant to be:
to serve, instead of being served –
a light for all the world to see.

So when I stumble, set me right;
command my life as you require;
let all your gifts be my delight
and you, my Lord, my one desire.

© *Christopher Idle*
Jubilate Hymns

Friday January 19   *1 Corinthians 1.26-31*

Manifested love

Paul presents the scandal of the ignominious death of a young man on a public gallows as the ultimate expression of God's unconditional love which is the heart of the gospel. Human 'wisdom' is about being in control and having power. But Paul is pointing to a mystery, a paradox at the heart of things which overturns human assumptions and aspirations, and replaces them with real wisdom. Paul tells these early Church members to look at themselves – an unprepossessing bunch of very ordinary people (nothing changes) chosen by God. Power-based wisdom, so loved in Greek thinking, and expressed in eloquent oratory, is foolishness compared with God's plan to restore, through the cross of Christ, people's broken relationship with him – the possibility of a new community through and in Christ. Human wisdom has proved futile. God has taken the initiative. Christ has made the self-offering and through him we can have the righteousness and holiness whereby we can at last approach God. So if anyone is to glory, 'let him glory in the Lord'.

✳ *O God, help me to walk in the boots of the miner, the*
shoes of the trader, the mocassins of the trapper, and
the sandals of Jesus the Master. Native American prayer

Saturday January 20   *1 Corinthians 3.1-9*

Starting from a different place

After the high theology of the preceding chapter, Paul comes down to earth and addresses the reality of the limitations of these new Corinthian Christians. They are as babies in their spiritual development and unable yet to receive the insights or digest the deep truths that sustain the mature Christian. To achieve this maturity, they have to shift their ground from human values and lock their hearts, minds and wills into God's thinking – then they will start to understand and grow up. This means redefining what life is for, with the cross, not themselves, at the centre. And that can only make sense in spiritual terms. Idolizing favourite preachers is a worldly idea – preachers are only of value in that they are chosen by God to carry his word and have accepted their call. It is God who makes the Church grow – the amazing thing is that he let's us help.

✳ *My talents, gifts, and graces, Lord,*
   Into thy blessed hands receive;
And let me live to preach thy word,
   And let me to thy glory live;
My every sacred moment spend
In publishing the sinners' friend.   Charles Wesley

For personal reflection or group discussion

Do we have difficulty in accepting that God seems to act in ways, and work through people, we might not think suitable? Think of some – either different sorts of Christians or maybe non-Christians. What does it mean to be open to God using you?

ACTION

Take a risk – trust that love will work, even though it may mean getting tough, losing face or getting hurt.

Finding the right help

If you find you cannot cope with the notes in this book, please try IBRA's other publication: *Light for our Path*. This follows the same scheme of readings, but the notes are briefer, written in simpler language and may be more helpful especially for those who are at the beginning of their spiritual journey.

If you wish, you may return this copy and a copy of *Light for our Path* will be sent to you free of charge.

GLORY OF GOD – stay with us

Notes based on the New International Version and
the Edição Pastoral (Portuguese) by

Joanildo Burity

The author is a lay Presbyterian and political scientist living in Recife, Northeast Brazil. He works in the 'borderline' of the evangelical and ecumenical movements trying to help foster ways in which Jesus' presence in the world may be signalled by the communities of his disciples.

What does it mean to recognize God with us today? We Christians affirm Jesus to be the self-manifestation of God, the closest possible way that God could have come to be human. And as Jesus' disciples we are called to continue his work and be the living sign of his presence among humanity. That was his prayer and his promise for us. That should be our prayer to him, for without the presence of God with us the journey is pointless and fraught with frustration.

3rd Sunday after Epiphany, January 21   *Exodus 33.12-23* *

My presence with you

The people of God had been stubborn and unbelieving, and God had already told them that he would send his angel before them to fulfil his promises, but he would not be with them. But Moses felt that could not be God's final word, for the whole purpose of the journey was to count on the accompanying presence of God. If people were to remain on their own – despite their swaying loyalty – what would happen to their hope that the future could bring about the promise? Life was hard enough as it was. If they could not have God as their fellow traveller, there would be no way to be sure of his promise. Mediated as the experience of that company might be – through Moses and the cloud – God's goodness, compassion and forgiveness were to become signals of his presence, his glory.

* *God, be our company in the journey ahead.*
  Without your presence among us,
  your people lose their way.

Without your compassion flowing through us
your people are no different from any other.

Monday January 22   *1 John 1.1-4 ***

That there may be fellowship

For the Johannine community, from which the next few texts
sprang forth, Jesus was the bodily, human, visible self-
manifestation of God. It is he who, in himself, and through his
words, made Life known. And this life, which is God's own, has
been handed down to us through Jesus, his first witnesses, and
all those who came after that down to ourselves. The historical
experience of God's presence is in the message we hear and in
our own lives.

The Word has been sent by God that we may live out the
same fellowship that exists between the Father and the Son.
Such a communion is more important than any other criterion of
God's presence among us: if we participate in God's fellowship
all barriers and hierarchies are broken between us. Horizontal,
love relationships will be our witness to the life of God among
us.

✳ *Father, thank you for your life manifested in Jesus*
that we may have fellowship with you
and our brothers and sisters.
Help our community ties to express this communion
that we can be true witnesses of your Son,
the living word of life.

Tuesday January 23   *John 2.1-12 ***

God is with us

Because God manifested himself in Jesus as a true human
being, he assumed the whole of our historical condition. Thus,
the celebration of life is more important than restrictive rituals
and institutional rules which insist on places and distinctions for
identifying God's presence. Just as the stone water jars used for
purification rites were to hold wine for the wedding guests, so
God's manifested life has a strong bearing on our life here and
now. It is more than this but not opposed to it. Just as important:
Jesus reduces the material nature of religious symbols and
practices to their right proportion: they are to be pointers, signs
of God's presence in Jesus, releasing life, not confining it. They

are signs *for* his disciples, helping us to believe that God cares for us in our own settings, despite our limited views of the sacred and the profane, the pure and the impure, the proper and the improper.

✳ *Lord, thank you for being in our 'wedding parties',*
in our concrete situation,
and there revealing your glory to us.
Liberate us to welcome signs of your presence anywhere,
taking them as moments of recognition
of your care for us through Jesus Christ,
who wishes to transform our needs into enjoyment and
life.

Wednesday January 24   *John 17.1-8*

Eternal Life: knowing God in Jesus

The Johannine community had very simple and powerful ideas about God's relationship with humankind: Jesus is not simply another messenger or an angelic agency, but God's self-manifestation as far as this could take place among ourselves. He brings a message of life and fellowship with God, and wants us to experience this in community. Knowing God through his Son Jesus is to prove his glory, his presence; it is to have eternal life. Being in relationship with Jesus is to participate in his life and the work he did for the glory of God. Here, the Son's 'descent' and 'ascension' become clear to his disciples: Jesus must go (i.e. die) that he may come back to his disciples, (i.e. resurrected and as the Spirit) and 'stay' in them. And so they can really testify, upon receiving the word, of Jesus' origin in the Father.

Obeying, accepting, knowing with certainty, believing: that is how we acknowledge that God in Jesus is among us, giving us of his own life.

✳ *Father, we thank you*
because having eternal life is knowing you
in and through Jesus and so being in fellowship with you.
Remain in us and with us. We welcome your glory.

Guard them in your name

With the ascending movement of the Son back to the Father, his disciples are called to continue his work, making him 'present' in the world. Hence Jesus' petition that the Father may guard them in his name. 'Guarding in the Father's name' means keeping them identified by the name of the Father, and under the protection of the Father.

Thus, even if Jesus must go, his disciples can remain 'guarded in the Father's name'. They do not live in a friendly world. The Johaninne church suffers persecution from a powerful community. Millions of disciples of Christ today are cut off from the resources of 'development'. Even when they feel excluded by the unfriendliness and irrelevance of the institutional churches, or deprived of a decent quality of life, these disciples are under Jesus' request. They are explicitly told not to abandon the 'world', but to trust in God's protection. There is to be no stepping back, no giving up. It is in this very world, from within, that they must witness. There they will be protected from the evil one: consecrated by God's word, historically manifested in Jesus. Now it is in their hands to continue God's self-manifestation in Christ.

✴ ***Protect us in your name, Holy Father,***
   so that we can worthily continue in this world
   the work of Jesus.

Unity to let the world know God in Christ

We are bearers of God's glory, if we preserve the fellowship that exists between the Father and the Son. Unity is mutual – between the Father and the Son, and between God and the disciples. The unity of God needs to be reflected in the life of the Christian community so that the world may accept Jesus' witness. The fellowship of Jesus' disciples is the key to the world's access to God's manifestation to humankind. It is the concrete sign of God's glory among us, in all the differences that make us truly human: gender, ethnicity, cultures, languages, forms of worship and beliefs. This not only accredits Christian witness in the world, but is the condition for God's revelation in Christ to be accepted as such in the first place. That is why Jesus did not wish to leave us alone: it is such a responsibility, that we need to be with him where he is, and have him in our company wherever we are.

✴ *Lord, we have not been able to balance all our differences*
and remain true to the unity
which alone can help the world believe in you
and your Son, whom you sent.
Stay with us, wherever we are, and unite us.

Saturday January 27   *Psalm 46*
Refuge in trouble

For many Christians today life is under siege. It is as if God's life abundant can only be experienced by very few people. The enemy comes right to the entrance of our besieged town and says: 'No way out; not even a God may save you now.' His logic is implacable and perversely simple: 'I alone hold the key to your future; make a bargain with me or die.' It seems quite like Jerusalem under Sennacherib, c. 701 BCE (cf. 2 Kings 18.13 to 19.37), which is probably the setting for this Psalm. Before his superiority and expertise, there was not much to expect: surrender or trust their God to deliver them. And as they bordered despair, a pest struck the Assyrian camp killing thousands and forcing the rest to withdraw. God made the war cease, liberated the life-giving running water to the people and reaffirmed his commitment to them. How counter-factual this seems to be: have we already fallen to 'Sennacherib'? Or are we still under siege, which at least means God has not forsaken us?

✴ *Lord, give us strength to resist the sacrificial logic*
of the powerful forces that produce death
and humiliate your children in our world today.
Be with us, that we may have hope and fight on.

For personal reflection or group discussion

1. For many, the presence and knowledge of God (his glory) is thought of in terms of a privileged access to spiritual truth or experience. But reading the texts above, do we not have a rather different picture: that since the 'ascension', it is within and through the fellowship of disciples that Jesus is to be found? What would it mean then, in that light, to pray for him to stay with us? What implications to the community of disciples would that bring?

2. How do you relate to three of the motifs in these texts:

- God our fellow traveller in life's journey;
- his communion with the Son being expressed through Christian fellowship;
- and God being our protector from the 'siege' waged against his people by the 'system'?

What would God's presence mean in each case?

ACTION

A great number of Christians all over the world have struggled, for decades now, to connect the effectiveness of their witness to the need for unity amid their differences. How could you help to strengthen this movement so that the world may see God's union with his Son in the Jesus event demonstrated in the lives of Christian communities?

INTERNATIONAL APPEAL

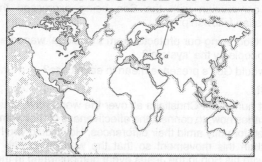

IN FIVE CONTINENTS YOU WILL FIND CHRISTIANS USING IBRA MATERIAL.

Some Christians will be using books and Bible reading cards translated into their local languages whilst others use English books. Some of the books are printed in this country but more and more of the books and cards are printed in their own countries. This is done by the IBRA International Fund working through churches and Christian groups and Christian Publishing houses overseas.

Each year we receive more requests for help from the IBRA International Fund, with greater emphasis on helping our overseas friends to produce their own versions of IBRA material.

THE ONLY MONEY WE HAVE TO SEND, IS THE MONEY YOU GIVE

SO PLEASE HELP US AGAIN BY GIVING GENEROUSLY

Place your gift in the envelope provided and give it to your IBRA representative,

or send it direct to
The IBRA International Appeal,
1020 Bristol Road, Selly Oak,
Birmingham B29 6LB, Great Britain

THANK YOU FOR YOUR HELP

AND SOLOMON IN ALL HIS GLORY?

(1 Kings 3-11)

Notes based on the Revised Standard Version by

Albert Friedlander

Rabbi Albert H Friedlander is minister of the Westminster Synagogue in London, and Dean of the Leo Baeck College, a rabbinical seminary training Reform and Liberal rabbis. His latest of many books is RIDERS TOWARDS THE DAWN which deals with post-Holocaust theology within Christian and Jewish communities. Recently he was elected Honorary President of the World Conference of Religions for Peace.

The book of Kings is a strange text. On the surface, everything is straightforward. It is a history of the kings of Judah and Israel, records actual events, and its narrative is supported by independent records outside the Bible. There was a time when modern historians tended to dismiss much of it as fiction or 'typically Oriental exaggeration'. A biblical archaeologist, Nelson Glueck, then explored Palestine using the Bible as his guide. He discovered the stables of Solomon, and the copper mines near the Red Sea, exactly where the biblical text had suggested. Now historians do accept these accounts as authentic history.

But the book of Kings is more than history. It is a religious text. It not only describes the rulers and courts of that time; it also judges them. The story of Solomon and the two mothers is not necessarily a court case: it is a text of religious instruction, and tries to see the Solomon behind the historical traditions. And so we read these texts as part of our religious quest, striving to understand how God's teachings manifested themselves in biblical days, in the palace or in the villages of an ancient land where the people felt close to the Divine word.

If only we had one wish

... what would that wish be? Looking beyond this world, we might say 'Salvation!' If we limit ourselves to the present, we might say 'happiness'. But then we still have to consider how happiness is to be achieved. We know enough of the world around us to see that riches and power cannot guarantee it. Throughout the Bible, we find mothers praying for their children, fathers placing their future into the hands of their sons; but tragedy often strikes. Solomon saw that riches, power, and children had not secured happiness for his father. Sons had died, sometimes in an act of rebellion against the king, their father. The people had turned against David; and his dream of building the Temple had failed. So Solomon asked for wisdom, and an understanding heart. God granted that wish, and Solomon found that he could judge wisely. And he built a Temple where all could pray to God and find happiness. Understanding our neighbour's grief and our own needs is the way which leads to happiness.

✳ *God, grant me strength to understand myself,*
   and wisdom to know my neighbour's pain.
   Let me make each day a building stone
   of a small sanctuary in which I can pray to you
   and find my happiness
   in the shared prayers of my family and friends. Amen

What is a judgment of Solomon?

We have often heard the story of the two mothers and the child, and misunderstand it. Even when we know that the cruel judgment – to divide the child in two – is intended as a test, the story seems a mockery of justice. If the judge's decision is not carried out, the very process of justice is challenged and weakened. If the child is killed, the mother will be destroyed. But as onlookers, we are only confused because we do not know where to look.

Don't look at Solomon, the judge. The story is not about him but about the mothers. And try to understand both mothers, particularly the wicked one who lost her child but yearns to hold a son to her breast. How many babies are stolen in the year by distraught and confused women? We must condemn them but pity them as well. And it is the other mother who instructs us, who is willing to give up her life as a mother, so that her child can live. We can appreciate Solomon's wisdom, but we must learn from the mother what parental love means: it includes the bitter lesson of letting go in order to keep our child.

✳ *My God, we live in troubled times.*
Violence confronts us every day,
and we wonder about the future of our children.
Help me to help them in every way.
Let them know that I love them,
and let them love me when they walk their own ways;
and may all ways lead us to thee. Amen

Tuesday January 30   1 Kings 4.20-34

How should a king live?

Is it wrong to say that royalty should live in luxury? But what is kingship? In the Bible, it represents a link between God and the people. In our own lives, the crown is a dream cherished by the nation and the individual citizen. In all our sanctuaries, we include prayers for the royal family – the 'loyal prayer' – in our worship. We pray that our rulers may show wisdom in leading the nation in the company of their advisers; and we pray for their happiness. Do we want to make this dream of ours small and tatty? 'And Solomon in all his glory', as he is described in this passage, is placed in a magnificent setting. We might say: 'he does us proud!' And the people 'ate and drank and were happy'; that, too, is part of the dream. But what matters most is that Solomon reigned in wisdom – the hope we express in our loyal prayer.

✳ *Grant us magnificence within our world, O God.*
Give us dreams, and models, and hopes
in which our country will fulfil its potentials.
Give us models in which we can discern
greatness and goodness.
And give us the compassion to see flawed humanity
in those who lead us and to recognize ourselves in them.
May our dreams unite us, both high and low. Amen

Are we more creative in war than in peace?

There are those who claim that war stimulates industry, inventions, and makes progress possible. Space travel or Teflon frying pans are end products of war. Our Bible text has a different message: David could not build a Temple in a time of war. Now, surrounded and encouraged by peace, Solomon could build a worthy sanctuary in Jerusalem. David had been at war with his neighbours. Solomon, the man of peace, could call on his neighbours to send the finest supplies. Cedars of Lebanon could travel along the sea in the ship of Hiram of Tyre. And the people of Israel took the task upon themselves to build a house of peace where all could join in worship. It is true that in a time of war we are more aware of dangers threatening us from the outside, and that we join together to defend our land. In peace, we may grow sluggish and care less for the welfare of the people. Then leaders arise and place a greater goal before us, and we can awaken and be worthy of the vision which arises in a time of peace.

✳ *O God of peace and compassion, let us search*
  for the time of peace in which noble dreams come true.
  Let us not be afraid of war, but let us love peace:
  not by might, and not by strength, but by your spirit,
  according to your word. Amen

How much planning is needed?

Architects cannot construct buildings without blueprints. The laity may stand alongside and admire, or we may be totally bewildered. What is all this business? 'The vestibule in front of the nave of the house was twenty cubits long' ... 'the lower story was five cubits broad, the middle one was six cubits broad ...' How dull a text! But then: 'neither hammer nor axe nor any tool of iron was heard in the temple, while it was being built.' There was a hidden plan behind those blueprints.

I recently visited Vienna, and saw the Breughel painting of the Tower of Babel. The more one studied it, the more one realized that there was evil intent behind the building. But Solomon's Temple was built to achieve peace. The rabbis tell us that no tools were used that could be used for war; no implement of iron was permitted. If the Temple was built for peace, God would dwell with the builders. And so it was. The elaborate structure needed master builders who would walk with God. We must not only look at the plan, but at those who fulfil it.

✴ *God, make us instruments of peace.*
Give us plans which do not pander to our pride,
but recognize our need to pray with others and to you.
May our human plans lead us into the plan of peace
you have prepared for us. Amen

Friday February 2   *1 Kings 6.15-38*
Gilding the lily
'And he overlaid the whole house with gold, until all the house was finished.' Pure gold, and cherubim, and palm trees and open flowers, and olive wood, and ... But how necessary was all this? The quiet dignity of a Quaker room of prayer, the simple beauty of a village church, the reverent attitude in a Hassidic prayer room – all these are just as much places of prayer as Solomon's glorious Temple. Once more, to answer this we must not look at the building but at the builders. Those who shared in the building, including Hiram of Tyre, wanted to give the best they had for this task. Just so, Moses had to stop the Israelites in the wilderness from giving more and more in the building of the Tabernacle. But both Moses and Solomon knew that the people wanted the finest place of prayer possible – not to impress God, but to remind themselves of the need for sacrifice and prayers. Meanwhile, no matter how lavish the exterior might become, the innermost chamber, the Holy of Holies, stayed empty. God did not need to be impressed.

✴ *God, make us not proud but humble in our prayers.*
May they not become our adornments, our decorations;
but let them be the finest which we can offer you.
A broken and a contrite heart you will not despise –
and you will discern the gold in our words. Amen

Saturday February 3   *1 Kings 8.1-21* *
You must earn your inheritance!
'Now it was in the heart of David my father to build a house for the name of the LORD, the God of Israel.' Sometimes our parents want to achieve their dreams and ambitions through us;

then, they can destroy their children and themselves. Often they have noble dreams and visions for the world, and want their children to share in them. The greatest gift David gave to Solomon was not the crown, but the dream of the Temple. It was a noble vision, but not enough in itself. Solomon had to understand why David failed; and he had to learn how he might succeed in making that dream a reality. It had to reach out towards God; it could not be an act of self-aggrandizement; and it had to reach out towards the rest of the world, as well.

Often we take our parents' gifts to us – gifts of wealth or gifts of spirit – and misunderstand them wilfully. In our Bible readings, we come to an appreciation of the spiritual values and religious practices which filled our parental homes. If we discard them, or follow them mechanically, like robots, we have thrown away our birth-rights. But the example of Solomon might show us how to accept the gifts of the past and realize them with a joy which will move through the generations.

✻ *God, make us grateful for the dreams of the past.*
   Teach us that the generations are linked together
   in search of thee, and that our pilgrimage leads us
   to acts of fulfilment which honour our parents
   and transmit their gifts to our children.
   Help us to be part of that chain of transmission. Amen

For personal reflection or group discussion

What significance can a central place of worship have in the life of a village, town, city and nation?

Isaiah (2.1-4) pictured all the nations coming to Solomon's Temple. What is the significance of his vision today?

9th Sunday before Easter, February 4   *1 Kings 8.22-34*
Education Sunday

Teaching the noblest prayer

Solomon's prayer of dedicating the Temple is more than an address directed to God. It is also a total admonition to the people standing in the gates of the Temple, a teaching all the more powerful because it is an act of worship. In Jewish tradition, the synagogue has always had three interlocking functions: it is the house of prayer, the house of public assembly, and the house of study. In today's reading, Solomon has assembled the populace together because they have to share this basic experience of a people – it is they who are dedicated as much as the sanctuary. And Solomon instructs them in the nature of divinity: God cannot be contained in any sanctuary. But the people can enter it and learn to pray. They can discover that their sins will be judged as individuals; that the community which deserts God fashions its own punishments; and that even natural calamities can be related to their shortcomings.

At this moment, in this prayer, the people discover the meaning of religion.

Let us always pray for understanding as we strive to teach others. Let us be tolerant to those who wish to learn, and let us remember how often our place of worship becomes the place of education, the sanctuary of the open mind which can receive new truth and return to ancient insights.

✳ *Help us to study and to teach,*
to teach and to study, O LORD. Amen

Monday February 5   1 Kings 8.35-43

Loving the stranger

When we join in prayer with others, many barriers which separate us from other traditions and peoples can be overcome. We must not make our house of prayer a fortress against everyone else. Solomon's words are crystal clear: 'When a foreigner ... comes from a far country for thy name's sake ... and prays towards this house, hear thou in heaven thy dwelling place, and do according to all for which the foreigner calls to thee ...'

The house of prayer is not a private club from which we can exclude the stranger. Our sanctuaries do not only serve our private needs. As Solomon's prayer indicates, the Temple was there to proclaim God to all the world, and to bring others to the knowledge of God. Israel could bring its anguish and suffering to God – famine, plague, or illness, every affliction. God was to hear in heaven, and forgive. But all humanity suffers, and cries to God. The sanctuary brings us together as comrades in suffering who can find help. When we open ourselves to one another, we open ourselves to God.

✳ *God of compassion and love,*
help us to learn that our way towards you

begins through the pain of our neighbours.
When we share with them, and can pray with them,
we are truly part of a community at prayer.
Help us to pray with others, O God. Amen

Tuesday February 6   1 Kings 8.54-66

What happens after prayer?

When Solomon had finished his prayer dedicating the Temple,
he turned to the people and blessed them. The dynamics of
worship have not changed since that time. We reach out in love
and reverence to the symbols of our faith; and the sanctuary
becomes a holy place. Then, at the end, the officiate turns
towards us to bless us. 'The Lord our God be with us, as he was
with our ancestors,' we are told. When we leave the house of
prayers, we carry our experience of worship with us, into daily
life. Prayer must be more than a moment of respite in a quiet
place. It is an instruction which will now accompany us: 'Let your
heart therefore be wholly true to the LORD our God, walking in
his statutes and keeping his commandments, as at this day.'
Our biblical account showed as an eight day celebration (during
the Festival of Tabernacles) which marked the unique event of
the completion of Solomon's Temple. The people went home
joyfully and glad of heart for all the goodness God had shown
them. Now, 3000 years later, the memory of that joy gives light
to us.

✳ *LORD, let my prayers not cease*
when I leave the house of God.
My thoughts in daily life, and my actions in my home
must reflect the joy I feel in the sanctuary.
May each moment I spend in the sanctuary
remain an abiding inspiration in my daily life. Amen

Wednesday February 7   1 Kings 9.1-9

The burden of chosenness

Solomon lives in history as a great and wise king, the builder of
the Temple in Jerusalem, the author of wisdom literature
(credited with writing Proverbs and Ecclesiastes), renowned for
the celebration of love and marriage (the Song of Songs). He
was surrounded by riches and crowned with great success. God
promised him that the line of Kingship established with David
would continue for all generations – unless 'you and your

40

children turn aside from following me'. This dark note is struck at the moment of his greatest triumph, when the Temple is dedicated. Solomon understands his own weakness, and the flaws of the people who will follow him. Chosen for a special task, he knows there are times when he will fail. Already he has been impatient with his people, demanded too much from them, taxed them too highly – all of it in pursuit of the task for which he was chosen. And he senses that the future is dark, and that the people will stumble from the way that has been chosen for them. There will be exile, but also redemption; the task of being God's servant will be fulfilled – but at the end of time.

* *God, give us tasks in life.*
We know that we will fail at times;
but what is life if we do not have a special purpose,
if we are not chosen for a task?
Deep within me is an awareness that I am unique,
as every person is a unique event within the universe.
Grant me to know where my task lies
and where I will go, so that I can accept the joy and pain
of my own way towards you. Amen

Thursday February 8   *1 Kings 10.1-13*

In praise of wisdom

Quiz programmes are still our favourites. We enjoy contests where the wise are defeated and only the fittest survive. That is the story of Solomon and the Queen of Sheba, even if a successful trade negotiation hides behind the events. 2,000 years ago, the rabbis told the story of the bee which stung Solomon, and asked to be forgiven. 'I'll help you some day,' it promised. 'How can a little bee help a wise and powerful king?' laughed Solomon. But when the Queen of Sheba came, she showed him a huge tent filled with flowers. 'Only one flower is real,' she said. 'The others are artificial. Find the real flower!' Solomon was puzzled; but then the bee appeared, buzzed through the tent and lit on one flower, without the queen noticing. 'That is the true flower,' said Solomon, and the queen was duly amazed. And Solomon learned that the small can help the great, and the simple the wise. And to this day the biblical text stirs our imagination and leads to new stories.

* *God, give us wisdom without arrogance,*
and understanding linked with humour
so that we can see small victories and defeats

41

in due proportion.
Let us celebrate the wisdom of the heart and mind,
so that life is bearable
and challenges are always ahead of us. Amen

Friday February 9   *1 Kings 10.14-25 and 11.1-13*

The material the spiritual

One of the last books to be written by the psychiatrist-philosopher Erich Fromm was entitled *To Have or to Be*. Surely, the text we confront here is a perfect example of the way in which possessions can overwhelm a person and remove the inner core of one's identity, as taught by Erich Fromm. All the possessions of King Solomon are described, with the ships from Tarshish bringing 'gold, silver, ivory, apes, and peacocks ... so that he excelled all the kings of the earth in riches ...' And Solomon 'had seven hundred wives, princesses, and three hundred concubines; and his wives turned away his heart.' For Solomon, sadly, wives were also possessions; and he became, as it were, possessed. He now judged by materialistic standards, as other kings. He permitted the pagan gods of the world around him to become part of a sacred land which had declared its allegiance to the One God of Creation who could not be seen by human eyes. And so, 'Solomon did what was evil in the sight of the LORD.' The end result was predictable. Solomon's great and wealthy kingdom disappeared after his death, and only Judah and Benjamin remained true to his son. The other ten tribes became a new kingdom, and eventually disappeared.

But the spiritual inheritance survived to guide us; and, in that fashion, Solomon is also part of our world.

✷ *God, make us grateful for our possessions.*
Let them not rule us, and make us aware
of the true standards of life
which we discover in the life of the Spirit.
Let us not think of others as though we owned them,
and let us acknowledge that we are the stewards
of what you give us.

The captains and the kings depart

Historians think highly of the first Jeroboam, who was a good general and an able ruler of the ten-tribe state of Israel which he established (later on, Jeroboam II was an even greater king). As far as the Bible is concerned, Kings are puppets in the hand of God, actors upon God's stage. Outside Israel, the people viewed their kings as sacred or as gods (Egypt and Babylonia); but the Israelites knew that they did not follow the law of the kings, but the law of God. Prophets proclaimed God's law to the king, as we saw in Nathan's message to David. Here, Jeroboam meets the prophet Ahijah, who tells him God's wishes. Part of the historical drama planned by God is unfolded to Jeroboam, as it had been to Solomon; and both can only conform to the role set out for them. Great actors can transform their parts, as we see when we study David and Solomon.

✳ *God, give us courage to play the parts which come to us*
   in the drama of life.
   May our entrances and exits be placed into sun-lit days.
   Yet, if we must walk through the valley
   of the shadow of death,
   let us know that you are with us. Amen

For personal reflection or group discussion

How is wisdom applied to the stewardship of power and wealth? What outstanding events would the Old Testament historian record in your country today, and what judgment would he pass on the people and political leadership there?

ACTION

What practical steps can you take to become a more effective citizen?

Reading the Bible with the blind

Could you spend some time daily or weekly to share the reading of these notes and Bible passages with a partially sighted or blind person?

DARKNESS AND LIGHT

Notes based on the Good News Bible by

Stella Bristow

Stella Bristow is National Secretary for the Women's Network of the Methodist Church in Britain, a movement which seeks to encourage, enable and equip women to take their full part in church and community. She is currently Vice-President of the Methodist Church.

Most images that come to mind when we speak of darkness are negative. We speak of going through a dark tunnel, forgetting that tunnels are often built that we might travel safely and quickly across difficult terrain. Though we cannot see the light at the end of the tunnel, it does not mean that it is not there, but that for the present it is hidden. Uncomfortable though it is, we all go through dark times. It is unavoidable. Jesus who knew the ultimate in darkness, in the garden and on the cross, struggled with despair, shouting out in anguish when he felt utterly deserted by God. It was not until Easter morning that the light was seen.

For the darkness of waiting
Of not knowing what is to come
Of staying ready and quiet and attentive
We praise you O God.
For the darkness and the light are both alike to you.

From All Desires Known, Janet Morley (SPCK)

8th Sunday before Easter, February 11   Job 23.1-10 *

Where are you God?

Job's so called friends and comforters load him with guilt and despair, undermining his faith by inferring that he deserves his suffering. Job cannot believe it but cannot make sense of what is happening to him. It is not fair that in his desperate struggle with the big issue of suffering, God seems to be absent. No wonder Job groans.

Job seems to have one thing wrong though. We do not have to vindicate ourselves by reasoning with God – he knows every

44

step we take. Job, blinded by despair and anguish, uses up energy in rebelling and complaining, searching for a God who is already surrounding him in his darkness.

You do not need to look for me my child
For I am already here surrounding you in your darkness.
The light you seek is not yet visible,
so feel for me in the depth of your darkness,
for light and dark are both alike to me.
Do not rave and kick against me,
for my arms cannot hold you whilst you struggle.
Be still and know that I, your God, am with you waiting
to carry you towards the light.

'God is nearer to us than our own soul. Because God is the ground in which our soul stands and God is the means whereby our substance and our sensuality are kept together, so as to never be apart.' *Julian of Norwich*

✳ *Think of a time when you felt a deep despair, when prayer was difficult and God seemed silent. What did you do? Light a candle for someone or a situation you know where all seems dark and hopeless.*

Monday February 12 Psalm 143

Deep need

When we go through dark and difficult times, we often scrutinize the past to see where we went wrong. It is easier to endure suffering if we can see some definite cause and effect. The 'why me?' and 'what did I do to deserve this?' type of questions reflect our deep need to confront God for an answer.

David at his wits end calls out to God for help. He just cannot endure anymore, but like Job he feels God is playing hide and seek with him.

There are similarities between the Psalmist and Job:

● both feel life is unfair.

● they know this suffering is undeserved;

● both begin to wonder if they have offended God in some way and search the past.

In asking for protection, however, the Psalmist tells God what he thinks he ought to do. 'If you love me – kill my enemies and destroy all my oppressors' – is there any other way? Do we pray for ourselves with any regard to the consequences for others?

✷ *O God,*
you have searched the depths we cannot know,
and touched what we cannot bear to name:
may we so wait,
enclosed in your darkness,
that we are ready to encounter
the terror of the dawn,
with Jesus Christ.   Janet Morley in All Desires Known
(SPCK)

Tuesday February 13   *John 5.1-18**

Comfortable darkness

Why, I wonder, does Jesus bother to heal this man? Is he irritated by his complacent attitude and acceptance of his situation? The man seems content to remain as he is – perhaps the prospect of full health frightens him. He will no longer be able to hide behind his disability as an excuse for inactivity. Perhaps his friends are at fault for giving up on him when a miracle is not immediately forthcoming. One by one they forget to visit, leaving him to slip further into darkness and apathy. Whatever the circumstances, it is Jesus who takes the initiative, who sees the potential yet to be realized. Jesus never gives up on people, and says, 'I CAME TO BRING LIFE, LIFE IN ALL ITS FULLNESS.'

● Is there someone you know who is cut off from the outside world because s/he is house bound? Is there something you can do?

● Do you use old worn out excuses when God confronts you with new challenges?

✷ *God, you call us to leave the familiar and travel new*
pathways with you. Give us courage to risk the unknown,
and to step out confident that you will provide us with
manna for our journey.

Wednesday February 14   *John 8.12-20*

Walk behind the light

Jesus is in the Temple, perhaps in the court of women, watching the lighting of the candelabra, symbolizing the pillar of fire which went in front of the ark to light the way. Jesus' claim is challenged. Self testimony is not necessarily untrue provided it is built on true self knowledge, but Jesus also claims his heavenly Father as witness.

'As God is my witness ...' We hear it exclaimed when others want to impress us with their honesty or when we have challenged their testimony with the words 'Prove it!' But there are some whose way of life and faith is a living proof. The light shines from them. They, like Jesus know where they come from and where they are going. Are you one of them?

'Let your light shine before others, so that they may see your good works and give glory to your father in heaven'

Matthew 5.16 (NRSV)

✳ *Lord, you placed me in the world*
To be its light.
I was afraid of the shadows
afraid of the poverty.
I did not want to know other people
And my light slowly faded away.
Forgive me, Jesus.

Peggy M. De Cuehlo, Uruguay
From Your will be Done (Christian Conference of Asia)

Thursday February 15   Psalm 139.1-12

He knows me so well

I still remember, as a child, being told by an adult who was trying to encourage me to 'own up' to a certain misdemeanour that God knew everything about me, and that I could hide nothing from him. I expected an interrogator's searchlight to fall on me and expose all! That someone knew my inmost thoughts and actions was very frightening! This Psalm has a little of that fear about it, but also the comforting knowledge of a God who knows us because we are his creation. He is responsible for our being and delights in us.

From the darkness and security of the womb, a woman brings forth her child. She examines each finger and toe, in order to know and delight in that creation, which is now exposed to the light of the world. The cord is cut for an independent life, but that knowledge and love, there from the earliest moments, will continue and the child grows. Can we expect less from our heavenly Parent?

* *After darkness, light;*
   After winter, spring;
   After dying, life:
      Alleluia!   *Fred Pratt Green*

Friday February 16   *James 1.2-5 **
The light is diffused

The Christian community to whom James writes is scattered over the whole of the known world. Yet some of the words in this letter seem rather thoughtless. James is not saying that there is virtue in adversity but that, when it occurs, it should be faced, and that God is there to give generously and graciously whatever we require to endure. But it is difficult to say that to people who are going through a dark period in their lives, especially when everything is going well for us.

I remember once being invited to visit a young woman and her mother in their home in a slum dwelling in India. They lived in appalling conditions with hardly any material possessions. She welcomed me with open arms and seemed almost unaware of the great contrast between us. To me she was living in darkness produced by poverty. Yet her face shone. 'God is so good,' she said. I could only admire her faith which overcame such adversity without bitterness, and question mine.

* *Thank God for those people who have shed light into the dark recesses of your life making you question attitudes and lifestyles.*

Saturday February 17   *1 John 1.5-10*
All consuming light

If possible light a single candle and reflect upon the way it gives light. Then read the Bible passage.

In order to provide light, a candle gives itself. It is literally consumed as the flame burns. It is not still either. The flame is constantly moving, as if seeking out the darkness. If we pick up the candle and move with it, other areas are touched by its light.

Jesus Christ, Light of the world, gave his life in order that our darkness and sin could be overcome. We no longer walk in darkness, but have the light of that love. As disciples we are called to give light to others and that will require not just observing the light, but taking it up and enabling it to spread, and in doing so we will be giving of ourselves. We will be consumed by the light.

Watch the sunrise one morning. See how it reveals the landscape. What are you able to see that you could not see before? What areas of your life need illuminating with the light of God's love?

✴ *Go in peace to the place where our God has given you responsibility. Go with the light of faith burning brightly, confident that God will nourish you in word and sacrament all the days of your life.*
    Liberating Liturgies, Women's Ordination Conference, USA

For personal reflection or group discussion

Take a close look at the weekday activities of your church. Ask two questions of each: why do we do this? and does the activity bring light, or might it bring darkness in some area? *e.g. make people feel guilty ...*

ACTION

Cut out some negative stories from national and local papers which depict darkness and despair. What needs to happen in order to turn the situation into one of hope and light? Write your thoughts underneath the paper cutting. Is there some way in which you can act (by a letter of protest to the authorities, or of support to the person(s) experiencing darkness?

LENT – GOD'S CALL TO RESPOND

1. Responding to hunger

Notes based on the New Jerusalem Bible by

Sheila Cassidy

Sheila Cassidy, a specialist in Palliative Care at Plymouth General Hospital (UK), has worked for many years with people dying of cancer. In her spare time she preaches, lectures, broadcasts and writes books. Her writing is deeply influenced by her involvement with suffering both in cancer wards and in her personal experience of imprisonment, torture and solitary confinement in Chile in 1975.

We look at hunger: our longing for food, for love, for sex, for happiness, for God. Our physical hungers we share with animals: they are an integral part of our make-up. After all, if we hungered for neither food nor sex, the human race would perish! Our spiritual hungers are different: they distinguish us from all other creatures and they manifest themselves by an intense yearning which drives us on to search for the true, the beautiful, the absolute, for the ultimate meaning of life.

Unlike physical desires, this spiritual hunger is never wholly satisfied, for, as Augustine puts it: 'our heart is restless' until it rests in God. And, yet, miraculously, there are moments, when like Moses, we glimpse the back parts of God, and know that the search is 'worth the candle'.

---

*7th Sunday before Easter, February 18   Deuteronomy 8.1-6 ***
God trains his people
The theme of this passage, that God trains us by leading us into the desert, is a familiar one. Hosea's promiscuous wife, lured by God into the wilderness so that he may speak to her heart (Hosea 2.14), is a metaphor for the people of Israel and for

ourselves. In illness, bereavement, redundancy, stripped of all our support systems, naked to the desert winds, we are particularly vulnerable to God's scary world. Terrified, we wrestle like Jacob with the mysterious stranger, and emerge, wounded, limping, muttering to ourselves 'the Lord was in that experience, and I didn't realize it.'

The greater teaser is whether God *inflicts* suffering on us as a way of purifying us, or whether it is inherent in the desert experience that, stripped of much that clutters our lives, we are able to see essential things more clearly. A 13th century Rhineland mystic seems to go along with the notion that God *permits* hard things to happen to us: 'The faithful God often lets his friends fall sick and lets every prop on which they lean be knocked out from under them ... For the more helpless and destitute the mind that turns to God for support can be, the deeper the person penetrates God and the more sensitive he is to God's most valuable gifts. Man must build on God alone' *(Talks of Instruction No 19, Meister Eckhart).*

✳ *Oh wild God of the desert,*
  call us, draw us, drive us into the wilderness
  so that we may catch a glimpse
  of your wondrous beauty,
  and know the touch of your hand.

Monday February 19   *Matthew 4.1-4 ✳*

Not by bread alone

Jesus the Carpenter, preacher, prophét, pastor, had to learn about God the hard way: in the desert. Although without sin he was still open to temptation, a man like us in all things.

We don't often think of Jesus being tempted, because it is so easy to confuse Christ, our Lord, the pure and holy One, with Jesus of Nazareth, the itinerant preacher who died on the cross and so *became* the Christ. Jesus of Nazareth was a man who, like the prophets before him, felt that he was being called by God for a mission. How easy it is for those who have this sense of destiny to believe that they are especially good or especially holy, when the reality is that God so often calls the frail and the wounded, the earthen vessels, so that *his* power may be manifest in them. The temptation to trust in their own power rather than God's is the temptation of all such men and women. They, above all, need to spend their statutory forty days in the wilderness while they learn to say 'no' to the triple lure of power, self-reliance and idolatry. It is there that they learn that it is not honour nor temporal riches which will sustain them but utter dependence upon God.

✳ *Lord our God, gentle prophet, loving Father,*
give us this day our bread for survival,
and our wine for rejoicing,
but keep us ever mindful that without your Word,
your life within us, we will die of starvation.

Tuesday February 20   John 6.1-15 *

Jesus' picnic

These Gospel stories have onion layers of meaning, endless depths. As I read the story today, I am reminded of two favourite sayings. One is, I think, Chinese: 'It's better to light a candle than to curse the darkness.'

My first acquaintance with this sentiment was in Chile where I worked alongside those who were trying to alleviate the suffering of the poor and oppressed in a vicious military dictatorship. I worked in a small shanty town clinic, bringing comfort to a few of the more desperate people. Some would have mocked my efforts as merely a *parche*, propping up a crumbling regime, prolonging the people's agony by postponing the day the regime would be overturned by the desperate masses, unable to endure their hunger a moment longer. Such theory has a sinister logic, but works only from the safety of office desk or a Marxist armchair. Faced by a starving woman and her fainting children, all one can do is divide up one's lunch and pass the fragments around.

The other saying I found on a headmaster's desk, and for me it contains the essence of the Gospel story:

✳ *'Love is like a basket of loaves and fishes.*
You never have enough until you start to give it away!'

Ash Wednesday, February 21   Job 24.1-12

Hunger unsatisfied

Job, the good man, the pious, God-fearing archetype of respectability, learns the hard way what the poor have always known: that God is not 'just' (by our standards), that he does not answer prayer the way we would like.

If God were just, then the poor would be cared for, the sick healed, the wicked punished. Alas, life is not like that. Job learned, as we learn in our own tribulation, that God is wilder and more mysterious than we care to imagine: that children die of cancer, women starve to death in Ethiopia and that Thomas Merton – monk, sage and priest – was electrocuted ignominiously in his bath.

This probably sounds blasphemous, but it is true. Oh, how we would like it to be otherwise! Our inclination is to run to God like a child to his or her parent, begging to be saved, to be comforted. Our God, of course, is too small. We naively think that God is our colour, our creed, our class: a white blue-eyed God for Anglo-Saxons and a black brown-eyed God for Africans. I repeat, God is not like that. He (she) has neither creed nor colour, is not a partisan God. If we pray for rain, for our child to be saved, we do right, providing we do not think we can manipulate God. He (or she) is not a marionette to dance to our tune. We pray out of our *own need*, not because God needs our instructions on how to manage the universe. By praying, by offering sacrifice, we acknowledge our state of utter destitution before the Lord of all creation. And then if we listen carefully we will hear him speak to us from the heart of the tempest (see Job 38) and tell us, to our utter amazement that he loves us.

✱ *Lord of the universe, scary, wondrous God,*
  we know you are out there, in here, somewhere.
  We are hungry, lonely, frightened, muddled.
  Show us your face.

Thursday February 22   *Matthew 6.1-4* ✱

True generosity

Last week, in a moment of generosity, spurred on by guilt at having spent too much upon myself, I gave a cheque to my parish priest in response to an appeal on behalf of the hungry.

'Who shall I make the cheque out to?' I asked, wondering idly if my friend X was still working for the said charity and hoping he would be impressed by my donation.

The priest hesitated, and then said, 'Make it out to the parish. It will make *our* gift look better.'

'Well!' I thought. And then I realized that the parish, catering mainly for impoverished students, had precious little to give and I was happy to augment their donation.

53

But why did I even think it would be nice if someone thought I was generous? The only person I should care about is God, and he knows the state of my bank balance better than my accountant. I have always had this struggle about giving. I like to give gifts to my friends and family, and hear them say, 'Are you *sure* you can spare it? You are generous!' Sorry. I am only doing the beginners' course in gospel holiness, and I'm not at all sure that I will pass my exams!

* *Generous God, teach me to give –*
without batting an eyelid or wanting thanks –
from the amazing store of gifts which you
have freely given me to share with all your people.

Friday February 23   Matthew 6.5-15 *

Praying in secret

This passage reminds me of Fr. Michael Hollings, chaplain at Oxford University, from whom I learned to pray when I was an undergraduate. He was a very attractive personality and I, worshipping the ground he walked on, wondered what made him so special and found that it was his passion for God. Attending early morning Mass, more out of hero worship than devotion, I found that he was always there praying in the chapel when I arrived. Anxious, as always, for a kind word, I came earlier each day until I found that he opened the door about forty minutes before Mass was due to begin. Thereafter I too arrived forty minutes early, and the two of us kept silent vigil before the altar. I found this early morning watching difficult, and would have to hold on to my chair to stop myself from walking out in sheer boredom. Later, he gave us some talks on prayer, and I learned that he did not spend his time before the altar *talking* to God but *listening*.

Over the years, my prayer too has changed so that I also sit and listen in the early mornings, keeping vigil, waiting on God. My guess is that this is what Jesus did during those nights of prayer on the mountain: sitting, kneeling, aching, sometimes bored and stiff, but somehow knowing that God was there and that this was time well spent.

Thirty-five years later, Father Michael still sits in the dark in church, huddled in his black cloak, stiff with sitting still. I'm glad he does it in a public place, though, because if he'd shut himself in his room, I might never have learned how to pray.

✳ *Holy God, we praise your Name.*
And we thank you for all the men and women
who have taught and inspired us over the years.
Fill us with your light and love
so that we too may lead the way.

Saturday February 24   James 2.14-17

Faith without good deeds is dead

One of my favourite religious observances is the saying of a
'grace', a prayer before meals. I am an enthusiastic cook and an
even more enthusiastic eater, so it seems only fitting to say
thank you to God in the same way that we thank the cook.
Generally speaking, I like to make my prayers up rather the way
I cook, throwing in whatever is to hand and seems right for the
dish, although I have no problem with prepared prayers from
those to whom improvisation does not come easily. One thing I
can't stand, however, is the sort of prayer that goes, 'We thank
you Lord for this fine dinner, and oh, by the way, give food to
those who haven't got any!'

How God must grit his teeth when he hears that one, for did
he not make it abundantly clear (through the prophets, through
Jesus, Paul, John and now James), that he expects *us* to use
the gifts he has given us to look after the widow and the orphan,
and to feed the hungry out of our own larder. The following
prayer (though often attributed to Mother Teresa) was written by
a monk, Father Tom Cullinan:

✳ *Make us <u>worthy</u> Lord to serve our fellow man*
who live and die in poverty and hunger.
Give them, <u>through our hands</u> their daily bread,
and through our understanding love
*   bring peace and joy. Amen to that.*

For personal reflection or group discussion

Reflect: 'Bread for myself is a physical thing; bread for another a
spiritual.'   *Nicholas Berdaeyev, Russia*

ACTION

IBRA helps people in over five continents to grow in their
understanding of God's Word. Look again at page 32, and, if
you have not already done so, send a donation to help to satisfy
the hunger.

LENT – GOD'S CALL TO RESPOND

2. Responding from the wilderness

Notes based on the New Jerusalem Bible by

Joseph G Donders

Joseph Donders, a Dutch Roman Catholic priest of the Society of Missionaries of Africa, is Professor of Mission and Cross-cultural Studies at the Washington Theological Union. He was formerly Head of the Department of Philosophy and Religious Studies and Chaplain to Catholic students at the State University of Nairobi, Kenya.

Traversing this world to our final destiny is heavy going. There are dangers on the road and deserts to cross. Conflicts and misunderstandings abound, and it is often difficult to find our way in the dark. Water is struck from rock; living bread is provided; strangers become friends; the way to the promised land is found, and peace is made. Thanks be to God who remains true to us, asking us to be true to God.

1st Sunday in Lent, February 25   Exodus 17.3-7 *
Water in the desert

Their way through the wilderness made them weary and thirsty. The adventure they engaged in, when deciding to follow their God, was more than they could bear. They dreamed about those they left behind, eating and drinking, carousing and frolicking to their heart's content. They complained and challenged, not only Moses, but God.

Add a few words to the term 'wilderness' above and the picture changes: 'Their way through the wilderness *of this world* had made them weary and thirsty.' We are then no longer only speaking about them. We begin to speak about ourselves, and our pilgrimage in this world. That is why it is good to know that

God did not leave them alone, striking water from rock. We, too, can rely on God. Our thirst for the kin(g)dom of God will be quenched. The desert will bring forth its justice (Isaiah 32.16).

✳ *Do not retreat into your private world,*
That place of safety, sheltered from the storm,
Where you may tend your garden seek your soul,
And rest with loved ones where the fire burns warm.
Kathy Galloway, 1989, from Bread of Tomorrow,
Edit. Janet Morley (SPCK/Christian Aid)

Monday February 26 *Exodus 20.1-17 **

Living bread

It seems to be no help to comfort our hurting selves and others with the ten commandments. Yet, why are we hurt, and why are we bruising each other? Is it not because our culture has been chipping away at those two old tables with their divine directives cut in stone? Is the wilderness we inhabit not due to lack of respect for those laws, that allowed God's people to overcome the confusion in which they lived so long ago?

Jesus told us to be more alive than stones; to be like salt and yeast. He warned us, however, not to destroy the Law. As Paul wrote, 'The law was our schoolmaster to bring us unto Christ' (Galatians 3.24, AV). Which does not mean that we have nothing to learn from the Law. The Law remains, but we should serve it up in a new way, like living bread, that supports us all.

✳ *It is not a matter of taking a lot of crushed rock*
broken commandments down other people's throats.
Instead, it is humbly slicing and serving up 'living bread
in two tablet sized loaves.'
Jack Hayford, 'Removing the cobwebs from the
decalogue' (Ministries Today, July/August, 1992)

Tuesday February 27 *Deuteronomy 10.12 to 11.1*

Stranger no more

Did you ever end up in a strange country without knowing anyone? Many do. For refugees and immigrants in our midst, society is often like a bureaucratic and social jungle. You get a taste of it, when you lose your money and documents in a foreign country, and have to help yourself in a language you hardly speak.

The wayfarers in the desert had once been badly treated strangers in Egypt. God helped them out of their troubles, and travelled with them on their escape, asking them to draw the conclusions of what God had done for them. They should love God with all their heart, and, like God, love the others, especially strangers: 'Love the stranger and give him food and clothing, for you were once strangers in Egypt.' This is a command we should take seriously in our church communities. Were we not once lost in the world, until God found us?

✱ *Churches are receiving [immigrants] with open arms, but then they are asked to serve in the kitchen rather than in decision making committees. Andres Tapia,*
　　　　Vivos los Evangelicos! (Christianity Today, Oct. 1992)

Wednesday February 28　　　　　　　　　　　*Matthew 4.5-11 ✱*
What is the use ?
Satan tries everything to get Jesus on his side and to waylay him: wealth, fame and power. Jesus is careful not to be caught. His answer is simple. Jesus' answer is God – there is no way but God's.

It is a simplicity well expressed in *Repentance*, a Russian film made just before that country began to change. At the end of the film an older woman asks the heroine: 'Tell me, does this street lead to a church?' 'No,' she replies, for it reminded her of the tragic events of her childhood and the church that was blown up. The last words of the film are those of the astonished old woman: 'What is this street for then, if it does not lead to a church?'

It was Jesus' answer as regards the quest for fame, wealth and power.

✱ *Turn us again from our captivity,*
　and restore our vision,
　that our mouth may be filled with laughter
　And our tongue with singing.
　　　　Janet Morley, Bread of Tomorrow (SPCK/Christian Aid)

Thursday February 29　　　　　　　　　　　*John 2.13-25*
Throwing out
Jesus did not just *purify* the Temple when he made a whip out of cord. He threw them out, the sheep, the cattle, the

moneychangers and the dove vendors.

It is interesting that he singled out dove sellers. They are the only ones he addresses. They were selling pigeons and turtledoves for the sacrifices of the poor. Did Jesus remember the story Mary and Joseph told him about his own presentation in the Temple? How they had only been able to pay for a pair of turtledoves (Luke 2.24)?

Jesus' protest is not just against the Temple's commercialization and its exploitation of the poor – 'devouring the property of widows' (cf. Mark 12.40) – but against the whole sacrificial system of the Temple. He explains his confrontational behaviour by calling the Temple 'My Father's house'. It is the first time in the Gospel of John that he identifies God as his 'Father'. The 'Father' we have in common is a kinship that should shape our lives, and make any commercialization or exploitation of others impossible.

✳ *Our Father in heaven,*
   may your name be held holy,
   your kingdom come,
   your will be done
   on earth as in heaven.   *Jesus (Matthew 6.9-10)*

World Day of Prayer, March 1   *Hebrews 4.12-16* *
God calls us to respond

She had been living for too long with her problem. She thought she was alone in this. It made her sick to think of it. Then she told her story. What an immense relief it was to hear that she was not the only one. Her friend had been going through the same thing. This is the comfort the letter to the Hebrews offers us. We are not alone. Christ is the One who knows our innermost thoughts better then we do ourselves. He can tell us in all honesty: 'I went through the same thing and I overcame it!'

Today, throughout the world women are coming together to pray, using prayers prepared by the women of Haiti, one of the poorest countries in the world. In their prayers they share their need for justice and peace with the One who sympathizes with all of us in our need.

✳ *God our guide, we live in hope for the future;*
   Difficult days lie ahead,
   but we believe that in the end, with your help,
   we shall overcome.   *Alain Rocourt, Haiti*

The making of peace

God's reconciliation with us in Jesus Christ means that 'the old order is gone, and a new being is there to see'. Belonging to Christ we share – in some sense – in God's righteousness. That sharing is the reason why we should follow the pattern God sets for us. This means that we ought to relate in a new way, not only to God, but also to each other. We should no longer 'consider anyone by human standards' (verse 16) but by God's standards.

Paul implores us to live up to this newness. He warns us not to let the 'acceptance of this grace come to nothing' (6.1). Receiving this gift is accepting the task of peace making. We should forgive each other. Humanity needs this reconciliation more than ever. Too often we were divided against each other, worse than wild animals in the wilderness. Reconciliation is the only way to overcome the horrors we inflicted on each other in the past, to survive the present, and prepare for our future.

✳ *The mark of community – true biblical unity – is not the absence of conflict, but the presence of a reconciling spirit.*   Bill Hybels, quoted in Leadership, Winter 1993

For personal reflection and group discussion

1. Is Jesus' saying, 'Be perfect as my Father is perfect' Matthew 5.48) ever an admonition you take seriously as a motive to act?

2. Does your following of Christ influence you in your public life as far as your political choices are concerned? Can you explain your answer with some examples?

ACTION

Have a conversation with someone in which you explain how you react as a Christian to the immigration and refugee issue in your country and your local community.

LENT – GOD'S CALL TO RESPOND

3. To blindness

Notes based on the New Revised Standard Version by

Jane Wallman

Jane Wallman, an Anglican priest in Woodbridge (UK), is a part-time research fellow at the University of Birmingham developing an understanding of Christian thought from the perspective of disabled people. Born visually impaired, Jane uses a guide dog.

The next time you find yourself in a busy place, pause for a moment and shut your eyes. In a few seconds, a sense of disorientation compels you to open your eyes and reassert your independence. The world of a visually-impaired person is small. It stretches as far as a cane will reach or a guide dog will lead. It contains much that is unidentifiable, frightening and inconclusive.

John Hull in *Touching the Rock* writes frankly about the difference losing his sight made to him as a committed Christian. Helen Keller's philosophy of life summed up in Anna Sullivan's biography of this deaf-blind woman, perhaps captures best the essence of a life without visual images: 'Life is a daring adventure or it is nothing at all.'

2nd Sunday in Lent, March 3   John 9.1-12 *

How were your eyes opened?

The blind man, at his regular spot, waited for donations. A familiar figure, caught-up in his interior world, non-productive in society's eyes, known for his disability and not for who he was – the story he had to tell.

Jesus was quick to dismiss any connection between sinfulness and disability. He stressed that the man had been born as God intended him to be so that God's own power might be displayed. The man received from Christ the gift of sight. He did not seek the gift, but he did recognize the uniqueness of the giver and accepted his part in enabling Christ to fulfil his destiny as Messiah. He defended Jesus to those who were curious. Once blind, he was now a physical manifestation of the Light of the World illuminating and energizing every aspect of life. He seized, with all his heart and mind, new life with God.

✳ *God of darkness and light,*
touch me gently, speak to me softly, and guide me
on the path towards your healing and love. Amen

Monday March 4　　　　　　　　　　　　　　　　*John 9.13-34* *

Let him speak for himself

The man's change of circumstance defied conventional teaching. It spoke of power, mystery and energy. The Pharisees failed to see the truth. As the man told his story with conviction and simplicity – so the Pharisees' shallowness was exposed.

The man who was identified by what he lacked, was suddenly known by all he had gained. He faced the Pharisees and explained the nature of Jesus as he then understood it – Jesus was a healer working through God's power and blessing. Change is painful. The Pharisees returned to their trusted Law. The man, healed, faced disbelief in others, yet still chose to embrace new life.

Change is about perceiving an opportunity and daring to risk engaging with the new and different; turning from the darkness to the light.

✳ *God of love,*
let my lips speak of all you have done for me.
Let my voice sing your praise.
Let my heart yearn to be what you would have me be
and let my mind long to pray. Amen

Tuesday March 5　　　　　　　　　　　　　　　　*John 9.35-41* *

Jesus found him

The blind man never once sought Jesus. Thrown out by the Pharisees, he was told in no uncertain terms that either he or his parents had sinned. The man could not fail to be hurt and dejected as those in authority reduced his dignity and worth once again. An old, familiar pattern within him – feeling set apart and seen as different – returned. Although physically healed, he was still regarded as an outcast. The thing he had most wanted brought him pain as well as joy.

Jesus sought him out. Jesus recognized his need before he saw it in himself. Jesus drew the man on in his understanding. The man recognized the invitation and fell on his knees: 'Lord, I believe.'

✳ *Light of the world,*
you know our needs before we cry to you.
You know our hopes before we dare to dream them.
Find us and fill us with your light and love.

Wednesday March 6   Mark 4.10-12
Seeing is believing
My father was a professional magician. He did impossible tricks with playing cards, coins, and all sorts of things. He often said: 'The quickness of the hand deceives the eye.' The harder you look to see how a trick is done, the less likely you are to discover! We all know that awful feeling when we lose something important. I've learnt, as a visually-impaired person, that searching is often frustrating, so I sit down and work out a timetable: when did I last have it? What happened next and so on. In the quietness of reflecting, the object is usually found.

The blessing of spiritual insight is a gift that God gives to those who are devoted followers. On our faith pilgrimage it is all too easy to become caught up in the searching for greater vision and fail to see the bountiful joys our limited 'vision' is already showing us.

✳ *O Thou who hast given me eyes*
to see the light that fills my room,
give me the inward vision to behold thee in this place.
             C Devanesen, India – Morning Noon and Night (CMS)

Thursday March 7   Revelation 3.14-22
What are you looking for?
I have yet to meet a blind person who does not long to see. Blindness makes you vulnerable. You are public property. You have little privacy. You are a pull on the resources, an object of concern and care. You are the sum total of what others suspect you cannot do.

Laodicea was charged with being 'blind and naked', vulnerable in the midst of greater strength – the power of God. 'Blindness' here is used in an insulting way; it is not a means of greater stillness and insight, but the inability of a community to see the error of their ways. Here, the writer assumes that physical sightlessness equates with an inability to see truth – stumbling in the path of God. The writer's image is not a helpful one. In reality, if you don't know where you're going, a blind person is one of the safest people to guide you: s/he knows every centimetre of the route!

The charge against Laodicea and each one of us is that we allow pride to get in the way of our love of Christ and action in his name.

✳ *The things, good Lord, that we pray for, give us grace to labour for.*

St Thomas More (1478-1535)

Friday March 8   *2 Kings 6.8-17* ✳
Standing in the need of prayer
Fear causes blind spots in all of us. Elisha's servant faced his own fear – that he might be captured by the enemy. He returned panic-stricken to his master. It was Elisha's prayer that the servant would see things in perspective that turned the story round.

The able-bodied often pray for the less able. In this story the power of intercession is in mutuality, recognizing the often hidden prayers of other people and folding them into our own prayers for ourselves. Elisha's prayer that his servant's eyes would be opened to see the massive power and strength of God's own army was also a cry that Elisha would himself trust the 'chariots of fire' and not visualize a city in destruction.

Look not only for support from those who seem stronger and better, but also to those who seem weaker and more vulnerable.

✳ *Open my eyes God,*
to see the potential and not the problem,
to spot the opportunity and not halt at the obstacle,
to gaze on difference and make it my own.   *Amen*

Life in Christ

Light and dark are powerful images of good and evil; life with Christ and life outside the community of the faithful.

For a person who cannot see well, the contrast and definition of light can be distorted. Light can be diffused or a pinprick of perception in an otherwise dark panorama. Light can actually blind rather than help to locate where a person is. Light is most effective as a metaphor for illumination; for focusing the truths that no one can actually see; a metaphor for viewing the universe; a vocabulary for framing and responding to the question of all time: why?

The light for all Christians is the light of firsthand encounter with Christ. We are encouraged to be comfortable with our experience, to be courageous in sharing, to delight in life and so point others to the power of God's interaction with creation.

✳ *May the light of God dance in my heart,*
the warmth of God sparkle in my eyes
and fall from my lips,
the energy of God make me open to wisdom and love.

For personal reflection or group discussion

God promises that he will bring good news to the poor, free the oppressed and restore sight to the blind (Luke 4.18). How can I award more dignity and mutuality to those who are different from myself? To those who frighten me or make me feel uncomfortable?

ACTION

Make an effort to talk to people with disabilities. Get to know each disabled person as an individual. Try not to assume too much or ask too many personal questions. When I am asked , 'Why are you blind?' after three minutes acquaintance, I often feel like asking the enquirer something equally personal in retaliation! Don't be put off by your own awkwardness or uncertainty. People with disabilities are used to dealing with non-disabled peoples' anxieties. Award the person with disabilities the same level of dignity, independence and courtesy you would give to your greatest friends. Allow them to tell their story and inform you. Enjoy sharing your true self with them.

LENT – TREE OF LIFE

Notes based on the New English Bible by

Desmond Gilliland

Des Gilliland is an Irish Methodist minister, now retired. He has been a missionary in China and Hong Kong. In Ireland, alongside his circuit ministry, he has been chaplain to Dublin Universities and Secretary of Committees on Social Welfare and World development. He also writes verse and has used some of it to illustrate this week's theme.

A tree is a living organism in which the diversity of underground roots, trunk, branches, twigs, leaves, flowers and fruit are held together by a mysterious life-force to form a harmonious unity.

Humankind longs for such a unity. Significantly the Bible begins with a story of innocent unity in Eden,

> Adam and Eve in total harmony.
> Love, work and play, inseparable.
> The forbidden tree and the Tree of Life
> Easily acceptable with all the rest.
> Looking at his planet's life
> and at the pair in their contented mood
> God loved the world that he had made,
> and saw that it was good.

Our theme is also **Paradise – Lost and Regained.**

3rd Sunday in Lent, March 10   Genesis 3.1-13

Unity shattered

In *Paradise Lost* Milton sets the root of discord further back – in heaven itself, in Satan's choice of pride and power instead of mutual love, and we take up the theme as a contrast to Eden's harmony:

> How different from that happy pair
> Was he whose pride
> Could not find peace in heaven itself,
> Where, within the harmony of mutual joy
> God ministered to all his heavenly ones,

The serving source of every perfect gift,

Such benevolence humiliated Satan.
He could not bear to be beholden.
Nor could he see in heaven's loving service
Anything but slavery. He made his choice.
To be great was to rule and to command!

So he rebelled, and even in defeat
Chose the harsh littleness of ruling hell
Before the greatness of forgiven share
Within the free heaven of the Father's love.

For Adam and for Eve, God knew
The time must also come to choose
Or else be discontented with their Eden there
And take the Satan path of self and pride.

✱ *'Choose you this day whom you will serve' (AV).*
Lord, help us as we make the choice
every hour of every day.

Monday March 11   Genesis 3.14-24

The nature of loss: division

The serpent's foremost task was to divide
The minds of those for whom all life was one;
To sunder labour and pleasure
In those for whom both work and leisure
Were twin companionable gifts of God.

To those already in God's image made
He sketched a demon God of power and pride.
'Assert yourselves. You too can be as Gods.
The way lies open now for you to choose!'
They chose so-called divinity and found
but dead-sea fruit on Eden's ground
and all creation trembled at their loss.

Eden was shattered. But evil and good
Battled on Earth together. Could
A new Adam choose a Tree of Life?
Restore lost unity? Lead the Rebel Race
Into a new Eden state of *conscious* grace?

67

* **Lord God, we thank you that you did not leave us
but through your covenants with Noah and Moses
and the message of the prophets,
you gave us a Messiah, a new Adam for all humanity.**

Tuesday March 12   *John 15.1-10*

The new Adam – the Tree of Life

At one leap we have skipped the long centuries of the Old
Testament and find Jesus speaking of himself as a Tree of Life.
We are invited to find our lost Eden by sharing in the life of the
vine. But does the miracle really work?

I thought to muse upon the theme
And soberly reflect upon the plan
Of restoring our lost Eden by the scheme
Of setting God's own image in a perfect Man.
But turning to the Gospel writings found
Not mere conjecture or a hopeful dream,
But cries of certainty from all around!

Constant usage blunts the shock of wonder
As the writers seek to catch the glory
Of their sure belief within a net of words
Sketched to breaking by the amazing story.

'In the beginning was the Word', with God,
All things that live were alive with his life
And that life was the light of all creation
And the Word became flesh and dwelt among us.
Adam's children still would not receive Him,
Seeking still a king of serpent power and pride,
But to those who were tempted by his goodness
To take the fruit of the Vine of Life,
To them he gave again the heritage, lost in Adam,
Of bearing the image of the sons and daughters of God.

* **O lift us up, strong Son of God;
Restore your fallen race;
We who have lost your image shall
Regain it by your grace.**

© *Cyril Hambly*

The new life is for sharing

Life in the.Vine, like that of Eden – and Heaven – was not a life of individual bliss but of shared and serving joy. In this passage the fruit of the vine is seen in terms of mutual love. In all the Bible, holiness is social holiness. The covenant with Noah envisages a harmony, a SHALOM which includes all living things and the planet itself.

> The world is still a garden, an Eden blue and green
> Where still we stand before the tree of serpent knowledge,
> Believing still the ancient evil myth
> That good life comes by force and greed
> And exploitation of our planet home.
> The Tree of Life offers instead its fruit
> Of peaceful knowledge, of a planet shared,
> Offers the Jesus way of Truth and Life
> Where we, united in a holiness of mutual love,
> Take on the image of the servant Lord.

✴ *Lord, how realistically do we pray*
'Thy will be done on earth as it is in heaven'?
At what cost to ourselves?

The Tree of Life in the Early Church

Paul had a painful experience of the Tree of the Knowledge of Good and Evil. In the tension between right and wrong he had committed himself to what was good, to the perfect moral law. He had taken on evil and fought it, and was defeated.

> 'The good that I would I do not: but the evil that I would not, that I do ... Wretched man that I am! who shall deliver me ...?' (Romans 7.19 and 24 AV)

Deliverance there was. In the Cross, a baleful Tree of Death, he finds, with all Christians not only a Tree of Life but a Tree where God's love is poured out in redemption from the burden of sin.

> 'See from his head, his hands, his feet,
> sorrow and love flow mingled down ...   *Isaac Watts*

That hymn has an unlikely parallel in a song by Johnny Cash:

> 'From his hands down ... from his feet down ...
> from the crimson dew the Tree of Life grew.'

Paul found salvation in the Cross. He also saw the new life as **a recovery of Eden**. 'As in Adam all die even so in Christ shall all be made alive.'

✳ *Jesus Christ, whose life poured out on a cursed tree,*
   your blood sets me free and makes me whole.

Heaven after a right choice was made!

Here we are in a region beyond time, in a vision of perfection where Eden is not only restored but surpassed. William Blake wrote *Songs of Innocence* and *Songs of Experience*. In Eden the song was of innocent unreflecting pleasure and unity. In this passage the song is of experience, of full knowledge and understanding. Among those in heaven were ones who had 'passed through the great ordeal' and washed their robes and made them white in the blood of the Lamb'. Now all is complete and the scene is one in which the new Eden has a River of the Water of Life, and Trees of Life for the healing of the world, where the people of heaven with the name of God on their foreheads see God face to face. Unlike some other parts of Revelation it has a quietness which I feel is true to the way of Jesus.

The Gospel says he made himself of no account,
As always, showing us God's image in a servant form
And in the end laid down for us his very life.
Even when he broke the grave he did not come in pride:
Unaltered still the quietness of his servant way.
Be not afraid. It is just myself, he said.
Glory there was, and they beheld it, not assertive, but
Born of his inner self, as unforced as the fragrance of a
      flower.

What was true on earth is true in heaven. It could not be that he should lead us into the new Eden like Lucifer, with force and pride.

✳ *O lowly majesty,*
   Lofty in lowliness
   Blest Saviour, who am I
   To share thy blessedness?
Yet thou hast called me, even me
   Servant divine, to follow thee.

George Wallace Briggs

Journey's end

We have come all the way from Eden to the vision of Eden
restored in these last verses of the last book in the Bible. It is a
joyful conclusion. We all love a victory. We must, however,
remember always that this is a victory of suffering love which
emptied itself, taking the form of a servant. That is the sort of
community which has been created. In heaven the authentic
symbols are still the wounded hands and feet of Jesus, and the
towel and basin for humble service. Those in heaven are those
who have entered by repentance and forgiveness into a society
of mutual serving love.

We tend, I believe, to see heaven's victory in our usual sense
of wiping out opposition and celebrating triumph in a final form.
Such a triumphalism is natural and creeps into our hymns and
sermons. But such a triumph would be far too easy for God.
Less than the blink of an eye could accomplish it and it would
not be victory in God's terms. Coercive power is rather Satan's
role. The Tree of Life – whether the Cross or the True Vine,
leaves each one of us to choose. That is not a way which offers
a tidy solution but an open-ended one, a Kingdom in which
God's will is freely done.

So we move forward. The last words of the last book in the
Bible are movingly relevant and very simple:

✳ ***The grace of the Lord Jesus be with you all.***

For personal reflection or group discussion and
ACTION

The theme of the Tree of Life includes all time, all creation and
all the history of God and humanity. We have applied the
principle of serving love rather than dominion both to God and
ourselves as the list of true reality. Is this acceptable to us? Do
we feel that in our own lives we need to *win*? cf. 'Blessed are the
poor in spirit for their's is the Kingdom of Heaven' (Matthew 5.3
– AV) – and the Tree of Life!

71

LENT – SET APART

Notes based on the New International Version by

Ebere O Nze

Eberechukwu Nze, a Nigerian theologian who has travelled widely and represented his Church in many international conferences and seminars, is Principal of the Methodist Theological Institute in Umuahia, Abia State, Nigeria.

'Set apart' suggests a sense of sacredness, the idea of holiness, set apart for a specific purpose. The level of sacredness depends upon the use to which a person's life is put, and the sanctity of a holy object or place of worship depends on the attitude of the worshippers.

Christians have been described as 'people set apart'. Jesus chose and nurtured twelve men for a specific task, to hand down the faith, and this role has been bequeathed to all of us. Lent is a period re-appraisal when we seek to become more aware of the demands of the gospel. As you read and meditate upon this week's passages, may the Lord sanctify your life for holy use. Amen

---

4th Sunday in Lent, March 17   John 12.1-8 *

Set apart for reciprocity

Notice the extraordinary hospitality given to Jesus at the home of Lazarus in Bethany. They gave a supper in honour of Jesus. Martha served, Lazarus stayed at table with Jesus to show his gratitude for having been raised from the dead, and Mary anointed Jesus with a costly perfume. On the contrary, Judas protested, and his protest must have been in line with the attitude of the chief priests who resolved to do away with Jesus.

To which group do you belong? To reject Jesus here on earth is to miss him in heaven, and to show hospitality to him is to prepare to sup with him eternally. Let every act of yours today be a means of showing love and gratitude to Jesus, for he raised you from sin and death and pointed you to the path of salvation. As God's people, we are set apart to reciprocate the loving act of God in sending his Son to give his life a ransom for many. That is why the Church set Sunday apart as a day of worship and rest. Every aspect of our worship must be a means of thanksgiving for God's great love for all people.

✳ *Our dear Lord,*
continue to knock at the door of every heart
that we may learn to welcome and sup with you
all our days.   Amen

Monday March 18   John 12.20-26 *

The death that makes us different

One of the main truths of our faith is the paradox that only by death comes life. Jesus emphasized this when he said, 'I tell you the truth ...' (verse 24). Experience has shown that the more we seek to be satisfied by material things, the more they do not satisfy and the more we seek them. Jesus uses the example of the seed which has to rot and die to bring forth new life. Like Jesus we must shed and bury personal aims and ambitions, pride and earthly desires before we can live the real life in God in whom we will find eternal security.

These words follow the arrival of some Greeks who wanted to see Jesus (verses 20-21). Not only is the writer of the Gospel pointing to the universal mission of Jesus, but through Jesus' answer (verses 22-26) implies that this letting go of life involves the shedding of national pride to enter fully into the richness and variety of God's world.

✳ *Our living Lord,*
who has chosen us to share the life you offer,
take from us those desires
that strengthen only the flesh,
that we may share in the joy of your Kingdom.   Amen

Tuesday March 19   John 12.27-36 *

Refined by suffering

Jesus was deeply troubled at the prospect of pain, but because he came to do the will of his Father, he subjected himself to suffering so that God might be glorified. Here again he spoke of the universal significance of his death (verse 32). Notice the crowd's failure to understand him. First of all, what was for Jesus a high moment of affirmation from God (verse 28) was for most of them nothing more than a rumble of thunder (verse 29). And his words about being lifted up as the supreme sacrifice were lost on them, and so they retreated to 'what the Law says' (verse 34). And Jesus, becoming more deeply involved in confrontation, went into hiding (verse 36), knowing the loneliness of standing by the truth.

We can only win with Christ if we suffer with him. Achievements are never exciting unless they have been struggled for. Triumph is not without a cost. Although we hold on to this life, it causes us pain to subdue it. Jesus shows that suffering, pain and death refine us to become people of the Kingdom. To win with Christ, you must fight the battle with the strength he supplies. Human strength causes tension while the strength of Christ gives certainty and light. Have you been refined by the Spirit of God?

✴ *Good Lord, may your strength give us courage*
to endure whatever suffering we may encounter today,
that we may win with you.   Amen.

Wednesday March 20   1 Samuel 9.27 to 10.7 *

Set apart for leadership

After the corrupt leadership of Samuel's sons, the people of Israel asked for a King, like other nations. Saul's anointing was not a public occasion; it was too sacred for that. In Old Testament tradition, anointing signified separation to the Lord for a particular task and a divine equipping for it. Samuel's question, 'Has not the LORD anointed you leader over his inheritance?' affirmed the appointment. Whenever God calls anyone, he equips and offers signs of his support. Leadership of any kind, whether religious, social, political or academic should be understood as God's appointment (see Romans 13.1).

Saul had been looking for his father's asses, but found a kingdom! A simple agricultural man was elevated to kingship (1 Samuel 2.6-8), chosen by a compassionate God to become 'a new Moses', to deliver his people from their new enemy the Philistines. 'God is with you,' said Samuel, and the onrush of the Spirit's power in his life made him no longer recognizable as the son of Kish. His future kingship was a sign of God's promise to be with his people.

✴ *Lord, may your constant presence guide us*
as we use the authority you have given us.   Amen

We also are God's anointed

Paul had promised to visit the Corinthians and later changed his mind, so as not to cause them pain (verse 23). They had accused Paul of vacillating, saying that if they could not trust his promises how could they believe the gospel he preached. Paul replied that we can rely on God. God is faithful and never changes. There is no vacillation in Jesus, and the message which the apostles had preached is as faithful as Jesus Christ, the 'Yes' of God.

Although the Corinthians were slandering Paul, yet the truth is that the trustworthiness of the messenger affects the message. The Christian's daily life and demeanour promote or retard the effectiveness of the gospel to the hearers. How then do you convey the gospel to those who are thirsty for the Word? Remember you have been set apart to do this. Learn to look beyond the messenger to see Christ who never changes. He has set his seal on us by the power of the Holy Spirit. This is his guarantee.

✻ *Our faithful, gracious Father,*
who remains the same and never changes,
pour your Holy Spirit into our hearts,
that we may depend upon your eternal changelessness,
and serve you with confidence, in Jesus' name. Amen

God acts alone

In symbolic language, this prophet of post-exilic Judah asks, 'Who is this ...?' 'It is I, speaking in righteousness, mighty to save', says a warrior who symbolizes the glorious victory obtained over those who have committed excessive cruelty against God's people. But as the warrior continues speaking, it becomes clear that the speaker is God himself (verses 3-6). For only God could vindicate his people, and redress the injustices done to them by Egyptians, Assyrians, Babylonians and their ancient enemy the Edomites. Bozrah was the capital of Edom where victory had been won over the Edomites who had triumphed in the destruction of Jerusalem by the Chaldeans (Psalm 137.7).

God, who is a God of judgment and redemption has been faithful to his side of the Covenant. But he is God of all and judges both the enemies of his people and members of the restored community who disobey and do not trust God's power to save. Where do you see God at work vindicating nations and communities in the world today?

✻ *Lord God, through faith*
we have received the seal of the Kingdom
and belong to the company of those you have
*   vindicated.*
May the joy of knowing your power be our strength
and may we always depend on this. Amen

Saturday March 23   *Colossians 2.8-15 **

Set apart through baptism

In this week's notes, the expression 'member of the Kingdom' has been deliberately used to remind us of the special role Christians have been called to play. In a corrupt world where ideologies tend to erode the truth of righteousness, Christians need a mark by which they can be identified. During the time of Paul, there were false teachers who demanded that Gentile Christians should be circumcised to set them apart as God's chosen people.

Paul goes deeper to explain that circumcision does not remove the part of human nature that sets us against God. Through baptism, a symbol of spiritual circumcision, we are buried with Christ and raised with him through faith in the power of God who raised him from the dead. If anyone is in Christ, that person is a new creature and a Christlike quality of life will be the mark of his or her faith. Is this the mark of yours?

✻ *Our heavenly Father,*
you have called us to be redeemed by your Son.
Make us faithful to your call,
in Christ our Lord. Amen

For personal reflection or group discussion

Read Ephesians 4.14-16. What are the implications of growing up into Christ?

Assess how far your local congregation has maintained the qualities of the Early Church as recorded in Acts 2.41-47.

ACTION

How can we become more like the first Christians? Make your own plan of action.

LENT – SHOW US THE FATHER

Notes based on the New Revised Standard Version by

Melvyn Matthews

Melvyn Matthews is the Vicar of Chew Magna with Dundry, two villages south of Bristol. Here he is the pastor to working and retired professional people in a strikingly beautiful rural setting. He has worked as the Director of an ecumenical centre for reconciliation and peace and has written a number of books on prayer.

You probably know that when Greek tragedies were performed the players wore masks and that in the dramatic traditions of other cultures, such as the Indian Kathakali or the Japanese Noh plays, the actors are heavily made up. When we come to St. John's Gospel, and in particular to the passion narrative, we might feel that we are entering the same sort of world, where Jesus is a divine figure moving with great dignity to his death, but able to soliloquise about it as he goes. The human elements of his person are hidden behind or underneath the divine being who is there playing out the drama. The mask has replaced the man. Here is the divine Son of God who moves with wonderful pathos, but total control, through the drama of death which was prepared for him from the beginning, and so returns to his divine home.

But there is more to it than that, for here too we have the man, the archetypal man, going slowly and inexorably back to the Father. He has come from God and is returning to God as John so frequently says.

This is the way we must all go if we are to return to the Father who made us and set us on our journey. These passages are not just about Jesus, but also a set of images about us, and our destiny. What we are reading about is the human journey through betrayal and death back to God. As somebody once said, – 'everyone in the world is Christ, and they are all crucified'.

Christ the scapegoat

Just as the raising of Lazarus (11.1-44) merges into the raising
of Jesus, so the plot by Caiaphas to kill Jesus moves very
quickly from the political to the theological. The elimination of
Jesus is seen as politically expedient – it will save the nation
from disaster – but the ostensibly political statement, 'It is better
for you to have one man die for the people than to have the
whole nation destroyed' (verse 50) is also a statement about the
redemptive power of Jesus' death, and these implications are
immediately drawn out by the Evangelist. As so often in John
everything runs into everything else – Lazarus merges into
Jesus, and the political and theological merge into each other.

Those in political positions should remember that theology is
never very far away. Any decision to sacrifice one person for the
sake of the whole has theological implications. Christ the
Scapegoat prefigures all other scapegoats and gives pause, or
should do, to those who would create them.

Jesus withdraws and remains with his disciples. The word
'remains' (verse 54) is a deeply Johannine word – he knows
what is going on but he rests in God.

✴ **God, when conflicts arise,**
  help us to rest in you
  rather than fuel the flames of division
  and make scapegoats where we need not.

The glory of it all

Each of the Evangelists record the story of Jesus' entry into
Jerusalem, and so it has deep and rich significance. It refers
back to the prophet Zechariah (9.9) and on to the triumph of the
Messiah. The particular point that John makes is that the
disciples did not realize what was going on at the time. They
only realized its significance after he was 'glorified' – that is,
after his death and resurrection, when they were able to look
back on the events of his life and see them for what they truly
were.

When we have been through the death and resurrection of
Jesus, taken it into ourselves and understood its 'glory', then the
events of our own life will make more sense than they would
otherwise do, because they will be seen to be part of what God

is doing in us. Everything will then be seen to have a glory. As the Psalmist says 'In your light we see light' (Psalm 36.9).

✴ *God, give us the confidence to look at our lives*
through the glory of your cross and resurrection
and so to see the true pattern which you have woven.

Tuesday March 26   *John 13.1-20* *

The glory of serving one another

In his account of the Last Supper John does not show Jesus as sharing bread and wine with the disciples and uttering the words of institution, 'This is my body, this is my blood ...' Instead he describes the washing of feet and talks about the necessity of mutual service.

It is as if John is saying, 'Do you really know what the eucharist means? If you are more concerned with what Jesus said rather than what this event means, then you may well have missed the point. It is the meal at which our participation in the witness of Jesus as the servant of all becomes real.' If we celebrate the eucharist and do not serve each other then the eucharist has had no meaning. Jesus himself said that we should first be reconciled to our brother and then offer our gift at the altar (Matthew 5.23-26). John's description of the last supper embodies that teaching. The Church has consistently risked losing its hold on Jesus' teaching at this point because of its need to argue about proper words and proper authority.

✴ *God, give us grace to know to whom we truly belong*
and when we share the bread of your life
and the cup of your passion,
make us one in mutual service in both deed and truth.

Wednesday March 27   *John 13.21-28*

The glory of self sacrifice

Here the slow dramatic nature of John's passion narrative is clearly seen, for the divine Jesus is filled with knowledge about who will betray him and gives the piece of bread with slow meaningfulness to Judas Iscariot. Judas' disappearance into the night of betrayal is immediately contrasted with Jesus' words about how the glory of God is manifest in his person – the drama is complete. The important thing is not to allow our modern suspicion of the dramatic nature of John's narrative to obscure just what it is that is glorified or what is significant. What is being glorified is the acceptance of suffering and loss. The true way to greatness is not through splendour but by the humble acceptance of what we are and of what sacrifice God calls forth in us. What is glorified is the way of love and self sacrifice, not the way of power and control – that is the way which Judas has espoused.

✳ *God give us grace to live by the truth of love*
   which may be hidden but which is the true glory.

Thursday March 28   *John 18.1-11* *
God's love of peace
Once again a dramatic incident is portrayed by John. Jesus says 'I am he' three times, and the soldiers fall to the ground as if struck down by some divine power. The original incident would have been dramatic but John brings out all the power of a moment of recognition of the divine. But it is not power that Jesus seeks but peacefulness. Jesus seems to move through these incidents with calmness and great insight into what is happening. He is in supreme and calm control. He demonstrates his concern for peace and lack of panic by his request for the freedom of the disciples and by telling the disciples themselves to put up their bright swords. These concerns are the true concerns of God – love for others and love of peace.

✳ *God, give us the same calm*
   in dealing with the hurly burly of life
   that Jesus showed at his passion,
   that we may see what is happening through your eyes
   and not our own.

Friday March 29   *John 18.12-27* *
Our frailty
It is interesting to pick out some of the details of the denial of Peter which have been highlighted by the Evangelist. In the garden of Gethsemane Jesus had said 'I am he' – three times. In this Gospel this is immediately followed by Peter's threefold denial, 'I am not'. This highlights the Evangelist's concern to show that Jesus is divine, while Peter, like us, is all too human and frail. Perhaps also the repeated references to the fact that

Peter was warming himself (verses 18 and 25) are intended to show that Peter at this point was part of this world, along with the slaves and the police, finding the comforts of this world more important than acknowledging the divinity of Jesus.

✳ *God, our frailty is like Peter's, often all too evident.*
Give us courage to follow you to the end
and to remain with you
even when we have to lose this world to do so.

Saturday March 30   *John 18.28-40* *

The struggle between life and death

In the dialogue with Pilate, Jesus is once again shown by the Evangelist as calm and regal, fearless in the face of interrogation and calmly asserting that his kingship – in implied contrast, of course, to that of Pilate – is not of this world. Jesus asserts that he is concerned not with political struggles but with the struggle between the power of God and the power of this world, between darkness and truth.

It is worth remembering that for the Evangelist the truth is not something which is said so much as something which is done. And Jesus, in the deed of his death, is finally doing the truth of God, loving his people until the end. Because Pilate cannot see that, and is merely concerned with trying to sort out political intrigue, then Jesus always replies and behaves as if he were somewhere else, in the realm of the deeper struggle for the truth of God.

✳ *God, help us to see beyond the struggles of everyday*
into the struggle between life and death,
so that we may set our hearts
where true joys are to be found.

For personal reflection or group discussion

Think of an occasion when you felt that a conflict you were involved in was 'cosmic' in scope, and raised issues of great importance. Reflect on how you behaved and whether you were so much part of Christ that you could see what was happening through God's eyes rather than your own. What lessons can you learn?

Here is the man

The writer of John's Gospel makes it clear where the blame for Jesus' death lies, and it is not with Pilate. Time and again Pilate tries to push the accusation back to 'the Jews' but in the end he gives in. 'The Jews' – and we should be careful not to see these references as encouraging anti-Judaism in our own day – have added a charge of blasphemy (verse 7). Perhaps they hope that such a charge will make Pilate think that Jesus is one who will cause civil disturbance. So Pilate asks Jesus, 'Where are you from?'. Like any apparently innocuous question in this Gospel, this is not without rich significance. The Evangelist has already made it clear (e.g. 13.3) that Jesus came from God and is on his way back to God. Jesus' silence only reinforces that belief. And so John's theological understanding of the origin and destiny of Jesus is borne out by the actual events which he records.

But Jesus is not just 'from God' as if he is some divine being. John also makes it clear that he is 'the man' as Pilate says 'Here is the man' (verse 5). Martin Luther's hymn picks up this theme when it says Jesus is 'the proper man'. He is the one who stands upright when we do not, the one who is really man as man was intended to be. Some see here a reference to the myth of the primal man. Perhaps we should just say that at his trial Jesus is 'everyone' and includes us all, staying true to God on our behalf and in our place, and that we can see our proper reality in him alone.

✴ *God, we know that Jesus stood accused,*
and that whereas we would be guilty
he stands free and true.
Help us to see ourselves in him,
to be free with him and so return to you.

Everything is full of God

The narrative continues full of hidden meanings. Pilate's apparent error in making the inscription say 'Jesus, king of the Jews' reveals the theological truth about him. The Jews, meanwhile, do not want to admit this truth and so try to persuade Pilate to say, 'he said that he was the King of the Jews'. Once again external events are understood by the Evangelist to illustrate the hidden truth about Jesus.

Similarly, Jesus' seamless robe symbolizes the unity of the people for whom he dies – '... so that they may be one, as we are one' (17.11). Psalm 22, which is quoted here, is a messianic psalm and shows that even the soldiers, in working out how to divide the garments of Jesus, are caught up in the messianic event. John's view is that if this is the deed of God, who performs his deed of truth in Jesus, then everything connected with this event is mysteriously significant. For modern readers these hidden meanings in actual events may become a little difficult to swallow and we may yearn, perhaps, for the plain truth. Did it happen just like this? Is not the link between event and symbol becoming a little overstrained?

Reflection shows that nothing ever happens 'just like that'. Every event is full of significance for each of us. In the light of John's narrative and the Gospels' interpretation of the death of Jesus, we are faced with two alternatives: we can either believe that nothing which happens is of any significance at all, and all is a tale told by an idiot, or we can trust that everything that now happens is full of God, and nothing is outside of his divine care.

✱ *God, enable us to see your hand at work in all things and draw us closer to yourself.*

Tuesday April 2   *John 19.28-42 ✱*

A sacrifice of praise

And so Jesus dies. He says that his work is finished. This is not a cry of despair or a last exhausted gasp, but a deep cry of triumph. The Word of God has completed the work he was sent to accomplish. The death is the final act of triumph. It should be stressed that, in John's account, Jesus is always seen to be in control, an agent and not a passive recipient. Notice how John makes this very clear in the narrative by omitting references to Jesus having to give up the cross to Simon of Cyrene. The text says clearly that he carries the cross himself (19.17).

We might be used to thinking that Jesus dies and then waits for the triumph of the resurrection which reverses disaster. John makes it clear that the cross is not something which has to be reversed but which completes, and the resurrection is the sign that that has been done. Cross and resurrection are not two distinct theological moments in John, but are both indicative of the triumph of Jesus. As the Anglican Book of Common Prayer has it, this is 'a sacrifice of praise'

* *God, help us to know that Jesus gave his life for us*
  by giving up ourselves to you in a sacrifice of praise
  and thanksgiving, every day. Amen

Wednesday April 3   *Isaiah 50.4-9* *

A sacrifice of dignity

In several places in John's Gospel there are references and allusions to the servant passages in Isaiah, of which this is one. The first Christians found that the events of Jesus' passion were so perfectly mirrored in these poems. This one reflects the Johannine understanding of Jesus, the regal one, stoic at his death, in control of what is going on and able to point out to those who have eyes to see the true meaning of what is happening to him.

The dignity of the passion is always a dignity for others. In Primo Levi's account of his time in Auschwitz, there is a story of the old Jew who, even when there was no water, insisted on going through the motions of washing. When asked why, he said that there was no point in behaving like animals when we were really men. This incident gave Levi courage to fight on in the face of death.

* *God, give us courage to face death and may we know*
  that our courage is never for ourselves alone
  for in you we are all one. Amen

Maundy Thursday, April 4   *Jeremiah 31.31-34* *

A renewed love of God's law

This is the new commandment which Jesus gives to his disciples. Reading this passage enables us to realize that maybe he was quoting it directly at the Last Supper. This puts into context all of John's strictures against 'the Jew', which must be modified by understanding that Jesus was sharing with his disciples the faith of his ancestors as he understood it. 'The Jews' of John's Gospel were not 'the Jewish people'. At several points in the Gospel it is clear that there is a distinction between the two. Rather they were those who misunderstood what their faith was about. What crucified Jesus was not Judaism – which gave us Jesus himself as well as this wonderful passage about love – but a lack of perception of this prophecy from Jeremiah and, in the circumstances of the time, an unwillingness to put it into practice. Marcus Borg, in *Jesus – A New Vision*, (SPCK

1993) challenges our common assumption that Jesus was the founder of Christianity, and suggests that this is not historically true. 'Instead, his concern was the renewal of Israel.' He wanted the Law to be written in people's hearts. The task of Christianity is no different.

✳ *God, awaken us where we are blind to true religion;*
replace our hearts of stone with hearts of flesh
and write your new law of love on our innermost hearts.

Good Friday, April 5   *Colossians 1.18-23* ✳

The arms of love

When Jesus dies on the cross what sort of sacrifice is he making? This passage shows us that he is not a sacrifice to appease the anger of a righteous and wrathful God – such views are grotesque – but a total self offering, a self offering in love of which we are a part. He gathers us into himself by being the proper man, the inclusive man, of which St. John hints, and offering us in his body on the cross in praise and love to God. His work is the work of reconciliation, bringing back into unity that which – contrary to God's will – has become separate.

In the face of family estrangements those who bring the most unity are not always those who try to bring the parties together. They are those who, by their deep inner joy and unity with God, the source of their being, reach out to all members of the family and enable them by that joy to drop their differences. Jesus does just that. He reaches out to all of us from his life in God and enables us to share in that source of life. He brings a rich, deep unity where there was division. This reaching out is effected on the cross. It requires arms so long and a wait so long that he breaks with the load.

✳ *Here is God, no monarch he,*
throned in easy state to reign;
here is God, whose arms of love
aching, spent, the world sustain.   *W H Vanstone*
from Love's Endeavour, Love's Expense (DLT)

Holy Saturday, April 6   *John 14.1-14*

Sharing Christ's journey

At the end of Matthew's Gospel the angel tells the women at the empty tomb that Jesus will go before them to Galilee. In John's

Gospel Jesus himself tells all the disciples that he is going before them to the Father. So John sees the journey that Jesus and the disciples are engaged upon as cosmic rather than local. For him it is a highly symbolic journey from God, through betrayal and death, and then back to God.

First, John believes that this cosmic journey is contained in the local journey. He sees more in the local happening than the other Evangelists. Secondly, he is quite clear that all the disciples are on this journey with Jesus. His is not just an indicative journey, pointing where we might go, but an inclusive one, gathering us with him on the way.

✳ *God, give us eyes to see that the journey we travel*
is also Christ's journey to the Father
and give us grace to share that journey with him
with open eyes and expectant hearts. Amen

For personal reflection or group discussion

Reflect on incidents in your life, or your community, when peace and reconciliation were required. How did the protagonists behave? Did they tinker with things, negotiate over little issues, or did they reach back into the deep personal resources with which God provides each person and so bring peace from a deep well of life within them? Try to see what stops people from acting as Jesus did at his trial and what forces them to act like Pilate.

ACTION

Make a study, over the next month, of incidents in your newspaper where efforts at reconciliation succeeded. Work out why this was the case.

EASTER – Jesus comes to meet us

Notes based on the Revised English Bible by

Jan Sutch Pickard

Jan Sutch Pickard is the Editor of CONNECT, a Christian Magazine linking faith and action, as well as the yearly PRAYER HANDBOOK used by Methodists in many places. She is a lay preacher in the New Mills circuit in the Peak District (UK), and a member of the Iona Community.

Easter is a time of profound experiences for Christians, of stories and images which not only recreate the experiences of the first Easter, but link them to struggles and signs of hope in our everyday lives. Prepare for the next two weeks' notes by reading the first five verses of John's Gospel.

These readings and reflections begin 'while it was still dark' – in confusion and uncertainty. Gradually, as first one and then more of Jesus' followers encounter the risen Christ, it becomes clear that 'the light shines in the darkness, and the darkness has never mastered it'. But how do we communicate this conviction, and the way it changes our lives? Through many words, Gospels and epistles attempt to capture the reality of the Word, which was with God from the beginning, who is still coming into our lives and offering new life.

Easter Day, April 7   *John 20.1-18 **

While it was still dark

The resurrection story, shared anew each Easter, still has power to surprise us with its mystery and joy. It starts with things half-seen, scarcely understood: 'While it was still dark'. Mary, glimpsing the stone rolled away from the tomb, runs to tell the disciples. They rush and peer in, seeing the empty shroud glimmering in the first light, and return home believing that something tremendous has happened but unable to find words for it. The record here states that men 'saw and believed', since a woman's evidence was not acceptable in law.

Meanwhile Mary, weeping outside the tomb, sees angels and expresses her confusion. She sees Jesus, and does not recognize him, a dim figure in the half-light. Recognition comes when he calls her by name: with his loved voice and his affirmation of her as a person. But she is not allowed to touch him, to cling or to stay with him. Instead she is told to 'go' and share the good news with others. We know that the resurrection day has dawned, in all its unambiguous glory, when she tells them confidently, 'I have seen the Lord.'

✳ *Are there times in your life when you have moved from doubt to joyful certainty? Have you ever wanted to cling on to an experience, and yet needed to let go of it, to move on, or share what you have learned with others?*

✳ **Loving Lord,**
in the dark of the night we fear we have lost you,
on the edge of a new day we feel your presence.
May we hear you call us by name
and go to share your good news with the world,
in the light of your love. Amen

Monday April 8   *Matthew 28.1-10 ***

Do not be afraid

Matthew's version of the resurrection story has a different emphasis. There are two women – two Marys – not one. No disciples are mentioned here. There is cause for fear: armed guards at the tomb, then a violent earthquake, heralding an angel who rolls away the great stone, while the guards fall to the ground in terror.

The angel's words to the women, 'You have nothing to fear' echo the words of the angel to Joseph (Matthew 1.20), 'Do not be afraid to take Mary home with you to be your wife.' Or the angel to the awe-struck shepherds (Luke 2.10), 'Do not be afraid, I bring you good news.' As in John's account, the women are told to go – and on their way they meet Jesus. They fall and clasp his feet, with mingled joy and awe, and again are told, 'Do not be afraid,' and 'Go and take word ...'

✳ *What are you afraid of, just now? How would the words 'You have nothing to fear' set you free? What would you want to share with others?*

✳ **Do not be afraid for I have redeemed you.**
I have called you by name. You are mine.

He answered me

This jubilant song of pilgrims nearing their destination contains phrases which vividly describe stages in the pilgrimage of each of our lives. Reflect on what these words mean to you:

'When in distress I called to the LORD,
he answered me ...' (verse 5).

✳ *Offer to God that distress, which opened you to his love.*

'The Lord is my refuge and defence,
and he has become my deliverer' (verse 14).

✳ *Give thanks for places of refuge and times of deliverance.*

'The LORD did indeed chasten me,
but he did not surrender me to death' (verse 18).

✳ *How were you chastened? How has it changed you?*

'It is good to give thanks to the LORD,
for his love endures for ever' (verse 1).

✳ *What signs of God's enduring love do you see in your own life and in the world around you? What other phrases in the psalm are especially meaningful to you?*

✳ *You are my God and I shall praise you.*
My God, I shall praise you in my heart;
with men and women everywhere I thank you
because your love endures for ever. Amen

The taste of truth

An ancient Passover tradition, observed in orthodox Jewish households, and enjoyed by children, involves searching for any traces of yeast – or things made with yeast – to get rid of them. The first Passover was such a hasty meal that there was no time to let the dough rise; so the people ate unleavened bread. Leaven, which is recycled from one batch of baking to another, thus became a symbol of a way of life which was left behind.

Leaven (or yeast) is a great agent for change. Jesus compared the Kingdom of God to yeast (Luke 13.20). But here it signifies something different: 'the leaven of depravity', old and pervasive habits – a way of life which we need to leave behind if we are to follow Christ. Paul's picture of the Christian community – people changed for ever by Christ's sacrificial death on the cross – is of simple nourishing *matzos* crackers, or unleavened bread, fresh from the oven, tasting of God's truth.

✴ **Thank God, naming them, for those you know whose lives have the 'taste of truth'.**

Thursday April 11   *Romans 6.3-11 ***
Alive to God
On the banks of a slow-flowing river in Sri Lanka, people gather for a baptism. The place is a tea-estate, and the crowd mostly Tamil labourers from the estate. In the 'line-rooms' where they live, a group have been meeting to study the Bible and learn about the Christian faith. After a year the young minister, who has been meeting with them, felt they were ready to make a public confession of their faith. On the river banks stand men, women and children – families who wanted to take this step together. Their Hindu neighbours are also there, watching with gentle curiosity. The minister scrambles down into the muddy river, and one by one the people join him, waist deep in the water. They are immersed and come up dripping to change, behind a palm-leaf screen, into clean white shirts and saris. A young boy stands in the river, his eyes wide and anxious as the minister prays over him. He goes down and the water closes over his head; then he comes up, laughing with surprise, shaking the shining drops from his hair in joy. What has happened is a mystery. There are many ways his life could change – and go on changing. But right now he is alive to God.

✴ **Jesus, our brother, your death set us free from our sin;**
may we turn away from all that denies your love;
alive to God, may we begin a new life. Amen

Friday April 12   *John 20.19-23 ***
Peace be with you
What makes you afraid? Write down, or name aloud, some of the situations, or things, or people that you fear. Name them, and then put them – and yourself – into God's hands.

The disciples were afraid. They huddled together 'behind locked doors'. Sometimes we find safety in the same way, literally. Sometimes we 'lock doors' in our minds to stop ourselves from thinking about things that worry us.

The disciples had tried to shut the doors on all the terrifying events in Jerusalem. Suddenly Jesus was in their midst, surrounded by their fear, but greeting them with the word 'Peace', 'Shalom', 'Salaam'. When he showed them his wounds they saw it really was Jesus, and were filled with joy. Again, he calmed their overpowering emotions with the word 'Peace': a greeting for those imprisoned by their fear, and for those confused by joy. The Holy Spirit at once began to work in the lives of the disciples. One expression of that is something which we may find surprising: the power to forgive.

✻ *What do you find hard to forgive?*

Write down, or name aloud, an experience or a person you need to forgive.

✻ *Put them – and yourself – into God's hands. Amen*

Saturday April 13   *John 20.24-29 **

You have found faith

At some point in the history of the Church, Thomas seems to have been re-christened! In John's Gospel he is called 'Thomas the Twin', but most people today would recognize him as 'Doubting Thomas'. *Do you think this is fair?*

'Seeing is believing' is a popular maxim in many parts of the world, and Thomas wanted to see and touch for himself. For him, learning was experiential. He wanted to believe that Jesus was alive, but he was not prepared simply to take other people's words for it. The turning point of the story is not Thomas's doubt, but his encounter with the living Christ. For Jesus understood his need, and came part-way to meet him. Although the Gospel says that Jesus invited Thomas to touch his wounds, we are not told that the disciple did so. His response of heartfelt recognition, on seeing Jesus 'My Lord and my God!' can be compared to Mary's 'Rabbuni!' (John 20.16). Jesus' words in verse 29 do not emphasize Thomas's inadequacy, but different kinds of faith experiences.

✻ *Without the face-to-face meeting of Mary or Thomas, as described in John's Gospel, how has the resurrection become real to you? Is your faith based on a different kind of encounter with Jesus?*

✻ *Living Lord, you come to meet us*
in our moments of doubt and despair;
we cannot touch you, but you touch each one of us,
different as we are, in the depths of our being
and you bless us. Thank you. Amen

For personal reflection or group discussion
Go back over some of the questions in this week's notes.

1st Sunday after Easter, April 14   *John 20.30-31* *
Many other signs

How quickly we come down to earth! During the last week we have focused on a series of resurrection stories. These two verses offer no further story to echo down the centuries. And yet they stimulate our imagination. 'There were many other signs ... not recorded in this book.' John's Gospel hints at resurrection stories current at the time but not recorded. In the Synoptic Gospels there are at most four more stories in different versions and combinations. So the 'many other signs' mentioned here, if they refer to other resurrection stories, have been lost to us. And yet, do we need more?

The Gospel writer suggests that the aim is not to catalogue or to write a comprehensive account of resurrection appearances, but to record a few of these 'signs' to help those far away in space and time to 'believe that Jesus is the Christ, the Son of God' and through that faith to find new life.

✳ *Which story has spoken to you most directly this week?*

The open-endedness of 'many other signs' may make us think of stories we have heard in other contexts, about God at work in people's lives, in human history, where love has triumphed over hatred, and over despair, hope.

✳ **Recollect one such story, and thank God for this and other 'signs'.**

Monday April 15   *John 21.1-14*
Gone fishing

Close your eyes for a moment and recall the many vivid images of this story. Open them again, and look for just a few. 'Gone fishing' is the sign Simon Peter might have hung on his door. During Jesus' ministry he and the other fishermen had left their nets on many occasions to follow their teacher: through neighbouring towns and villages, where Jesus preached and healed the sick; away to pray in desert places, where the crowds followed and were fed; to Jericho, to Jerusalem. Now, in the uncertain time after Jesus' death, living with the many questions of the resurrection, Simon falls back on a familiar way of earning his daily bread – and the other disciples follow him.

After a frustrating night of fishing and catching nothing, they follow instructions shouted from the shore, cast the net on the other side of the boat and immediately feel it fill with fish. John recognizes Jesus – either by his voice or because of this 'sign'. Peter translates encounter into action, leaping over the side and splashing to the shore. The others tow in the net, full of fish. Some commentaries emphasize the quantity, others the variety of the catch. It is significant that the net is not broken. If the disciples are to become 'fishers of men' then their way of working, while not perfect – what human institution is? – needs to be adequate to the task.

'Come and have breakfast': Jesus' greeting is as down-to-earth as the disciples' needs after a hard night's work. Metaphorical fish don't feed hungry people. We can almost smell the fish Jesus is grilling over a fire. As so often, he and his friends share food together; they encounter Christ in the breaking of bread.

✳ *Have you ever felt the presence of Christ in a similar situation – an act of hospitality, a time of fellowship, a simple meal, a few words, when a workplace or home or a picnic was transformed ?*

✳ *God of surprises, you meet us in the everyday,*
you fill our poor nets with your rich creation,
with your living Word to be shared.
Thank you for the many ways you welcome and feed us,
put us to work, fulfil us, and meet our deepest needs.

Tuesday April 16   *John 21.15-19 **

Do you love me?

A common conversation begins 'If you really love me you would ...' Young men and women use it to put pressure on each other. Parents lay a burden of moral obligation on their children. Children see how far they can push this argument with their parents. All this is not surprising, for love is a powerful emotion that binds us together while baffling us about how to express it adequately.

When Jesus asked Simon Peter 'Do you love me?' he was not putting pressure or a burden of guilt on his friend, but giving an opportunity to express this love. Some commentators see the thrice-repeated affirmation as a way of 'undoing' Peter's triple denial of Jesus. Our love needs to be expressed not just in our words but through our actions. Those actions need to be done not just liturgically, but practically, for our fellow human beings – the 'sheep' and 'lambs' for whom the Good Shepherd died, for whom the disciples take up the responsibility of caring. Responsibility for our actions, as part of God's work in the world, may expose us to blame, persecution and suffering – which is where this conversation between Simon Peter and Jesus leads. There will come a time when this most active disciple will be helpless; when, a leader of the young church, he will be led to his death.

✶ *What other people can you name, who have followed Jesus to the death?*

✶ **Lord, we love you. Help us to learn how to express our love in what we do for others, how to understand your love in what is done for us, and how to suffer whatever happens to us, for your sake.**

Wednesday April 17   *John 21.20-25 ✶*

Being witnesses

Think of a fellow Christian whose way of experiencing and expressing his / her faith is very different from your own.

✶ *When have you been most aware of your differences? How can you learn from and help each other?*

In this passage two disciples, Peter and John, are mentioned together (see also John 20.2-8; 21.7). Each time their actions are linked, while showing different reactions to what is happening. Both, we are told, ran to the tomb. John reached it first, but he did not enter. The bolder Simon Peter did so, and saw the linen wrappings, but no body. Then his friend followed, 'saw and believed'. We are told that 'The disciple whom Jesus loved' recognized Jesus on the shore and told Peter 'It is the Lord' – but it was Peter who rushed to meet Jesus face to face. As Jesus questioned Peter about his love, challenging him both to action ('feed my sheep') and to suffering, Peter saw John and asked 'What about him?' and received the answer '... what is it

94

to you? Follow me.'

This conversation seems to be related for a specific reason: to resolve an argument in the Early Church. Some had held on to the belief that John would not die until the Second Coming. When John died, what happened to their faith? But, the Gospel emphasizes, Jesus never promised that John would not die. God's purposes are sometimes mysterious to us. The important words are 'Follow me'.

Yet the text at this point also emphasizes that this Gospel draws on the authority of John's experience and vision and 'we know that his testimony is true'.

While there may be things in the Bible and in your daily life that you find puzzling or hard to understand, there will be some things you want to hold on to.

✷ *What experiences of God at work in your life would you want to share?*

✷ *Living Lord, may we – like John –*
bear witness to the light of your love. Amen

Thursday April 18   *1 Corinthians 15.1-11*

'The gospel that I preached'

Near the end of his letter to the Corinthians, Paul reminds them of 'the gospel that I preached ... which you received ... on which you have taken your stand.' He describes himself as handing on a tradition – a belief shared by the Early Church based on the experience of many, but not all: 'Cephas ... the twelve ... five hundred of our brothers ... James ... all the apostles'. He includes his own experience. He calls himself 'the least of the apostles' because he began by persecuting the Early Church – but he was enabled to change: 'by God's grace I am what I am.' Paul does not describe his encounter with the risen Christ, except in its impact on him. It began a new life for him, so was like a birth, but an 'abnormal birth' because of his history. It was the start of a ministry in which – by God's grace – he has been enabled to change many other people.

✷ *Who handed on the tradition to us? How much of their own experience did they share? Give thanks for these people. Do we see ourselves as part of that tradition? What do we have to share?*

✷ *Pray for courage and clarity in sharing the good news.*

Into a living hope
Here another writer sees all believers sharing the experience of
'a new birth into a living hope': not just the hope of a new life, but
an inheritance which will last.

In September 1994, at St Martin in the Fields Church in
Trafalgar Square, London, a 'living memorial' was dedicated to
those who died under the apartheid regime in South Africa. The
physical memorial is a small statue commemorating the
Sharpeville massacre. The more enduring memorial is a fund
for education of the children of the new South Africa; linked with
this will be the memory, not only of those who never received an
education which is one of the rights of citizenship, but also of
those who suffered, struggled, went into exile, prayed and
campaigned peacefully and painfully for change, forgave their
former oppressors and are now working with them. Among
these are many Christians, examples of 'faith which stands the
test'. From a land famous for its gold-mines, this is something
'more precious than perishable gold'.

The image of reaping a harvest (verse 9) also appears in
Psalm 126, which was read at that memorable and joyful
service.

✴ *Use Psalm 126 as a prayer.*

The enduring word of God
Members of the Early Church are reminded that through Christ's
death – a gift more precious than silver or gold – they have been
set free from the burden of their sins. They have learned the
secret for which prophets searched and 'that angels long to
glimpse': through Christ they 'have come to trust in God who
raised him from the dead and gave him glory' (verse 21). Amid
the many images of this passage is a phrase which we might
pass over, but which is worth further reflection (verse 13) 'Your
minds must therefore be stripped for action and fully alert.'

✴ *What does this mean for us? What kind of concerns
encumber our minds? How can we let go of them?*

Think of just one thing which preoccupies you, and prevents
you from praying with full concentration – it may be an anxiety or
something which gives you pleasure. Acknowledge before God
that it exists, then imagine that you are unwinding it like a scarf

from round your neck, and carefully putting it to one side. Let the knowledge of God's love and power enfold you instead.

✳ *Do you think this is what the epistle means by 'fix your hopes on grace'? If our minds are stripped for action, what is the action to which you are called, here and now? 'Love one another wholeheartedly with all your strength?' What does this mean in the Christian community of which you are a part?*

When all our anxieties and aspirations have run their course, God will still be there. When our words fail, the living Word prevails.

✳ *Living and enduring Word,*
you are the Gospel that was preached to us,
the One who comes to us and speaks to our needs:
may we share your good news
both with our words and through our lives. Amen

For personal reflection or group discussion

Look again at questions asked each day this week.

ACTION

Find a way of communicating something you have experienced or learned this Easter: sharing a thought or describing an act of worship to someone who was not there. Use any means: a letter, a poem, a contribution to a church magazine, a conversation in the street.

NEW LIFE – the book of Ezekiel

Notes based on the Good News Bible by

Simon Oxley

Simon Oxley is County Ecumenical Officer for the churches of Greater Manchester. He was formerly General Secretary of IBRA. He is a Baptist and began his ministry by serving churches in north-west England.

Against the background of the destruction of Jerusalem and its Temple, together with the death or exile of God's people, Ezekiel proclaimed a message about the renewal of worship and life. Rather than shift the blame for their fate onto others, the people had to accept responsibility. However the new life would not come about only through their own efforts. It was the work of the Lord. A strong sense of the power of God runs through the visions, dramatic actions, laments and spoken prophecies.

Ezekiel, born into a priestly family, was taken into exile by the Babylonians in 597 BCE. His prophetic ministry began in 593 BCE and continued until at least 571 BCE.

2nd Sunday after Easter, April 21   *Ezekiel 1.1-28*

The glory of God

Standing in the valley, it was an amazing sight to see the lightening flashing in the hills above. I could not tear myself away. Yet I also had a sense of fear that the natural power on show was beyond human controlling and potentially very destructive.

There is something compelling about the contemplation of God. We might describe it as 'the beauty of holiness'. Yet, at the same time, we have a sense of fear because God's power is beyond our understanding and control. It is not surprising that Ezekiel's vision of the glory of God began with a thunderstorm.

We have grown used to seeing God in terms of Jesus and we are right to do so. At the same time, we must recognize that there is something about God which is beyond description. The images Ezekiel used may seem strange to us, but they do give a feeling of the power and mystery of God.

* **Lord, you are close to me, like a friend.**
  Help me to respond gladly to your love in Jesus.
  You are beyond me
  and my words cannot begin to describe you.
  Give me the imagination to glimpse your glory
  and your power.

Monday April 22   *Ezekiel 2.1 to 3.9*

Called to be a living message

A renewed vision of God is also usually a call to renewed service. As a priest, Ezekiel already served God. Now he was to be a prophet – that most difficult of tasks, conveying an uncomfortable message to his people. We rightly honour those who are called to leave home and serve God in other parts of the world. We recognize the sacrifice they make and the difficulties they may face. We also need to recognize and value the call we all share to a prophetic ministry in our own neighbourhood. That is no easy task. People know who we are and what we are like.

In this passage we see the first of several examples of prophetic action in the book of Ezekiel. In eating the scroll, Ezekiel makes, in a dramatic manner, the message a part of himself. The message about God we convey is not just the words we speak but the kind of people we are. One of the purposes of daily Bible reading is to make the good news a part of us, so that the totality of our living proclaims God's love.

* **Lord, when people are hurting**
  I worry about finding the right words to say.
  Help me to demonstrate your love to them.

Tuesday April 23   *Ezekiel 3.10-27*

Actions speak

Walking through the housing estate was a depressing experience. The area looked neglected and run down. The patch of ground at the front of the church was covered with litter. A few weeks later, visiting the same place, there had been a dramatic change. The area at the front of the church had been laid out with flowers and shrubs together with a sitting area. What had been done was a message. No words were needed.

99

The task of the prophet or of any Christian communicator is not to pile words on words. It is to convey what they discern to be God's message. Ezekiel began his ministry in silent demonstration, bound and gagged. Words would come later, when the time was right. Ezekiel was not his own man to act and speak as he thought right. He was to be under God's control only.

What about our acting and speaking? Do we fall into the trap of presenting our hopes and prejudices as God's message to people?

✳ *Lord God, It is frustrating when my way seems right
and yours seems foolish.
Help me serve your interests and not my own.*

A prophetic demonstration

A large cage was placed on the ground in the market place, and a man sat in it. Passers by stopped to look. It was not a punishment by public humiliation but part of a campaign against unjust imprisonment. A dramatic demonstration can draw attention to a cause.

In his prophetic action, Ezekiel was doing this and more. He was drawing the attention of the exiles to the siege of Jerusalem. Many had been hoping for a speedy return. Ezekiel demonstrated that Jerusalem's agony would be severe and prolonged. This was not the activity of a fickle God. The tragedy for people remaining in Jerusalem, and the exiles, was that it was the consequence of their sin. It would have been easier to stand on the sidelines and condemn. Ezekiel's prophetic ministry was a painful identification with the sufferings of the people, even though they had brought it on themselves.

Many of us have taken the easier path of condemning an evil world from the safety of the sanctuary. Thank God for those Christians who have been prepared to pay the considerable cost of identifying with the oppressed.

✳ *Lord God, help me resist the temptation to give up
on the rest of humanity.
May I follow the way of your Son Jesus
in sharing the joy and the pain of all of human life.*

God at the centre

Ezekiel's prophetic actions were not simply visual aids. They were rich in symbolism. A shaved head was the sign of mourning or of being taken into captivity. What Ezekiel did with the hair was symbolic of the destruction of Jerusalem, and some of its inhabitants, with the scattering of the rest into exile. The real horror of the siege of Jerusalem was brought home in Ezekiel's words.

There was no mystery about what had gone wrong. Jerusalem was to stand at the heart of all human life as a witness to God. Its inhabitants' way of life was worse than those who made no claims to be God's people. This spiritual and moral disease destroyed the city.

Looking back across the years makes it easy to spot the problem. We have to recognize, though, that God expects the same in our churches. Our life is to be a witness to God. Ezekiel's words come to us as a warning of the consequences of not making our church life Christ-like.

✳ *Lord, thank you for putting your trust in us.*
We know we cannot live in your way on our own.
Remind us of your presence with us
and the unlimited resources of your love.

Being responsible

It's never our fault. 'I'm sorry I'm late, I got held up on my journey', or was it that we did not set out in time? It's tempting to make up an excuse rather than confess that we got it wrong. The people of Israel, said Ezekiel, had convinced themselves of good excuses to make to God. If they were found to have failings, it was always someone else's fault. Ezekiel hammers home the message that they could not blame their sins on their parents' sins, nor could they claim any virtue for their parents' goodness.

I am grateful for the Christian example of my parents but I cannot claim to be a follower of Jesus on the evidence of their faith. I am responsible for my response to God's love. When I get things wrong, as I often do, I must confess it to those I have hurt and to God. When I try to blame someone else, I make matters worse.

✳ *Father, all kinds of influences have shaped my life.*
   (Reflect on these)
   May your Holy Spirit help me to be creative and loving
   in all I am.

A new mind and heart

Some children suffer from parents with expectations. Whatever
the child does, it can never be good enough. There is only
criticism, never a word of praise. Constant failure leads to a loss
of self confidence. The child may give up trying to please the
parent and may become anti-social in all her behaviour.

Ezekiel's message about individual responsibility could make
us think of God as such a parent. The people of Israel and
ourselves seem bound to fail and suffer the consequences.
Looking at humanity and our own lives, are we trapped in a
never ending cycle of failure?

Ezekiel shows a way God offers us to break out – new minds
and hearts. We see this more clearly in the coming and work of
Jesus. This is no instant cure. Like a surgical transplant
operation, where the body's systems fight to reject the new
organ, we have continually to resist the dominant urge to be
selfish. God is with us in our struggle, and life lived in God's way
is possible.

✳ *Lord, I keep getting it wrong.*
   Even when I try to please you,
   I end up by finding a way to do what I want.
   Stay with me as I wrestle
   that I may let a new mind and heart take life in me.

For personal reflection or group discussion

1. This week, we have found several examples of Ezekiel's
   prophetic actions. What is the difference between these and
   a 'visual aid' used to illustrate a talk? What part can prophetic
   actions play in communication?

2. Pretend that you are a stranger to the area and walk past
   your church building. What 'message' does everything about
   it (not just the notice board) give?

Overwhelming grief

Every culture has its mourning rituals to help bereaved individuals and communities come to terms with death. When we do not encourage the bereaved to grieve thoroughly, we create problems rather than solve them. The death of a loved one brings a searing pain which has to be worked through and not suppressed.

In this passage, Ezekiel points to the destruction of Jerusalem, a calamity so great that even the normal rituals of mourning would be inadequate. The shock would produce emotional and psychological paralysis.

This passage is difficult. Are we to believe that Ezekiel's wife would die and Ezekiel be deprived of grieving simply as a means of offering a dramatic illustration for God's message? Is this the action of the One we know as the Father of our Lord Jesus Christ who sends his Son to die to save the world? To look for God and signs of the Kingdom in everything is surely right. We need to learn from bad happenings as well as the good. We do not have to say that God causes the bad to teach us a lesson.

✳ *Spend some moments praying for people in the news or known personally to you who are grieving.*
Pray that we may be spared the grief of seeing the good in our society destroyed by selfishness and foolishness.

Watching out

Those of us who drive cars are familiar with road signs. A lot of care is taken to design signs whose message can be seen at a single glance, but it is the responsibility of the driver to take notice and drive safely.

The task of the watchman was not the same as that of a guard or sentry. He was to call out a warning when he saw the enemy approaching. It was then up to others to take action. Ezekiel's role as a prophet included that of watchman – recognizing danger and pointing to new opportunities for God's people. He was responsible for giving a warning, not for whether people took notice.

We believe that we are called to be 'watchers' but may

confuse this role with that of armed defender! We are to watch for signs of hope and danger in the life of society, but we cannot protect God's Kingdom by forcing people to love God and their neighbour. All people are responsible for their own actions.

✳ *Reflect on where we should act to protect weak and vulnerable members of society and where we should leave it open for people to take responsibility for their own lives.*

Tuesday April 30   *Ezekiel 33.21-33*

Encourage action

'Speakers' Corner' in Hyde Park, London, is a place where anyone can stand and speak. Many stop and listen, though few desire to hear a life changing message. What for the speaker is a burning issue becomes for the passer-by a piece of entertainment. This is what happened to Ezekiel. Even though the message he proclaimed was one of condemnation of people's individual and collective sin, they loved to listen. Perhaps treating him as an entertainer was their way of not facing up to the truth about themselves and their situation.

There is a narrow dividing line between enjoyment and entertainment. We enjoy our relationship with God so we invite others to share that enjoyment. We should be creative and imaginative in proclaiming the good news but we are not in the entertainment business. Worship and evangelism are not to be judged by the loudest laughs or the biggest crowds, but by another kind of response.

✳ *Pray for Christian speakers that they can catch our interest and help us live out our faith. Pray that as listeners we may look not for entertainment but for changed lives.*

Wednesday May 1   *Ezekiel 34.1-10*

Leaders who fail

It is tempting for leaders to use power for their own good. We rightly get angry when we hear of politicians, leaders in commerce and industry, or even church leaders, who make their lives comfortable at the expense of others. It is an abuse of power. Ezekiel's condemnation of the leaders of Israel, who combined political and religious responsibilities, was the kind of story modern journalists love. The strong image of shepherds who eat the sheep rather than care for them would make telling headlines.

It is so easy to condemn leaders who fail without recognizing that our sins may be equally destructive. As Christians, we have been called to be the body of Christ in the world. We have been given the love of God and the power of the Holy Spirit for our task. Yet we tend to keep them for ourselves within the Christian community, as if we are afraid that there is not enough of God's love for everyone in the world.

✳ *Lord, we pray for all who are given authority and power*
that they may work for the good of all.
May we, your people,
learn to exercise a style of leadership which liberates us
for love and service to the world.

Thursday May 2   Ezekiel 34.11-31

The good shepherd

Terrible stories of physical and mental abuse of children by their fathers have come to light in England. This makes it difficult for many to have a positive image of fatherhood, or to know God as Father. We have to identify clearly what kind of parent God is to us.

In the same way, Ezekiel had to restore a strong positive image of God as the good shepherd. This conflicted with people's experience of human shepherds, particularly of the 'shepherds of Israel'. All around them were the consequences of the destruction they had brought on themselves. God was not the destroyer but the one who would heal and re-create. Ezekiel offered people living in exile a vision of how things would be under God.

We may be so disillusioned with the world that we no longer look for any vision. In fact, we may look for a vengeful God who will destroy all evil, presuming that others will suffer and not ourselves. God does not work this way. Although a good shepherd is not a familiar image to those of us who live in cities, we learn from Ezekiel and from Jesus how God works.

✳ *Good Shepherd,*
When we are divided, gather us together.
When we are hurting, heal our injuries.
When we are lost, show us the way.

105

Lead all people to the good pasture of your Kingdom.

Friday May 3   *Ezekiel 36.22-38* *

Return and renewal

Four years ago, I had the joy of returning to live in a part of
England I love. I had been away for eight years, and it was good
to renew friendships. But our different experiences in the
intervening years meant that all of us had changed. Life cannot
stay the same. Its pleasures (and its frustrations) are different.

Nostalgia is a dangerous emotion. We look back longingly to
a place or a way of life where we were happy. We think we can
go back and live as though nothing had happened in between.
But, for good or ill, everything and everyone changes. There is
no going back.

The people in exile with Ezekiel wanted to go back to the old
place and their old lifestyle. However, the vision offered them
was of a return which creates renewal.

God does not want us to recapture the past, however good it
was, but to co-operate in creating a new future.

✳ *Lord God, we look back*
to the story of your people long ago in the Bible;
to the story of your people in the Church;
to the story of our own life.
May these stories not make us nostalgic for the past
but confident to travel with you into the future.

Saturday May 4   *Ezekiel 47.1-12*

New life flows from God

On a visit to India, I was able to see for myself the dramatic
effects of irrigation. Next to parched land with sparse vegetation
struggling to stay alive there were fields green with fresh
growth. Water made the difference.

The final chapters of Ezekiel contain a vision of a new temple
in Jerusalem replacing all that had been destroyed. Ezekiel saw
the Lord returning and worship renewed. Today's passage has
the image, later taken up in Revelation (22.1-2), of flowing
waters bringing life.

When we talk about the role of the local church in the
community, we sometimes use the image of light shining in the
darkness. Here is an equally powerful picture for us to

contemplate: a life bringing, health giving stream flowing out of the worship of God's people. Water of life brings the green of fresh growth as it flows through the community. This is a vision for every congregation, small or large. In the end it does not depend on what we do. New life flows from God who is at the heart of worship.

✳ *Lord, you come like water to a dry and dusty land.*
Flow into the lives of ... (name people and situations).
Wash me in the power of your love.
Refresh my faith so that I may serve you.

For personal reflection or group discussion

Ezekiel was called to be a watchman (33.1-20). How do we function as watchers in the local church within our community, and in the churches nationally for society? What can help us to identify signs of hope and danger?

ACTION

Ezekiel gave us a picture of shepherds who ate the sheep rather than care for them (34.1-10). Get a copy of your church's Annual Accounts and see how much God-given resources are consumed by the congregation and how much in the activities of Ezekiel 34.4.

LOOKING AT . . . series
by Brian Haymes

- ADVENT
- THE CROSS
- EASTER & ASCENSION
- PENTECOST

Four books giving fresh insight into the main Christian seasons – for private study or as a resource for group discussion.

UK price: **£4.50** each *(Post/Packing included UK only)*

SPECIAL OFFER: £16.00 for the set

GLIMPSES OF THE SPIRIT

1. Sharing hardship

Reflections based on the New Revised Standard Version by

Jane Ella P Montenegro

Jane Montenegro, a Filipino, was gripped by Christ's liberating gospel in the Martial Law period. She moved into Christian Education within and outside the Church, working in both urban and rural areas. Today she facilitates workshops on liturgical renewal, children's work, and the empowerment of women. She is presently pastor of a mountain church while studying Asian feminist theology.

To commit oneself to the work of Jesus Christ for truth, justice and peace is to plunge into the darkness of life. It means being with the fearful, the ignorant, the anguished, the lost – victims of socio-economic, cultural, political exploitation. Sharing hardship means taking risks, extending into more complicated struggles, linking creatively with varied structures, with a deeper thirst for inner light.

Inspired by the Spirit of God, we work with those who share this passion for 'peace on earth, good will toward all humankind and creation'.

4th Sunday after Easter, May 5   *John 15.18-27 **

Sharing the burden of being hated

As a child, I believed that one must be submissive, at peace with everyone at home, school, church, among neighbours – everywhere. But later experience taught me otherwise.

At 16, a trumped-up letter destroyed my father's career, because he counselled against martial infidelity. Some years later, while in government service, our Faculty Club complained about salary deductions without prior consultation, and the Church has questioned other irregularities. In these painful events, interpersonal relationships were blocked, school and church authorities preached against each other, intrigues ran high and trust and friendships were broken. Certainly Jesus' admonition becomes an assuring reality. 'I have chosen you out of the world – therefore the world hates you.'

Will you follow the way of Jesus: being maligned, misunderstood and isolated? Will you lighten your anguish and burdens and let them be shared with others who seek truth and peace? Then together, we can grow in faith, by our shared struggle and hardships for Christ's sake.

✳ *O Spirit of Christ, come.*
Blaze this darkness among us with your truth.
O Spirit of Peace, come.
Heal our woundedness together. Amen

Monday May 6   *Matthew 10.16-23*
Living with death
Jesus tells his disciples how to live with death: to be wise and innocent among their persecutors, to be still and alert to what the Spirit wants them to say to the powers-that-be. They would be hated for proclaiming his name. They would run for their lives, escaping – if possible – premature death.

Almost 2,000 years later, these texts come alive to a mountain church in Mindanao. During the 1980s and until the early 1990s, this area of the Philippines was notorious as the 'killing fields' of peasants and other suspected rebels of the government of President Marcos. Soldiers and a para-military unit controlled this zone. Innocent farmers were beaten up or hacked to death while the perpetrators went free.

A community of faith persevered, encouraging one another in birthday serenades, Sunday School and worship, family rituals and thanksgiving celebrations. They learnt endurance from each other and shared their hardship in prayer. Their faith in Christ grew – despite the complex political ideologies and the preservation of national security.

✳ *O Spirit of Christ,*
may this shared experience of persecution
become my lesson of renewal
and commitment towards peace. Amen

The Spirit shares the hardship of the helpless

It is an old, powerful story, culturally and religiously rooted. It shaped the very core of their beings. It had been shared from clan to clan, generation to generation. It is the story of shared hardship among the weak and how the strong are toppled by God's mighty acts.

So it was with Moses and Pharaoh, David and Goliath, Esther and the King, and now Peter and John with the religious aristocracy. Neither imprisonment nor a ban on teaching about Jesus could stop them.

Contemporary events confirm for us the unpredictable movement of the Holy Spirit. The end of the Philippine Martial Law Regime in 1985 was a miracle of prayers, bread, flowers and songs surrounding government soldiers and tanks of war. Mandela's election to the Presidency of South Africa in 1994 toppled decades of bitter suffering under apartheid. This is the essence of the Kingdom. God shares the hardships of the weak and helpless and grants them victory in the end.

✳ *O empowering Spirit, let me be full of faith in you,*
  that in my weakness I may share
  in turning the world upside down for others' sake. Amen

Share to dare

The bonding of the apostles made them strong enough to dare to confront the Temple hierarchy. Most probably, they shared strategies and planned how to proceed with the proclamation of God's saving acts. Then, miracle of miracles ... ! More boldly and joyfully than ever they shared together, daring their opposers with the message of the Holy Spirit. Faced by the most powerful men in the land, they stood firm in their faith conviction.

Centuries later, this bold encounter with religious authorities has been shared by many women reformers and martyrs, as well as men, influencing them to act towards change, like Joan of Arc, condemned as a heretic and burnt at the stake. Melchara Aquina and Gabriela Silang became Filipino martyrs during the Spanish regime, and thousands more unnamed women and men have been persecuted, but the daring for the gospel's sharing has not been stopped.

The natural world shares our groans (page 112)
Woodcut by Boy Dominguez, the Philippines

* **O Spirit of power, help us to share and dare
for the transformation of Church and society today.
In Jesus' name. Amen**

Thursday May 9   *Romans 8.18-25*

The natural world shares our groans

I learnt to swim in a river teeming with small fish. The forest that I loved had giant trees with eagles, hornbills, orioles, colourful butterflies and insects with fascinating shapes. We ate upland rice that was black, pink, red or creamy white. Each variety smelt sweet and tasted deliciously different from the other. I would sing heartily, '...the valleys stand so thick with corn ...' My feelings were deep. I was very aware of my soul. God was everywhere!

Today, the river is dry. It is filled with junk and garbage. The giant trees have long been sold by a logging company to countries that do not cut down trees. There are no more eagles, nor hornbills that caw. Our variety of rice is decided by the International Research Rice Institute. How can I sing when the valleys are brown and the ears of corn have become like the fist of a child?

I feel an aching emptiness – a sense of loss. Will the deep feelings, a sense of connectedness to the earth ever return? Will learning again from indigenous old women be part of the answer and a sign of hope?

* **O Creator God, let me be courageous to redeem
one groaning piece of the earth as my offering to you!**

Friday May 10   *Romans 8.26-27*

The Spirit shares our weakness

Depay was heavy with child – her tenth when I met her. Pale and thin, she was stretching her crumpled skirt repeatedly, letting her women neighbours speak up for her. Two weeks ago, she and her husband Pedro had just sold their corn products and were going back to the farm when a man accosted them on the road, demanding their corn sale at knife-point. Depay pleaded for mercy. She was pushed violently aside. It happened so quickly. Pedro bled to death on the road. No one was willing to testify as witness. The roadside houses were closed. But in whispers, the village women identified the killer as a notorious military man who was absent without leave from his assignment. Yes, we can make the report for Depay to sign, but the police will only receive it. The village councillors cannot do much either. There is no justice.

✱ *O grieving Spirit of God, help us to discern*
   that you are here in our suffering and powerlessness.
   And teach us how to pray – in Jesus' name. Amen

Saturday May 11   *Revelation 1.9-20*

Sharing a vision of Christ

In Revelation, John transports us to his divine experience. He describes Christ vividly in minute detail: the colours, figures, numbers, metals, elements and vestments. One can smell and feel the flame of fire from Christ's eyes and the blazing rays from his face. His voice is multi-toned. Did it sound like a brook, ripples on a stream, a waterfall, the ebb tide on the shore, an undersea current, or the crest of ocean waves? Ah, what magical tones!

Hundreds more have had mystical experiences which they alone could fathom. What matters most is that after a spiritual revelation, we are converted by the Spirit – committed to bring wholeness to the world.

✱ *O Divine Spirit, forbid it not*
   that I should miss your revelation. Amen

For personal reflection or group discussion

What injustices are suffered in your country? To what extent have you shared them, and how costly has that been? When has the presence of Christ been most real?

ACTION

Find out more about the issues that affect the Philippines. Pray for Christians who witness in this situation.

113

GLIMPSES OF THE SPIRIT

2. Revealing truth

Notes based on the Revised English Bible by

Julie M Hulme.

Julie M Hulme, a writer and Methodist minister, lives in St Ives, Cambridgeshire, where her husband, David, is superintendent minister of the Huntingdon circuit. They have two daughters, Cathy and Debbie. For some years Julie has been following a call to live the ministry of word and sacrament as a life of prayer.

Through the life, work and person of the Holy Spirit, we discover God present in our everyday existence, sharing our struggles, heartache and difficulties, our joys, achievements and fulfilment. But God is not only at work in us in the present and for the sake of the 'now'. The Holy Spirit within us is always pointing us forward and onward, encouraging us to grow in wisdom, mature in faith, and deepen in compassion. The Spirit is at work in us and amongst us to reveal truth, and in doing so, to equip us for the future God desires for us. As the Spirit opens our eyes to learn more of the things of God, so we are transformed for worship, witness and service (see Romans 12.1-2).

5th Sunday after Easter, May 12   *John 16.1-11 **
The Spirit reveals the wrong

In this chapter, Jesus is preparing his followers not just for his own death, but also for the persecution they will endure when he is no longer with them. They must have no illusions about what they face, but he also wants to encourage them. They will have the strength, support, counsel and companionship of the Spirit.

But the Spirit is more than a friend and guide: the Spirit will reveal the wrong. Nothing will remain hidden. The world will know what is sinful, and will know that it has been judged. The righteousness of the Father, as revealed in his Son, will be acknowledged by all, and everything which stands against it will be condemned.

In a time of trial and danger this is both a warning and a comfort. We are reminded that the secrets of our own lives will be brought to light. And we are assured that God sees our suffering, and in due time the truth of it will be revealed and judged. Whatever evil is done to us because of our allegiance to Christ – whether harrassment, persecution, torture, even murder – will be brought into the light.

✳ *O God of Justice,*
stand with all who will this day suffer for what is right,
and may the truth of your love be revealed in their lives,
and in mine. Amen.

Monday May 13   *John 16.12-15*

The Spirit reveals the things of God

How can anyone ever come to the end of all that can be said or sung about God? There is so much grace and truth to be revealed (John 1.14-18; 21.25) that we cannot absorb it all at once. It must be revealed gradually or it will overwhelm us. Like rich food, the knowledge of God's wisdom, love and glory must fill and transform us slowly, throughout our lives, or it cannot be properly digested!

God knows that we are fragile creatures, easily broken, needing to be treated with the utmost care (Isaiah 42.1-4), and so it is with the greatest gentleness that the Spirit reveals to us the things of God. We must not become impatient or greedy. All that we need to know, all that we can understand, will be given to us.

And we are given a simple test to apply to any 'revelation' to discern if it is truly from God. Does it glorify Christ? For the Spirit does not usurp the authority of God, but in all things works within, and seeks to magnify the compassion, grace and glory of the Son, who himself was concerned only to point to the Father.

✳ *O God of truth, deal gently with my heart today,*
that I may be sensitive to the frailty of those around me,
and care for them with the tenderness of your truth
and the grace of your compassion. Amen.

The Spirit reveals joy

Shortly after my first daughter was born, I remember lying with her in my arms, unable to believe that such a wonderful creature had been entrusted to me. It was the deepest joy I have ever known. As a woman in labour I had not been able to see beyond my struggle and pain, but now I had entered a new life, a new relationship, and my suffering was no longer immediate or important.

There are times when the pain of the world presses in around us and we cannot see beyond it. There are times when our own wounds cause us so much suffering that we cannot believe any other life exists. And yet there is a deeper joy which runs like an undercurrent beneath the most troubled life, if only we can open up a well to find it, or let it rise to the surface of our lives like a spring of hope and refreshment. The pain of the world is real, but it is not the only reality.

The Spirit of God comes to reveal a joy which does not mock or deny our pain: it exists alongside and beneath the worst that can happen to us. It is God's new life, God's vision, which lifts us – not always out of our suffering – but within it.

✳ *O God of joy, come to my heart as light and life.*
   Transfigure all that is decay and difficulty,
   so that I may share your peace
   with all about me this day. Amen.

The Spirit reveals the Father

Again and again in John's Gospel, Jesus speaks of the closeness between himself and his Father. The Father is not hidden mysteriously behind symbols and story. Jesus is aware of the deep unity which binds them together in love and purpose.

This closeness remains, even as he faces the Cross. Indeed, the unity of Jesus and the Father will become even greater, because in dying on the Cross he is 'going to the Father.' Jesus wants his disciples to know that this intimate life with the Father will be theirs too, as they face their own time of trial.

It is this unity with the Father, through the Holy Spirit, which is the source of our peace and cheerfulness, even in the midst of much tribulation. Jesus' disciples in every age can know themselves to be held directly in the Father-love of God. Those around us may be scattered, but we can say, with Christ, 'I am not alone, for the Father is with me ...' (John 16.32).

✳ *O God of faithfulness, open my eyes to your grace;*
open my heart to your love;
open my life to your self-offering,
this day and forever. Amen.

Ascension Day, May 16   *Acts 1.1-11 **

The Spirit reveals the Kingdom

When will the Kingdom be restored? For the disciples, this is the most important question of all. But Jesus' response shows that this is a distraction from the task before them. The Holy Spirit is promised as the power to fulfil their true mission, to be faithful witnesses to Christ to the ends of the earth. Through their witness, the mission of Christ will continue (see Luke 4.14-21) and the Kingdom be revealed.

The Spirit gives strength and direction to our work and our witness. Without the help of the Spirit, we can make the mistake of looking for Jesus in the wrong places (Luke 24.5; Acts 1.11).

The Spirit is constantly at work in the present moment, revealing to us its potential in God's reign of love and glory, and calling us to be faithful witnesses to Christ in the place where we happen to be. We are not to become distracted by questions which do not concern us. It is rather through listening, obedience and faithfulness that the Kingdom of God comes amongst us.

✳ *O God of power,*
strengthen our hands to ready obedience,
and our hearts to praise,
that we may witness to your Son
wherever you ask us to be. Amen.

Friday May 17   *Daniel 7.13-14 **

The Spirit reveals the power of God

Daniel's vision is concerned with the basic question 'Who runs the world' or 'Where lies the ultimate power and authority?' He sees the rise and fall of mighty empires, symbolized as great beasts with powerful horns, but their ability to rule is taken away, so that though they may continue to survive, they can no longer inspire obedience or terror.

Compared with earthly empires, which only last for a time, God the Judge is the 'Ancient of Days.' God is the one who rules, and decides who has power on earth. He gives dominion and glory to the one whom he has chosen. This is the forceful contrast which lies behind Daniel's vision: the impotence of human power and the sovereignty of God.

The power given to God's Chosen One cannot fail, because it has no internal flaws or inconsistencies to weaken it. And it cannot be destroyed, because there is no power in the universe which can defeat it. The sovereignty and authority of God remain for ever, and it is within this power, and under this authority, that we stand.

✳ *O God our Judge, look upon us in your great mercy.*
Forgive our many offences against your holiness and love.
Renew us in your power
to live as your subjects, friends and heirs. Amen

Saturday May 18   *Romans 8.28-39* ✳

The Spirit changes us

God desires that we be conformed to the image of his Son, as brothers and sisters to Christ. This is a process of change. The full significance and power of God at work within us is revealed gradually as we grow in our calling, in our faithful dependence on God and in our freedom to reveal God's glory.

This is the work of the Spirit within us. As the Spirit reveals to us more of the truth – the truth of God, the truth of ourselves, and the truth of the world – so we are transformed.

Because we see the world as it really is, we gain confidence and courage in our discipleship. Because we are not greedy for spiritual things, we trust God to reveal what we need to know. Because we know joy, we are sustained in hope, even in the midst of great pain and struggle. Because we are united with the Father, we experience peace of heart and mind. Because we concentrate on being faithful witnesses to Christ, we see the Kingdom. Because we stand within the power of God, we know that nothing can stand against us.

✳ *O God of all truth, transform us by your love*
so that, confident in your powerful mercy,
and strong in your gentle grace, we may live

to your praise and glory, this day and forever. Amen.

For personal reflection or group discussion:

What qualities, activities and attitudes must we encourage, in ourselves and others, if we are to be open to the Spirit? How can we encourage others to experience God's truth, joy, love and sustaining power? What things get in the way and frustrate the Spirit? What is Christian humility?

✳ *O Spirit of Life,*
present with us in truth on the way,
speaking from our tradition,
nourishing our dreams,
leading us in adventure:
we adore you.
In you is the fountain of life:
In your light do we see light.

O Spirit of Life,
wild as the wind in high places,
breaking the walls of our love,
bursting our categories of hope,
carrying us beyond sight into faith:
we adore you.
In you is the fountain of life:
In your light do we see light.

O Spirit of Life,
merciful love of the Father,
compassionate service of Christ,
untamed communion of God with us:
gentle us into believing,
unsettle our certainties,
and strengthen us in the truth
in which we are held,
this day and forever. Amen

Julie Hulme
From Living Prayers for Today,
IBRA's new anthology of prayer (see page 49)

ACTION

Ask a more experienced Christian to pray with you and to help you discern any qualities, activities or attitudes which frustrate the work of the Spirit in your life.

GLIMPSES OF THE SPIRIT

3. Coming with power

Notes based on the Revised Standard Version by

David Bridge

David Bridge is the Superintendent minister of the Sutton Circuit (UK). His interests include the Church in Europe, the arts – especially cinema and theatre, and Christian apologetics. His most recent books, published by the Methodist Home Mission Division, are on the theme of apologetics: 'God of Science, God of Faith' and 'Letters to Rebecca'.

In recent years the Christian Church has paid increasing attention to the work of the Holy Spirit and many new and exciting things have happened as a result, not least the writing of new hymns and songs for worship and a rediscovery of the ministry of healing. At the same time there have been developments which have caused people to wonder how they can distinguish between the work of God's Spirit and that of other forces. We cannot say that something is of God just because it is unusual or mysterious. As this week we think about the power of the Spirit we shall consider how the Bible helps us to discern what is truly the work of God.

6th Sunday after Easter, May 19   2 Kings 2.1-15 *

Calling us to do new things

The theatre was full with the audience waiting expectantly for the curtain to rise. Then came the announcement, 'We regret to announce that owing to the sudden illness of' – and he named the star of the show – 'his part this evening will be taken by the understudy.' I wondered how the understudy would be feeling, eager for the chance to be in the spotlight yet aware of an audience disappointed and quick to make comparisons.

Elisha has mixed feelings as he walks with Elijah towards Gilgal. He is on edge so he snaps at those who tell him what he already knows, that shortly Elijah will be taken from him and he will be on his own. He knows that Elijah was inspired by the Spirit of God and he wants that same inspiration. It will not be enough to remember Elijah and try and imitate him; he needs to be empowered by the same Spirit.

God does not want us to be mere imitators of the past but to catch the spirit of faithful men and women who have gone before us. If we do only what has been done previously we shall be imprisoned by the past. If we are open to the Spirit we shall sometimes find ourselves being called to do new things. Our tradition is to be open to the possibility of change.

✳ *Think of the people whose lives have been an inspiration to you and thank God for them.*

Monday May 20   *Joel 2.28-29*

Overcoming barriers

I have a friend who is a distinguished television producer. Sometimes when he arrives at a studio where he is not known it is assumed that he is a messenger or has come to make the tea – because he is black. We have preconceived ideas about people, and those who do not fit those expectations are easily ignored.

Joel says that God's Spirit will inspire all people and disregard human distinctions. He will overcome barriers of gender, 'Your sons and daughters will prophesy', of age, 'Your old men shall dream dreams and your young men shall see visions,' and of class, 'even on the menservants and maidservants.'

These barriers still exist in most societies throughout the world. The contribution women can make is not valued as highly as men. People over a certain age discover when they apply for a job that no-one wants their experience. Those from humble backgrounds are perceived as having nothing worthwhile to say. Yet God's Spirit can inspire all who are open to him and we neglect the message they bring us at our peril.

✳ *Help me, Lord, to be open to your word whoever speaks it, and to listen with particular care to those I might be tempted to disregard.*

Inspiring organization

A woman sent a generous donation to a large national charity. With her cheque she enclosed a letter saying, 'This gift is on condition that none of it is used for administration.' She reflected a commonly held view that the work done by a Church or charity is important while the organization that supports the work can be dispensed with.

Christians sometimes contrast the spiritual life of a church with its structures, rejoicing in the former and disparaging the latter. This was not the view of St Paul who regarded administration as one of the Spirit's gifts to the Church (see 1 Corinthians 12. 28), nor was it the message given to Ezekiel through his vision of the valley of dry bones. What God's does to restore the people of Israel is both to build up the physical body and to give that body life. The body without the breath of life is dead, but the Spirit needs a body if God's work is to be done.

Every aspect of the life of the Church, its worship, its outreach and its administration all need to be inspired by the Spirit. Poor organization and unnecessary meetings hinder the work of God but good organization and purposeful meetings are necessary if Jesus' ministry is to be continued through the Church. 'God is not a God of confusion but of peace' (1 Corinthians 14. 33).

✳ *Almighty God, breathe your Spirit*
into the life of the Church and into my life.

Like living water

If a young man says, 'My love is like a red red rose', he doesn't intend to suggest that he is courting a scarlet rambler. He is using the language of poetry, which takes words that are commonplace but uses them in such a way as to point beyond their everyday meaning. The language we use about God is like this. Because God is a mystery we have to use words as signposts rather than precise descriptions. Biblical writers take words out of their own experience like 'shepherd' or 'king' to hint at the nature of God, and Jesus himself taught that the word 'Father' could help us to understand something of God.

When people did not realize that Jesus was using language

poetically, they were greatly puzzled by what he said. When Jesus speaks about going away his hearers take him literally. Then he speaks of living water as a metaphor for the Holy Spirit and people are confused, just as the Samaritan woman, whom Jesus met by a well, had been (John 4.1-15).

We use poetry and metaphors to speak about God because he is so much greater than we are and our minds can never dispel the mystery which surrounds him. In this way we remind ourselves that we can only approach God in worship and never on equal terms.

✳ Heavenly Father, may I never lose a sense of wonder when I think about you.

Thursday May 23   *John 14.15-31 **

Perceived through love

There is a difference between seeing and perceiving. You may pass important people in the street and see them clearly but you may not perceive who they are. A great many people in Palestine saw Jesus but only a few perceived that he was special. Jesus would not force people to recognize him, only invite them to see in him the nature of God.

Jesus is preparing his friends for the day when they will not be able to see him or hold his hand. Only when he is no longer physically with them will the Spirit be able to be present, not only with them but with all people. However the difference between seeing and perceiving will continue: everyone will see the followers of Jesus but not everyone will see the Spirit of God who empowers them.

God never coerces people, but only invites them. The power that the Spirit brings is not the power of a tyrant to compel submission; it is the power whereby Jesus' followers can continue his ministry so that others may have the chance, not only to see but also to perceive. Those who have love in their hearts will be able to see and perceive but those who are unloving will have great difficulty in recognizing the presence of God in their world.

✳ O God give me love that I may recognize your loveliness.

Bringing unity

Those who often travel on the underground in London learn to recognize signs that a train is shortly to arrive. The first indication is a gentle wind, followed by the sound of the wheels on the track. Then the train's headlights can be seen and finally the train itself comes into view. We can make an underground journey less boring by reminding ourselves of the experience of people on the day of Pentecost. Sound, light and wind heralded the coming of God's Spirit before it was possible to see those who were being influenced by him.

The unusual nature of the event attracted a crowd but Peter did not want people just to be impressed by a spectacle; he wanted them to understand what it meant. So powerfully did he present his message that he was understood by all who heard him, no matter what part of the world they came from. So the process begun with the building of the Tower of Babel was put into reverse.

God's Spirit unites those who are open to him. That is a test we can use to determine whether or not an event is truly inspired by the Spirit. When a new movement, however spectacular, causes barriers to separate godly people, it is most unlikely to be a work of the Holy Spirit.

✳ *All praise to our redeeming Lord,*
Who joins us by his grace,
And bids us, each to each restored,
Together seek his face.   *Charles Wesley*

Changing lives

We know from many references in Paul's letters that the Holy Spirit was one of the aspects of faith which perplexed new Christians most. We also know that it was a topic on which Christians were likely to fall out. There were serious conflicts in the churches in Galatia and these are evident in this passage where Paul warns his readers against 'biting and devouring one another' (verse 15) and against self-conceit, provoking and envy (verse 26).

Unusual behaviour like speaking in tongues did not appear to have any other explanation than the inspiration of the Spirit. Those who could speak in tongues began to be held in special esteem while those who could not were made to feel inferior. Ecstatic behaviour in worship was regarded more highly than controlling your temper or being faithful to your wife.

Paul leaves his readers in no doubt that they have got their priorities wrong. The important signs of the Spirit at work are lives that are growing to be more Christlike. God's most precious gifts are those which affect the way we live every moment of every day.

Paul's teaching on the fruit of the Spirit is as relevant in the last years of the twentieth century as it was in the first half of the first.

✱ *Holy Spirit, fill my life with your most precious gifts.*

For personal reflection or group discussion

1. What are the tests which we should apply to see if any new movement is inspired by the Holy Spirit?

2. What do long-established congregations need to learn from those that have more recently come into being and how can this learning process be encouraged?

3. What practical difference might it make to us as individuals and to the church as a community if we were to receive more of the 'gifts of the Spirit'?

ACTION

Discover if tensions have arisen among Christians in your neighbourhood over different understandings of the work of the Spirit. Consider what might be done to overcome divisions and to help Christians to learn from each other.

HAVE THE MIND OF CHRIST
The Epistle to the Philippians

Notes based on the Revised English Bible by

Edmund Banyard

Edmund Banyard is a minister and former Moderator of the General Assembly of The United Reformed Church in the United Kingdom. He has written both plays and worship material including TURN BUT A STONE, prayers and meditations based on the Joint Liturgical Group Lectionary (JLG2) and currently edits ALL YEAR ROUND for the Council of Churches for Britain and Ireland.

It is possible that Philippians contains fragments of more than one letter. There is, however, so much here that speaks to our own condition that it is immaterial whether or not it was all written at the same time. Paul is dictating, not from the calm of a study, but from the discomforts and restrictions of a Roman prison to a group of people he knows and loves; but they are human beings just like us, capable of plumbing depths as well as scaling heights. In these warm, often passionate words, we see Paul seeking to know the mind of Christ for himself in his own precarious situation, whilst at the same time pointing this little church to ways in which they must continually seek to discover the mind of Christ for themselves.

Pentecost, Sunday May 26   *Philippians 1.1-11*

A Spirit-filled church

Today we celebrate the gift of the Spirit at Pentecost (Acts 2.1ff); but this passage is testimony to the fact that the occasion recorded in Acts is no one-off experience. As we shall see later, this little group of Christians is not without its problems, but there are no qualifications to the warmth of Paul's greeting. The Spirit is actively at work among them; his prayers for them have good reason to be 'always joyful'.

Writing from prison Paul speaks of 'the privilege that is mine'; beyond the hardship and danger Paul sees the opportunity to defend and proclaim the gospel. Would you count this a privilege? Would I? Paul says the Philippians share his privilege, how? By helping him? Through the difficulties they themselves face?

Notice how Paul links the growth of love to a growth of understanding, with the implication that the more we love, the more we shall recognize the things that 'really matter'. How would you define today 'the things that really matter'?

✳ *Lord, may the spark of your love*
  grow brighter and warmer within us
  until it so fills us that we do indeed recognize
  and centre our lives upon things that really matter
  to the glory and praise of God.

Monday May 27   *Philippians 1.12-26*

Dying or living we are Christ's

As Paul goes on to say more about his imprisonment we get a clearer idea of what he means by 'privilege' (1.7). Christianity is being openly discussed and many hitherto secret Christians have been encouraged to proclaim their faith. On the darker side we are given an insight into the early seeds of sectarianism, but Paul refuses to be disheartened; if Christ is being presented then ultimately his truth must prevail. Not that Paul is indifferent to what is preached; he can be very vigorous in combating false teaching (e.g. 3.2).

As to the coming trial, Paul is ready to die, but sees so much work to be done that he thinks it must surely be God's purpose that he should be acquitted. Uncertainty remains, though he has utter confidence that whatever happens to him he will be safely held in Christ's hands. And isn't this the ultimate ground of all Christian confidence, not that we shall be preserved from pain or disaster, but that whatever happens, God in Christ will not let go of us?

✳ *Help us to know joy as a spring*
  always welling up within us
  and give us the power to dance through life,
  not as men and women who are blind
  to sorrow, misery or shame,
  but as those who know your victory over evil
  and over death and who cannot but rejoice.

127

Conduct worthy of the gospel

'Whatever happens' – here we come to the heart of what
Christian living is all about. It doesn't depend upon outward
circumstances but on your commitment and mine to the gospel
of Christ in good and bad times alike. Always aim to live
worthily! That Paul should write to this fellowship in these terms
reminds us that even the most sincere and committed people
need to be vigilant if they are to keep up to the mark.

Earlier Paul has written of folk around him being moved by
selfish ambition and mixed motives (1.17); in contrast he urges
Philippian Christians to remain united in the common purpose of
advancing the gospel. Actually he speaks of 'the struggle to
advance the gospel' which may be some encouragement in
days when, though for other reasons, we can still feel very much
up against it. He also urges confidence in the face of opposition:
confidence not in our own ability, skill or planning, but that, if we
faithfully play our part, we may safely leave the outcome to God.

✳ *Lord, we cannot know what lies before us this day,*
   but whatever awaits us, may we face it with confidence
   and may our conduct be worthy of the gospel, and you.

Our common life in Christ

Isn't this a marvellous passage, saying so much in so few
words? What we already enjoy in Christ is to be the spur to our
making 'our common life' even richer. Christian living is shown
to be a community experience where everybody's contribution
is valued. Could you say that this is true of the fellowship of
which you are a part?

Though we are encouraged to put the needs of others before
our own there is no room for false humility, nor any excuse for
sitting back and giving less than our best. Paul wants us to rise
to a genuine recognition of the gifts others have to bring, and to
rejoice that they have them to offer. This could mean in some
situations that we step down to make way for others; or we
might find ourselves taking on a fresh responsibility and so
releasing another to do something the church really needs of
him or her.

One way or another though, the emphasis is on coming to a
common mind and acting as a united body.

✳ *Lord, teach us the humility which does not underrate*
the gifts you have given us to use,
yet is able to truly welcome and rejoice
in the gifts you have given to others.

Thursday May 30   *Philippians 2.5-11*

An example to cherish

How do you react to the claim that 'At the name of Jesus every knee shall bow'? Do you think that non-Christians find this aggressive and threatening? Does it suggest some of the worst moments in the history of the Church?

But look at it in its context. The passage starts with Paul emphasizing the humility of Christ who, one with God, deliberately becomes, not only human but poor, claiming nothing for himself and dying the death reserved for the most despised criminal. Isn't Paul saying that this is where the true glory, the true nature of God, is revealed? If we are to enter into the life God has for us, we must first recognize the God who is with us in our weakness, the God revealed in Christ. So we have two tremendous thoughts to grapple with. The first is that our God is a God who is most surely with us when the way is hardest. The second, that we are called to make the way of humility our own.

✳ *Lord Jesus, you call us to follow in your way,*
to lose ourselves for others
that we may be at home in the eternal kingdom.
Lord, we would follow you,
but you know the battles we fight within ourselves.
Help us to discover the way of true humility.

Friday May 31   *Philippians 2.12-18*

Shine like stars in a dark world

'You must work out your own salvation ... for it is God who works in you.' A contradiction? Not really. If I say, 'God is at work in me so I don't have to bother' you would immediately recognize my folly. No, we have to fight our daily battles with the evil that so easily spoils our living and sometimes those battles can take all we have to give; yet isn't it your experience, that the more we are involved, the more we know that God is in the fight with us?

Paul refers again to the death sentence which possibly

awaits him. If he is to die it will be an offering bound up with their living witness; one will complete the other. And what lovely imagery we have here. 'You must shine like stars in a dark world and proffer the word of life.' Maybe the world is dark round about us: all the more need for us to shine like stars to light the path of others.

✳ *When the world is dark,*
We'll shine like stars;
When the world is false
We'll be true;
When the world is greedy,
We'll give way;
And when the world despairs,
We will renew.
... But only with your help, Lord.

Saturday June 1   *Philippians 2.19-24*

Dealing with practicalities

It is one thing to steel ourselves to meet a great challenge; it is another to face day to day problems and irritations. Yet it is with these that the larger part of the Christian conflict lies. In this passage some difficulties Paul is experiencing surface: 'they are all bent on their own interests' (2.21) and 'they' in this context are fellow Christians. Maybe Paul is going through a particularly black period, but he has earlier referred to Christ being proclaimed 'in a jealous and quarrelsome spirit' (1.15) so the Christian community with which he has contact in his imprisonment does leave quite a bit to be desired.

Timothy has been of great service to Paul and is ready to travel to Philippi. There's a depth of commitment here. No missionary society to provide backing! Timothy will have to work his passage. Faith is put to the test both in petty irritations and demanding tasks. How does our level of commitment compare with what we see here?

✳ *Lord, help me to recognize the fact*
that facing niggling daily irritants is just as important
as meeting great challenges when they come.
Grant me your help to confront and overcome both.

For personal reflection or group discussion

If Paul were writing to your church, for what in its life might he give thanks? – and what might he reprove?

Against all the odds Paul shows great confidence. What most assaults your faith? – and what are the grounds for your confidence in Christ today?

1st Sunday after Pentecost, June 2   *Philippians 2.25-30*

Expressions of loving care

Again the curtain is raised on the life of a small Christian community. Epaphroditus has come from Philippi with the support of the church there to give some service to Paul. He has been dangerously ill – and is there a hint of homesickness? How beautifully Paul expresses appreciation as he encourages Epaphroditus to return to Philippi. There's no hint that he feels let down, but just warm appreciation and commendation.

But with the departure of Epaphroditus and Timothy, Paul will lose two trustworthy helpers. In view of what he wrote in 2.21, he must surely wonder how he will manage after they have gone, even though it is planned that Timothy will return later. Yet if Paul has anxiety on this score he does not show it. He can show concern about the work of the gospel, but for himself, he is in God's hands and God will give him strength to meet each challenge as it comes.

✳ *Lord, we thank you for every time your love is expressed*
through kindly, self sacrificing acts.
Help us to appreciate the service others give
and use every opportunity to be servants for your sake.

Monday June 3   *Philippians 3.1-11*

A passionate declaration

After the first half of verse 1 this passage strikes a very different note. Paul's anger blazes out against those who attempt to tie the young Church into ancient ritual (in this case of course Jewish observances). This leads him to set out his own formidable pedigree which he has willingly written off in response to the call of Christ. It could have been no light thing to repudiate all that would have given him position and respect among his own people and instead be regarded by them as an outcast.

Paul speaks of his one desire 'to know Christ and the power of his resurrection' which for him cannot be separated from reaching out to bring others to the same knowledge – thus the anger and conflict with those who limit such a universal gospel. Are you aware of similar conflicts today? Are there inherited traditions you need, or maybe ought, to throw overboard? It doesn't hurt any of us to stop and face these questions.

✱ *Lord, strengthen my desire to know you*
and the power of your resurrection,
and stiffen my resolve to follow wherever you may lead
whatever treasures I may have to discard on the way.

Tuesday June 4   *Philippians 3.12-21*

Keep your eye on the goal!

Yesterday we saw the passion with which Paul attacks the narrow orthodoxy which is blind to the implications of the universality of Christ's mission. As he continues to write of his own inner struggles, Paul is led on to concern with other enemies – who 'make appetite their god'. This is highly relevant to the western world and its consumer society in the last decade of the twentieth century.

For most of us materialism is a far more dangerous enemy than over-zealous orthodoxy. Without realizing it we expect a certain 'standard of living' with endless updating of our homes as the norm. Yet the Christ we serve is to be found among the homeless, the hungry, the displaced and the misfits. Living as 'citizens of heaven' is not the same as having every modern comfort; nor is it any excuse for being blind to the needs of the rest of the world.

✱ *Lord we rejoice that we are called to be citizens*
of your Kingdom,
but save us from being so full of heavenly thoughts
that we are of no earthly use.

Love for the world starts at home

Years ago, I had my first taste of being on one of the central committees of the church. I travelled up from Derbyshire to meetings in London and found the experience quite exhilarating and the subjects discussed highly significant. But back on the train, getting ever nearer to home, the things I needed to do that night, or the people I would be seeing next day became far more important.

Paul has now to come down to niggling details and to address a particularly unedifying squabble. Two ladies have had a difference of opinion which has so upset things that news of it has been brought to Paul in his prison cell. If we knew the details we might well say, what a trivial thing. But it isn't trivial to the two concerned, or to others who have probably lined up behind them. How can it be tackled?

In a single sentence – 'I appeal to you both: agree together in the Lord'; Paul comes to the heart of the matter. If within the church we have fallen out with one another, or are in danger of doing so, then we need to make the effort to see how much bigger 'in the Lord' are the things which unite us compared with those which have come between us.

✳ *Lord, when we feel hurt, slighted, or misunderstood,*
help us to seek reconciliation,
remembering that you love us all
and that it is you we hurt most of all by our divisions.

Think on these things

For me this is one of the loveliest passages in the whole of the Scriptures, and for which I still turn to the Authorised Version. 'Rejoice in the Lord alway: and again I say, Rejoice ...' After the brief but searching appeal to Euodia and Syntyche, Paul lifts all thoughts to the heights.

Be joyful because you are Christ's, be considerate because that is his way, pray with confidence and trust and set your thoughts on the highest and noblest things and then, as inevitably as day follows night, the peace of God will be with you. Can Christians read such a passage together, pray and meditate on such things together and still remain divided? Did those two ladies whose difference had so upset the church in

Philippi come together joyfully into a new God given harmony? We hope they did; more important for us – does this incident remind us of any of our own relationships which need healing?

✳ *May the peace of God, which passeth all understanding keep our hearts and minds through Christ Jesus.*

Friday June 7   *Philippians 4.10-20*

God working in every experience

Earlier (2.26) we learned that Epaphroditus, who has come in the name of the Philippian church to support Paul, has been ill and is now returning to them. Now we discover that part of his mission has been to bring gifts to help Paul, and that this is not the first time that this church had so supported him. How gracefully Paul thanks them whilst declaring that he has learned to face all the ups and downs of life – and in terms of material well-being he has had more than his share of downs.

'And my God will supply all your needs'. Paul says nothing about all our 'wants'. The answer to heartfelt prayers can well be, 'No', or 'not now'; we are not likely to get all we want, but Paul, who knows both answered and unanswered prayer, says God will supply all our needs. In that faith he is ready to face all that life throws at him.

✳ *Lord help us to be generous to others and show us where our gifts should be directed, in sure faith that we have no occasion to be anxious for ourselves, but that all our needs will be supplied.*

Saturday June 8   *Philippians 4.21-23*

Greetings in and through Christ

In this brief final greeting Paul includes colleagues and 'all God's people'. 'Those in the emperor's service', who are specially mentioned would be imperial administrators, not confined to Rome, a Roman civil service reaching out across the empire, mainly made up of freedmen or slaves.

Paul is able to refer to the local Christian community without the pain he showed earlier concerning mixed motives (1.7) and those 'bent on their own interests' (2.21); but of course he had mentioned at the beginning (1.14) that most of his fellow Christians had been speaking the 'word of God fearlessly and with extraordinary courage'. Thus the picture we get both from the place from which Paul is writing – Rome? – and from Philippi, is of churches with vital, living fellowships, despite having individuals in their midst who gave cause for heartache.

Maybe you would like to think back for a few moments over what, for you, were the highlights of this letter in which we see the gospel declared in word and deed in very earthly situations.

✻ *Lord, may your grace indeed be at work within us, within the Christian church of which we are a part and within the lives of all we love and for whom we pray.*

For personal reflection or group discussion

It is very clear that whilst Paul's vision is nothing less than the salvation of the world he is still very conscious of inner struggle (e.g. 3.12ff). How far have we got his vision, or his determination to wrestle with evil within?

ACTION

Take a little time to look again at Philippians 4.8-9. Does it in any way strike a chord in your own heart?

LIVE AS GOD'S CHILDREN

Notes based on the Revised Standard Version by

Joseph Pungur

Joseph Pungur, a Hungarian minister of the Reformed Church of Hungary, now serves the Calvin Hungarian Presbyterian Church, Calgary, Alberta, Canada. He has also served as tutor at St. Paul's United Theological College, Limuru, Kenya (1976-83), as Professor at the Department of Religious Studies, University of Alberta (1984-92), and has written several articles and books in Theology.

'Know yourself!' said Socrates. This is the first step for each of us on the long road to becoming truly human. At some point we have to face the question: 'Who am I?' To find the right answer is essential to the meaning of our life, our value system and world view. There are as many answers as there are religions and philosophies, all of which provide contradictory answers. For Christians God's answer in the Scriptures states that we are God's children (1 John 3.1-2; Romans 8.16; Ephesians 5.1). God is our creator from whom we came and to whom we return. There are two life-determining consequences: the *promissiones Dei* and the *mandate Dei* – as classical theology calls them: the promises and the commandments of God. God calls us to be his children; and so we are to live as his children: walking with his blessings and in obedience to his will.

2nd Sunday after Pentecost, June 9   *John 3.31-36* *

A new quality of life

Almost all religions confirm the idea that we are the children of God. But there are degrees of belonging. Some may deny the existence of the loving care of God; some have only a thin philosophical knowledge of God. Those who follow Christ, says John, are the dear children of God for they believe in God wholeheartedly and follow the Son of God, God incarnate: 'He who comes from heaven ... whom God sent utters the words of God ... the Father ... and has given all things into his hand' (verses 31, 34, 35).

Christians come to God through their Mediator, Jesus Christ. The reward is tremendous: whoever 'believes in the Son has eternal life' (verse 36). We are no longer merely mortal, aware of the inevitability of death in all we do, but are given 'eternal life', a new quality of life which begins here and now, a new world view and new priorities. Be such a person!

✳ *Praise be to you, O Lord, who in the power of your resurrection gives us confidence and hope for the future.*
Amen. Yes, Lord, so says my heart.   Nigeria
                                 From Oceans of Prayer (NCEC)

Monday June 10   Habakkuk 2.1-4*

Living by faith

Habakkuk, just before Nebuchadnezzar of Babylon invades Jerusalem in 586 BCE, holds a dialogue with God – why is the tyrant Babylonia flourishing? In waiting for God's answer he utters one of the most profound, far-reaching and history-shaping statements: 'the righteous shall live by his faith' (verse 4). It played an important part in the teaching of Jesus, and in the theology of Paul and Martin Luther. Faith is vital for God's children.

First, in times of distress, trial and defeat when we do not understand why God allows these things to happen to us – as in the case of the prophet – we ask God and no answer arrives. Instead of resenting God it is right to keep an unflinching faith in God: for only through faith shall we survive bad times. Despite the odds, have faith in God. God's children will be proved to be right!

Second, what we did in evil times, we can do for our entire lives. Faith is one of the greatest of divine gifts, with love and hope (1 Corinthians 13). And 'This is the victory that overcometh the world, our faith' (1 John 5.4).

Third, through faith in the redemptive power of Christ we receive forgiveness of sin and the promise of eternal life (Galatians 2.16). By this faith we have the assurance of being the children of God (Galatians 3.16).

Eventually everything we possess will be taken away from us, gradually or suddenly: wealth, health, family, friends, even our lives – only faith abides to help us make the great leap from here to there, confidently and peacefully. Keep your faith for it will keep you!

> * *In God, whose word I praise*
> *in God I trust without a fear,*
> *what can flesh do to me?* Psalm 56.4

Tuesday June 11 Psalm 15

Living responsibly

The privilege of being God's children brings responsibility. Psalm 15 lists some golden rules of conduct for us: being blameless (verse 2), not doing evil to friends (verse 3), using our money in a responsible and ethical way (verse 5), making sure that those who carry responsibility for the community are men and women of Christian principles (verse 4), not committing slander (verse 3), nor breaking a promise (verse 4). Similar wise advice can be found in other Psalms and other books of the Bible (e.g. Proverbs, Ecclesiastes, Matthew 5-7), and Paul's letters (e.g. Colossians 3.18-25; Galatians 5.14-26 ...).

The overall rule for God's children is: 'Do not be conformed to this world but be transformed by the renewal of your mind (Romans 12.2). The conduct of God's children must be radically different from that of the children of the world. Why? Because only those who obey the will of God 'shall sojourn in thy tent and dwell on thy holy hill' (verse 1) – that is in God's Kingdom!

> * *O Lord God, set up thy kingdom in our hearts,*
> *that we may be true men and women*
> *and serve thee better as the days go by;*
> *through Jesus Christ our Lord.*
> The Bishop of Croyden (UK)
> From A Book of Prayers for Schools (SCM)

Wednesday June 12 Proverbs 10.1-17

Living wisely

Here the wise ethical rules of God's children are countered by the evil conduct of others.

Verses 2-5 present directives with regard to the right attitude of God's children towards work. They should not sit idly waiting for undeserved blessing, nor should they gain treasures by wickedness, for their good standing with God would be lost.

Verses 6-7 promise that God's children are under the blessings of God while the wicked ones will bear the consequence of sin, which is death.

Verses 8-9 state that God's children walk in the commandment of God and gain integrity and security; while wicked people go astray and ruin their lives.

Verses 10-14 say that God's children are peacemakers, love-givers and fountains of love. Wicked people are trouble-makers, hate-mongers and violent.

Verses 15-17 talk about the abundance of life as the reward of those who heed God's instructions, and sin is what the wicked gains. *But does it really work like that?*

Verse 1 says that 'a wise son makes a glad father' – likewise the children of God make God pleased. Here are two pathways. On which do you walk?

✳ *O Lord Jesus Christ, who art the way, the truth, and the life: suffer us not, we pray thee, to stray from thee who art the way; nor distrust thee, who art the truth; nor to rest in any other thing than thee who art the life.*

Erasmus, 1466-1536

Thursday June 13   1 John 2.22-29*

Knowing what you believe

In this passage John points out the divine side of being the children of God. First, he emphasizes that 'Jesus is the Christ' (verse 22). This means that Christ is the only Mediator between people and God. Consequently there is no access to God the Father except through the Son. He said that 'I and the Father are one' (John 10.30). In it lies one of the critical features of Christianity. Second, only those who believe in the Son have the Father also (verse 24) and the Holy Spirit too who teaches 'about everything' (verse 27). Third, God's children should be faithful to this vital teaching. John warns against those who 'would deceive you', and he admonishes: 'may this teaching abide in you' (verse 26). Only then 'you will abide in the Son and the Father' (verse 24), and this yields eternal life (verse 25). As it was in John's time, in our age too, there are many who question the foundations of Christian faith and try to minimize them. In the wave of new syncretism in which the vital role of Jesus Christ in Christianity is diminishing – the children of God should take the message of the apostle John with utmost seriousness!

* *O Father, my hope*
  O Son, my refuge
  O Holy Spirit, my protection.
  Holy Trinity, glory to Thee.
  Compline, Eastern Orthodox, St. Joannikios

Friday June 14   1 John 3.1-10

Becoming Christlike

John asks questions about some basic characteristics of the children of God, about their credentials, their mandate and their hope. To provide the clearest answer he uses the method of comparison: the children of God *vis à vis* the children of the devil.

First, John underlines that children of God are here because the Father called them so, and this is rooted in divine love (verse 1) – they 'were born from God' (verse 9).

Second, the consequences of being the children of God are that they enter into the evil-destroying work of Christ (verse 8). Because they are born of God, God's nature is in them and they do not commit sin again (verse 9). They do right including loving their brothers (verse 10).

Third, their reward will be apparent at the end: they 'shall be like him' – the glorified Christ (verse 2). If you are the child of God – live accordingly!

* *For beauty and gentleness we praise you, O Father,*
  For challenge and testing we submit to you, O Father,
  For victory over self and sin we pray you, O Father.
  Tonga, from Oceans of Prayer (NCEC)

Saturday June 15   John 3.1-8

A complete renewal

Nicodemus, a deeply religious and respected person, who had some burning questions and inner problems which prompted him to seek Jesus secretly, started with flattering words. But Jesus – having looked into his soul – cut him short and plainly told him: 'unless one is born anew, he cannot see the kingdom of God' (verse 3). For the children of God it is not enough to be born by 'flesh' only; to be born by Spirit is a must. Its human side is the conversion centred around *metanoia* – radical changes of thinking. Conversion is a process and it includes various stages such as the realization of lost status owing to sin, contrition, confession, and self-dedication to God. Classical theology distinguishes three elements in conversion:

1. the intellectual element, when one recognizes sin (Psalm 51.3; Romans 1.32);

2. the emotional element, when a person feels sorrow, for it is sin is by which life is ruined and God is hurt (Psalm 51.4; Hebrews 10.26-27);

3. the volitional element, when one wants to change its sinful state by seeking God's help, pardon and cleansing (Psalm 51.2,7,10).

Conversion may occur suddenly or through a long process. It may appear as human achievement but it is, indeed, the secret work of the Holy Spirit. No one can be God's dear child without being born anew!

✳ *Fire of the Spirit –*
moving and loving –
warm us and lead us,
encourage and change us.

Fire of the Spirit –
give light to our chaos,
drive out our confusions
and heal our hurt world.

Fire of the Spirit –
join us together,
dance in our churches,
transform our lives.

Jan S Pickard
From Oceans of Prayer (NCEC)

For personal reflection or group discussion

1. What does it mean to be children of God?

2. Can children of God expect God to give them preferential treatment?

3. What are the temptations of being children of God?

ACTION

Rededicate yourself to fuller obedience to God.

141

WOMEN'S VOICES

Notes based on the Revised Standard Version by

Clare Amos

Clare Amos is Editor of Partners in Learning, *an educational programme for all age-groups in the Church.*

From the context of a patriarchal society, the Gospels spotlight some exceptional insights from the voices of women. And part of the challenge they make to us today comes from the way Jesus responded to each of them.

3rd Sunday after Pentecost, June 16   *Luke 1.26-38*

The woman who listens

For today the only words we hear from Mary are a question (verse 34) and a simple statement of assent (verse 38).

Mary is an ambiguous figure for many Christians. It is not simply a case of historical disagreements between Catholics and Protestants, but the fact that her image has been used to cajole and encourage women to be submissive – and to reinforce the view that motherhood is (or should be) the 'raison d'être' of a woman's existence.

Perhaps one way forward is to compare the Mary we meet today with Eve: a comparison often made in Christian tradition. The Eve of Genesis listened to the wrong voice. Her own desires drowned God's words. She touched; she grasped; she was instrumental in setting human history off on the wrong track. Now it is through Mary's willingness to listen that history changes its course – and a new creation comes into being. If God is to begin to act we need to make space for him, to listen for him. Only thus can we too begin to give birth to the Word of God in our own lives.

✻ *Let us bless God for the women*
  who know what has been done to them;
  whose courage leaves them exposed;
  who, in fear and trembling and steadfast faith,
  proclaim the whole truth of salvation.
                    From All Desires Known, Janet Morley (SPCK)

The woman who speaks out

How dare she! Mary, a laywoman, proclaiming proudly that through her God's upside-down Kingdom is going to come into being! The answer in this Gospel batters our hearts with a vision that is liberating, exhilarating and desperately frightening to those of us who are counted among the world's and society's 'haves.' We will only get into the Kingdom (if we are lucky!) through beggars pleading on our behalf. And our invitation to God's banquet may well be withdrawn and given to others who cannot afford to feed themselves. The Song of Mary is perhaps the most revolutionary document in the New Testament: it is the programme for a revolution that Caesars and priests feared, and yet could not begin to understand.

A woman? Who better to sing this song? For she was poor – in a society where riches seemed to guarantee God's favour. She was a girl in a culture where the words 'Blessed are you, Lord God ... because you have not made me a woman' were part of a man's daily prayers. Now, pregnant and unmarried, she risked being cast out and scorned. Yet with her own exultation as the mother of God's Son she had become sacrament and symbol of God's new world, the time of grace of our Lord.

✳ *O unknown God,*
   whose presence is announced
   not among the impressive
   but in obscurity:
   come, overshadow us now,
   and speak to our hidden places;
   that, entering your darkness with joy,
   we may choose to cooperate with you,
   through Jesus Christ, Amen
                    From All Desires Known, Janet Morley (SPCK)

The woman who cares

This is not the easiest of stories for those who like their Jesus to be perfect! On the face of it Jesus' reply is racist and sexist – it is not fair to take the children's bread and throw it to dogs (would you like to be called a 'dog'?)

Yet the picture of Jesus here is one of the most attractive in the Gospels: it shows his willingness to learn from a most unexpected teacher: a woman who challenges age-old cultural assumptions and pet religious beliefs. We do not know what went on in Jesus' mind. But we may wonder whether – for the first time in his life in the Gentile city of Tyre – he was himself coming to a deeper realization of how widely his Father's love and care extended. Even Gentiles could eat at the banquet table in God's Kingdom.

What gave her courage to approach and tackle a stranger? It was love for her sick daughter. Through a mother's love for a daughter, a Son learned more of his Father's purposes.

✴ *O God whose word is life,*
and whose delight is to answer our cry,
give us faith like the Syro-Phoenician woman,
who refused to remain an outsider;
that we too may have the wit to argue
and demand that our daughters be made whole,
through Jesus Christ, Amen.

From *All Desires Known*, Janet Morley (SPCK)

Wednesday June 19   Mark 12.41-44

The woman who gives

A little old woman with little money did something that most people didn't notice. Of such, Mark wants to tell us, is the Kingdom of God. The seed sown through the preaching of the gospel of the Kingdom, begun in Galilee (1.14-15), bears fruit in the actions of a woman in Jerusalem. Mark cares deeply about 'little people' and suggests they have much to teach Jesus' close friends – those who should have known what he demanded. Jesus challenged his disciples with the need to give their all (8.35) and their response – bickering over who was the greatest – made clear their inability to 'hear' his message. But this woman had done precisely that: given away her 'very life.'

As the shadow of the Passion draws near, we wonder if the whole story of Jesus will simply end in failure – a failure made worse by the hopeless lack of understanding on the part of those nearest to him – as Judas betrays and Peter denies. But the story of this woman is a glimmer of hope that lights our way to the resurrection. She, like Jesus himself, gives 'all' and shows us that greed, fear and self-interest never have the final word.

* *Lord God, turn our eyes from the glitter and emptiness*
  of earthly wealth, and open our eyes
  that we may see your glory
  in acts of true goodness and sacrifice.
  And when you find us despising the lowly
  turn us back to the way of Jesus.

Thursday June 20   *John 4.5-15 **

The woman who struggles

Life was hard for this woman, until a stranger stopped one day
at the well she used. The well was deep; it was back-breaking
work to draw the water on which her family's existence
depended. And she had to go there at noon – the hottest part of
the day. If she went in the early morning, other women shunned
her, or called her names, and picked up stones to throw at her.
It was her reputation: she had had five husbands – some had
died, some she had escaped after they beat and abused her.
Now she lived with a 'protector' – and suffered the jibes of 'tart'
in silence.

Normally she hoped she would not meet anyone at the well,
but today there was a man sitting there looking as tired and
thirsty as herself. He was a Jew: she could see that by his
clothes. He was bound to ignore her, since she was a
Samaritan woman. But instead he asked for a drink, and when
she asked 'why', he started to talk, answering all those
questions that poured out of her frustration, tiredness and
unhappiness. She hadn't felt so human – in years: it was as
though she sat there drinking deep of a heady draught she had
not drawn – and which refreshed the depths of her soul.

After those few strange days she did not see him again, but
heard news of him from time to time. One day, about two years
later, grim news filtered to the town that he had been crucified –
in Jerusalem. She thought of him hanging on the cross in the
middle of the day, thirsty unto death, and remembered the time
he met her at mid-day and gave her new life and refreshment. It
seemed that the living water he offered had sprung deep out of
his side.

* *Lord Jesus Christ, increase our willingness to take time*
  to draw from the well of your grace
  that we may be healed by your love,
  grow in faith, and live by the values of your Kingdom.

The woman who questions

When she heard of his death she heard what had prompted it. She knew that some feared and hated him, just as deeply as she loved him. The final straw was his action in the Temple in Jerusalem – he charged in and threw out those who bought and sold there, who tried to exclude others – Samaritans, women, society's outcasts – from its hallowed precincts. The powers-that-be would never forgive him, for it challenged their prestige and self-interest to the core.

She remembered how they bantered about whether the Temple in Jerusalem was God's chosen place – or whether it was the Temple which soared above them, on the heights of Gerizim where her people worshipped. Jews and Samaritans had argued over this for centuries, and fought over it: but she and the Jewish stranger laughed together over the folly of those who tried to trap God in a building, or confine him to a place. 'Soon, soon,' he told her, 'the time will come when we will all worship God together, for God is spirit, breath, wind, who blows away the dead wood of our hatred, and will lift the roof off our temples that are so holy that they will not permit human beings to pray in them!' (see Isaiah 56.7 and Mark 11.17)

Priests of Gerizim hadn't liked that, nor, she supposed, had priests in Jerusalem. So he was killed: but she knew that was not the end. The living water welling up in her heart could not be quenched, even by death.

✳ *Spirit of freedom, whose hour is now come,*
blow away our dust, our despair, our divisions.
Give us a vision of the new earth
where a temple will no more be needed,
but cleanse our hearts
so that in them you can find your dwelling-place.

The woman who goes

She always remembered the moment she saw him, sitting by the well, like a dream out of ancient tales – a handsome stranger asks for water from a woman and takes her to be his bride (Genesis 24.15ff). But in the stories the woman was a young, innocent virgin, not the soiled goods that no good man wants to be seen with. But he had needed her; he gave her a task – and for that she was grateful.

His disciples had gone to buy bread, and when they came back their revered leader was talking to this disreputable woman. She could see they longed to ask what he was up to, but didn't dare. He was like that: gentle, with the kind of authority that brooked no unnecessary questions. He hadn't thought her questions were unnecessary – he answered them, even encouraged the asking.

He respected her as a person, not a channel for men's desires. He made her the messenger of his good news. She, the dregs of her city, became the one through whom their lives were changed. Why had they listened to her, when normally they turned their backs and stopped their ears? Was it the lightness of her step, the light in her eyes that commanded attention? They listened, and came to see for themselves – they made her Saviour their own.

Of course some belittled her contribution. And those disciples, years later, after his death, came again. They called it their 'Mission to Samaria'. Had they forgotten that Samaria had already received the gospel from a woman? And had they forgotten Jesus' story about sowing and reaping? How easy it was to claim for one's own the harvest another had planted!

✳ *Let us bless God for the women*
who have boldly touched our lives;
who have disrupted our use of power;
who have made us see what was hidden,
and feel in our bodies what it means to be made whole.
From All Desires Known, Janet Morley (SPCK)

For personal reflection or group discussion, and ACTION

Read again and reflect on Luke 1.39-56 from the point of view of your own culture and nationality. Make a list of the sayings and actions of Jesus which reflect his mother's sentiments in this great song.

THE WORK OF GOD

1. Breaking hostility

Notes based on the New Jerusalem Bible by

Brian Brown

Brian Brown was banned by his government when working for the Christian Institute in South Africa. He then settled in Britain and now serves as Africa Secretary for the Methodist Church Overseas Division (London).

He worketh still! Christians agree that God's work of breaking hostility was revealed supremely in the person of Jesus. But they often disagree as to how God works today.

In my homeland, South Africa, a miracle was seen in April 1994. The prophets of doom had declared the impossibility of peaceful change. They were wrong. The walls of apartheid crumbled and the world watched in amazement as a new, democratic nation emerged. The illustrative material for this week's theme (written in January 1995) relates to South Africa's miracle in 1994. It shows how God, who breaks hostility, is active in history.

4th Sunday after Pentecost, June 23   *Hosea 14.1-7 **

Cry, the beloved country

Hosea concludes his prophecy with a picture of Israel returning to God in penitence. The prophet who has grieved over his people's disloyalty anticipates national renewal under God. Sensitive spirits don't enjoy declaring God's unpalatable truths to a resentful and unresponsive people.

One of the greatest prophets in South Africa during the apartheid years was Dr C F Beyers Naudé, a church leader banned by the regime. His 'crime' was to be an Afrikaner who saw the incompatibility of the gospel with apartheid – long before his Church and people ceased their support.

I was with him one afternoon when a government newspaper

published a vitriolic attack on his person. Beyers had been called a communist, terrorist and traitor. In the intimacy of his office he broke down. They were not tears of self-pity. Quietly he sobbed, 'my volk, my volk.' Like Hosea before him he prayed for his people, and like all true prophets he looked in faith to God's gift of the new.

In the National Service of Reconciliation which followed the birth of the new South Africa in 1994, Beyers was asked to invoke God's blessing on all of its citizens.

✳ *Lord, fall like dew on all nations*
  that they may bloom like the lily.

Monday June 24   *Jonah 1.1-17*

Hating the evil – or its perpetrators?

'One settler one bullet' was a sentiment expressed by black hard-liners who had no desire to see a negotiated end to apartheid. Like Jonah, they wished to see the destruction of the sinners – to escalate hostility, not break it.

That both black and white were able to negotiate a new South Africa was due to the conscious effort of the majority to defuse the hostility. People like Lutheran Bishop Manas Buthelezi repeatedly stressed that he needed whites to attain his freedom – and that they needed him to attain theirs! Proclaiming the indivisibility of freedom was far removed from Jonah's 'us and them' mentality.

Most black people creatively spoke of being 'against the system' rather than against the whites who were the perpetrators of the dehumanizing system. Had this phrase of grace ceased, to be replaced by declaring hate for whites, the miracle of peaceful transition to the new would not have happened. The truth of freedom's indivisibility became self-evident for the millions of whites liberated from the shame and guilt of the old era.

✳ *Lord, may we hate evil*
  as we work to redeem the perpetrators of evil.

Tuesday June 25   *Jonah 2.1-10*

Repentance and the household of God

Before Jonah could obey God and help to change Nineveh, a 'down in the mouth' Jonah had to repent.

The household of God must always lead in repentance. During 1990, at the town of Rustenburg, leaders of virtually every major church in South Africa came together. As they observed a nation ready to self-destruct they had reason to cry out from 'the belly of Sheol'. Violence was escalating and a divided Church reflected the polarized society. Out of their distress, the leaders cried to God. The representative of the powerful and hitherto pro-apartheid Dutch Reformed Church declared; 'I confess before you and before the Lord not only my own sin and guilt, and my personal responsibility for the political, social, economic and structural wrongs that have been done to many of you, and the results of which you and our whole country are still suffering from, but vicariously I dare also to do that in the name of my church ...' The unity of the Church, forged at Rustenburg in penitence before Christ, became a potent factor in breaking hostility in South Africa.

✳ Lord, may your church say 'Sorry'
before asking other sinners to do so.

Wednesday June 26   *Jonah 3.1-5*

Let's talk – Now!

Jonah was amazed by the response of the people when finally he got round to talking to them.

In 1988, when negotiation and reconciliation were swear words in parts of South Africa, Stanley Mogoba, Presiding Bishop of the Methodist Church, challenged a gathering of eminent politicians, saying, 'We all know that negotiations are inevitable because no war ever ends without a peace conference. I offer the analogy of two fathers who are having a conflict. They say, "we want to fight," or even worse, "we don't want to talk to each other, we rather want our children to fight each other." And that of course is happening today ... People may continue to destroy one another for a long time to come. But at a certain point, they will have to sit down and talk. Now if one is going to have talks at sometime, why postpone them? Why kill first?'

This kind of seed was sown faithfully by Christians who were willing to swim against the tide in the dark years. In 1990, negotiations began for a new South Africa and with the talks came the breaking of hostilities.

✳ *Lord, if I need to talk to end hostility,*
  enable the talk to begin now.

Thursday June 27   Jonah 3.6-10 *

The splendour of sackcloth

The King of Nineveh was never more splendidly attired than
when in sackcloth. He was never more kingly than when calling
for a renunciation of evil and violence.

South Africa's ex-President, F W de Klerk, was called the
'lesser of equals' when he and Nelson Mandela were awarded
the Nobel Peace Prize. This was understandable. It was the evil
and violence of *his* party's policies which had to be repented of.
But although the lesser figure, nothing should detract from the
nobility of de Klerk's public penitence. It didn't come easily.
Initially he claimed that whatever hurt apartheid had occasioned,
its perpetrators had been sincere until deepening relationships
across the racial divide led to growing awareness of the enormity
of apartheid's evil. They learnt that to have 'sincerely'
dehumanized millions diminished neither the pain nor the sin of
those forty years. There is little virtue in the sincerity of error. De
Klerk's penitential declaration of the evil of apartheid contributed
to the healing of the nation. Apartheid's victims did not need to
see him humiliated. They did need to see his 'sackcloth'.

✳ *Lord, help us to wear less silk and more sackcloth.*

Friday June 28   Jonah 4.1-11 *

We can't have heaven crammed

Jonah was distraught. He'd relished the prospect of the
despised Ninevites being destroyed. Now, as he'd feared, the
'tender, compassionate God' had let them off the hook.

There are those today who can't tolerate the thought of
heaven being crammed. They accept that God wants everyone
to be saved and reach full knowledge of the truth but they then
imply that the divine will is constantly frustrated. Their God is
like a failed impresario, attracting only one in ten while the
Adversary pulls in the others.

In apartheid South Africa, the belief that God favours the
elect white few had credence for decades. This failed
nationalistic theology is now being re-interpreted; God's election
means responsibility for all not favouritism for some.

For the Jonahs who wish heaven to resemble an isolation ward, the tender, compassionate and accepting God is a disappointment. For those committed to breaking walls of hostility, God of Jonah declares them on the side of right.

✴ **Lord, it's great to know you don't wish anyone to be lost.**

Saturday June 29   Ephesians 2.11-22 *

Take courage

Mandela's inauguration as President of a democratic South Africa was a day for which millions had prayed and sacrificed. In that moment the old apartheid era died.

After the ceremony, Mandela hastened to a football stadium where a predominantly black South African team was to play Zambia. This in itself was a celebratory moment, ending the long sports' boycott promoted by black South Africans. The band struck up the people's hymn *Nkosi Sikelele*. Now, for the first time, it was an official anthem. Seventy thousand voices rejoiced. Then, to stunned silence, the anthem of the apartheid era was played – the 'oppressor's anthem' – sung in the language against which black youth had rebelled for decades. In response Mandela took the microphone. He chided the crowd for not singing 'the other national anthem'. He asked that they learn the words, reminded them that they were now one nation – and invited whites to learn the new anthem too. This courageous man had testified to the breaking down of barriers, the destroying of hostility, and the making of the two into one.

✴ **Lord, make us courageous to do the right.**

For personal reflection or group discussion

In the light of what God achieved through Christians committed to reconciliation and justice in South Africa, can it be said that Christianity and politics do not mix?

What insights gathered from South Africa would be relevant for other societies where hostility needs to be broken?

ACTION

List the persons mentioned as God's instruments in the week's notes and pray for them.

THE WORK OF GOD

2. Eternal life for all

Notes based on the Revised English Bible by

Salvador T Martinez

Salvador T Martinez teaches theology at the McGilvary Faculty of Theology, Payap University in Chiang Mai, Thailand. He was formerly Secretary for the theological concerns of the Christian Conference of Asia. He is an ordained minister of the United Church of Christ in the Philippines sent to the Church of Christ in Thailand as an international associate under the joint auspices of the United Church Board for World Ministries and the Division of Overseas Ministries (Disciples of Christ).

For many Christians, eternal life is something to be enjoyed in the future. For the writer of the Gospel of John, however, eternal life is also something we can and must enjoy here and now. Eternal life is God's gift to all who believe in the Lord Jesus Christ. To have eternal life is to enter into a new relationship with God, with others and with ourselves. To have eternal life is to live a life guided by the Spirit. It is a life full of new, exciting and creative possibilities. To have eternal life would be to have 'a new heart' and 'a new spirit within' (Ezekiel 36.26).

This was illustrated for us in last week's notes. The present writer now looks more closely at some of the theology that under girds this new life.

5th Sunday after Pentecost, June 30   *John 3.9-17*

Love and life

Jesus had explained how a person is born again 'from water and spirit'. Nicodemus asked: 'How is this possible?' Jesus' answer, which begins with a hint of sarcasm, is unequivocal: to be born of the Spirit is accomplished through the death and resurrection of the Son of Man. The phrase 'the Son of Man must be lifted up' refers to Jesus' death, resurrection and ascension – his cross and his glory.

This reading includes the best loved Bible verse for Christians of all time: John 3.16. Why is this verse so popular? Why does it appeal to young and old alike? This verse summarizes the whole Christian message of redemption. It tells us that God in his very being is love. It tells us of God's great love for humankind, that he gave his only Son, through whom there is eternal life for all who believe in him. To believe in Jesus is to believe the truth about God.

✳ *O God of love,*
   teach us to enjoy and to share the eternal life
   which you have so graciously given to us
   through our Lord Jesus Christ.

Monday July 1   *John 3.18-21*
Truth and life
The symbolic use of light and darkness for good and evil is common in Jewish Scriptures as well as in classical Greek literature. An evil doer avoids the light for fear that his works will be exposed. Dark places are invitations to crime. We are advised to avoid dark streets. It is safer to walk along a well-lighted street. Light exposes evil. Jesus uses this common understanding of light to show that those who reject God will be exposed when the light of revelation comes upon them (cf. John 1.4,5). Unbelief is the choice of darkness over light. Those who remain in darkness are condemned. All is not gloomy, however, for it is God's desire to save. 'Those who live by the truth come to the light.' Truth describes everything that belongs to God as opposed to evil. The emphasis is on living (doing) the truth. The person who performs truth comes to the light. That person's works are 'done in God' and the light makes this clear to everyone. The person who experiences rebirth in Jesus Christ lives by the truth and that person's way of life will show it.

✳ *O Lord of Light, let your light shine through us*
   that we may honour your name in all that we do.

Tuesday July 2   *John 5.19-24* *
Judgment and life
Accused by the Jews of breaking the Sabbath and making himself equal with God, Jesus repeatedly affirms the unity of his

154

actions with that of the Father's. Earlier in the Gospel, John made tremendous claims about Jesus – he is the eternal Word, he is the Messiah, the Son of God, the lamb of God. On what basis were these claims made?

Jesus claims that he is completely dependent on the Father. His will is the Father's will. The Father is the source of life and judgment. Both matters – the giving of life and bestowing judgment – are delegated to the Son who gives life and judges as he chooses. Those who accept the way of life that Jesus offers, and believe in God who sent him, have eternal life. Those who reject the life he offers are judged. Life and judgment are seen by the writer as both present and future. Here and now, those who believe are no longer under judgment but have 'already passed from death to life'.

Have we accepted the way of life Jesus offers? Has it made a difference to the way we live? Have we shared this new life with others?

✳ *O God our judge,*
 make our words and deeds reflect the glory and honour
 of your Son, Jesus Christ.

Wednesday July 3   *John 5.25-36 **

Death and life

Yesterday's reading showed us that the divine prerogative of giving life and bestowing judgment has been passed on to the Son. John's emphasis is on the present aspect of judgment and eternal life: 'Indeed it is already here.' Those who choose to remain in darkness receive their judgment and those who believe accept a new quality of life, here and now. Jesus uses the word 'dead' in two senses: spiritually (verse 25) and physically (verse 28). The spiritually dead come to life when they hear the 'voice of the Son of God'. The physically dead will come to life at the resurrection and will be judged according to what they have done in life. The choice depends on us. We may choose the way to life or the way to death. What do we choose?

✳ *O Son of God,*
 help us to choose the path that leads to eternal life
 and teach us how to help others to do the same.

Spirit and life

Some disciples became discouraged. They understood the implications of Jesus' words, but they found them difficult to accept. Many people are turned off by the Christian faith because it demands a total surrender to Christ, and a life based on a very high moral standard. Some do not have what it takes to be a Christian.

Jesus says that it is the 'spirit that gives life'; the flesh is powerless to accomplish anything. What did Jesus mean? What we do in the flesh is useless if it is not done for a higher purpose. Christ can provide that purpose for us. His words are 'both spirit and life'. How fitting is the answer of Simon Peter: 'Lord, to whom shall we go? Your words are words of eternal life.' Christ provides the true purpose for our life and the power to work it out (cf. Philippians 1.21).

✵ *O God's Holy One, help us to believe and to know*
   in the power of your word and spirit.

Faith and life

This passage begins with the often quoted saying that 'a prophet is without honour in his own country' (cf. Mark 6.4; Matthew 13.57; Luke 4.24). Unlike the other Gospels, the saying is followed by John's account that the Galileans welcomed our Lord. They had seen what he did in Jerusalem and that drew them to him.

The story that follows has some similarity with the healing of the centurion's servant in the synoptic Gospels (Matthew 8.5-13; Luke 7.1-10). But John's account differs in several ways. An officer of Herod's court came to Jesus to plead for the healing of his son who was at the point of death. It must have taken a great deal of courage for a high ranking royal officer to come to Jesus. And Jesus responded to his faith in a way that had never been done before or thought possible: Jesus healed his son at a distance. The officer believed what Jesus told him, and he and members of his household became believers.

How much faith do we really have in Jesus? The officer should be an example to us.

✵ *O God of mercy, how little do we really trust in you.*
   Forgive us. Teach us to fully trust in you.

Grace and life

Verses 14-17 are a supplication. The people plead to God to 'shepherd' (cf. 2.12) their nation, that they may 'graze in Bashan and Gilead' anew. They have been devastated and isolated, anticipating the desolation of their city. They recall the marvellous accomplishments of their ancestors and pray that God will lead them as he had led them 'out of Egypt'.

The second part is a song of victory. It begins with the declaration, 'Who is a god like you' – an apparent play on Micah's name that means 'Who is like Yahweh?' The song affirms that God forgives and forgets and does not retain his anger (cf. Psalm 30.5). Yahweh is different from gods of other nations. God's majesty is described in terms of grace and compassion, faithfulness and mercy. *Hesed* (Hebrew) means a love that is constant and steadfast; it keeps on no matter what happens. In spite of the horrible experience they have been through, they cling to the promises of God. Do we have the same faith in the God of grace and truth today?

✱ *O God of grace,*
  help us have faith that you love us in spite of ourselves
  and that you will be faithful and loving till the end.

For personal reflection or group discussion

What does it mean to have eternal life? How do we experience eternal life today, right where we are? How can we share our experience of eternal life with others?

ACTION

Who in your community are deprived or unable to experience eternal life? What can you do to help them?

157

FACING NEW CHALLENGES
Acts 21-28

Notes based on the Good News Bible by

David Dunn Wilson

David Dunn Wilson is Tutor in Pastoral Theology at Hartley Victoria Methodist Theological College in Manchester (UK).

'I myself will show him all that he must suffer for my sake.' With these disturbing words, God sent Ananias to greet Saul of Tarsus, so recently converted on the Damascus road (Acts 9.16). Very soon, Saul himself learned the truth of those words because when he began his work for Jesus it was like leaving a safe harbour to face the open, raging sea. New challenges swept down upon him like great waves threatening to drown his new found faith. In this series, we will be thinking about some of those challenges and, as we see the way in which Paul met them, perhaps we can learn lessons for our own Christian living.

6th Sunday after Pentecost, July 7   *Acts 21.17-26*

The challenge of compromise

In spite of the warm welcome given to Paul in Jerusalem, he is aware that the old argument about Jewish Christians and the Law is still unresolved. Paul has upset the Jewish traditionalists. How is he to still their criticism without sacrificing his own integrity?

The event illustrates the tension between the new and the old, which tests the Church in every age. Often, traditionalists tend to be defensive and resistant to change. Notice how fanatically they try to destroy Paul's credibility by exaggerating his faults! On the other hand, innovators tend to be impatient, seeing themselves as champions of progress and dismissing traditionalists as obstinate and foolish.

Paul's reaction is intriguing because, by submitting to the traditionalists' rules instead of attacking their errors, he risks being despised by both sides. The traditionalists might interpret his action as surrender while innovators may see it as treachery. Yet, for Paul, the enrichment of fellowship is more important than his own feelings or reputation. By compromising, he hopes to harvest for the church both the riches of tradition and the new vision of innovation.

✳ *Lord teach me to know when to compromise.*

Monday July 8   *Acts 21.27-36*

The challenge of violence

Paul's heroic compromise fails and it nearly costs him his life. When the fanatical mob drags him out of the Temple to lynch him, the Jewish authorities abandon him to his fate and slam the gates of the Temple. Knowing the risk that he is taking, Paul bravely faces the challenge of violence.

Today, Christians, like everyone else, experience the violence which is a sad part of our world, but sometimes, in addition, they must face persecution for being faithful to Jesus. This persecution comes in many forms including mob violence, denial of human rights, rejection by family and friends, verbal abuse and mental cruelty.

In whatever form the challenge of violence comes, Christians must confront it with Paul's spirit of realism, accepting that standing with Jesus in this world means confronting the violence of evil. Like Paul, we must understand that, at such times, 'courage' does not mean lack of fear but the receiving of God-given victory over fear.

✳ *Lord, give me courage to be faithful to you, no matter what the consequences may be.*

Tuesday July 9   *Acts 21.37 to 22.16*

The challenge of misrepresentation

Although rescued from the howling mob, Paul's troubles are not over. The Roman commander thinks that he has captured a notorious revolutionary and is understandably annoyed when he realizes that it is a case of mistaken identity. Grudgingly, he allows Paul to set the record straight – something which Paul often has to do during his ministry because he is continually misrepresented and misunderstood.

The passion with which Paul sometimes defends himself shows how deeply he feels the pain of being misunderstood. Misrepresentation can be as cruel as physical violence, and many modern Christians know the hurt of being caricatured as hypocritical and stupid when they do not deserve it. Paul's defence teaches us three important lessons about responding to the challenge of misrepresentation:

- it is controlled – he does not lose his temper or return abuse for abuse;

- it is factual – Paul sets out the simple truth of the situation;

- it is Jesus-centred – Paul humbly tells his hearers what God has done for him in Christ because, ultimately, it is what Jesus thinks about him which really counts.

✳ *Lord, if I am unjustly misunderstood,*
give me grace and skill to set the record straight.
If I begin to feel sorry for myself,
remind me that I sometimes misrepresent others.

Wednesday July 10 ·   Acts 22.17-29

The challenge of fanaticism

As Paul carefully tries to set the record straight, the mob erupts in terrible fury. A mob is more than the sum of its parts. It develops an irrational personality of its own. When normally reasonable people join a mob, they seem to lose their reason and are driven by their worst animal instincts. The challenge of fanaticism, which Paul encounters here, lies at the root of much modern violence, injustice and war.

'Fanaticism' is a respectable, religious word which originally meant a proper respect for the temple (Latin – *fanum*). How then does it turn the fervour of religious people into the sort of mindless brutality which threatens Paul's life?. The answer is complex but there may be a clue in this passage. Verse 22 says that the trouble begins when the people stop listening to Paul. Perhaps that is always when the trouble starts – when we stop listening to other people and assume that they must be wrong and that we must be right. Once we believe this, it is easy to think that it is our duty to silence ideas that differ from our own. Beware! There is a 'fanatic' lurking inside most of us!

✳ *Lord teach me to hold my convictions humbly,*
to defend them bravely
and to respect the convictions of others.

The challenge of controversy

Is it by accident or design that Paul focuses upon the resurrection of the dead, the one subject which he knows will set his accusers at each others' throats? As an advocate, he certainly knows how to exploit the weaknesses of his opponents, but this is not mere legal skill. Paul is taking his stand upon a matter of principle.

Paul's reaction to the challenge of controversy is worth noting. He neither seeks it nor avoids it. When he says, 'I become all things to everybody' (1 Corinthians 9.22) he does not mean that he tries to please everybody by agreeing with them.

Some people seem to thrive on conflict but most of us would rather avoid controversy at all costs. Paul reminds us that, whether we like it or not, there are times when we must stand up for truth even if that means becoming involved in controversy. When we face this challenge bravely, we can be sure that, like Paul, we will hear our Lord's encouraging voice saying, 'Don't be afraid!'

✳ *Lord, I prefer a quiet life without controversy:*
   when I have to give it up, give me courage.

The challenge of hatred

In the readings for yesterday and today, we glimpse two kinds of hatred. The first is the animal fury which is capable of tearing Paul to pieces (verse 10), the second is the cold, calculated hatred which is ready to starve to death rather then let Paul live. Different though they may seem, they share the same intensity. Hatred may begin as simple dislike but it soon becomes an obsessive desire to harm and is focused on its victim with the precision of a laser-beam.

If hatred is to become truly potent it must distort the image of its victim, magnifying faults and blotting out all redeeming features. That is why hatred makes such an effective political weapon against minority groups and why there are so many places where the church suffers because it stands with those who are hated.

Like Paul, we know that, on a personal level too, hatred is perfectly capable of killing without remorse – but beware, 'hatred' is merely 'dislike' grown ripe! When we dislike somebody it is easy, almost without being aware of it, to set in motion the process of distortion which becomes self-destructive hatred.

✳ *Lord, there are some people that I find it hard to like. Help me to look at them through your eyes of love. Save me from hating others, even if they hate me.*

Saturday July 13   Acts 24.1-27 *

The challenge of the 'religious talker'

In verses 24-26, there is an interesting cameo of a Roman governor engaged in long conversations with Paul. At first sight, Felix appears to be an earnest enquirer but he is soon unmasked as an unscrupulous dabbler in religion who will discuss it but has no intention of being changed by it.

We probably know people like Felix for whom religious faith is an intellectual game. Paul once called them 'the skilful debaters of this world' (1 Corinthians 1.20). If ever they suspect that debate might lead them into costly decision, they too 'become afraid' (verse 25) and change the subject. Witnessing to such people can be frustrating and, unlike Paul who has no choice but to appear before Felix, we have to choose whether or not to continue our discussions with them.

Although it can be very time-consuming, it is normally better for us to continue our discussions. Conversion can be a long and intricate process and, at least, we can ensure that the 'religious talker' keeps on thinking about religious truth. It is a small price to pay for the privilege of being used by the Holy Spirit to lead somebody to faith.

✳ *Lord, give me as much patience in seeking others for you as you needed when you were seeking me.*

For personal reflection or group discussion

What are the challenges to faith which confront me personally at this time, and what does Paul teach me about dealing with them?

The challenge of opportunity

Paul is assured that he will bear witness for Christ in Rome itself (23.11), but the opportunity comes in the strangest way. When cornered by the plotting of the Jews and the deviousness of Festus, Paul turns adversity into opportunity and uses his Roman citizenship to appeal to Caesar. Thus Rome itself will ensure that he is carried to his goal in safety!

Paul knows that Christians must seize opportunities for spreading the gospel, even when those opportunities come in the most unexpected ways. Jesus himself urges his followers to seize opportunities with all the 'shrewdness of the people of this world' (Luke 16.8) and his words still apply to us. Successful businessmen spend their lives making circumstances work for them, and we must be just as astute in making circumstances work for Christ.

God has given us the 'building blocks' of life – time and people – and he wants us to use them to the full. We must create opportunities to spread the gospel and to serve our neighbours in Christ's name. We need to approach every situation positively and with expectation.

✱ *Lord, life is short and precious.*
  Prevent me from littering it with lost opportunities.

Monday July 15 Acts 25.13-27

The challenge of power

There is a striking difference between the interminable private discussions between Paul and Felix and the picture presented to us now. In verse 23, a scene of magnificence confronts Paul when he is brought into the audience hall. All the trappings of imperial power are here, political authority, legal control, immense wealth and military might. In contrast, Paul stands in the dock – just one man and, if tradition is to be believed, physically not very impressive.

The confrontation seems symbolic for, in every age, the faithful followers of Jesus have found themselves standing over against the world's power-structures. Paul wrote to the Corinthian Christians, 'From the human point of view few of you were wise or powerful or of high social standing' (1 Corinthians 1.26) and that is still often true of Christians. What is more, history shows us that when the Church is nearest to worldly power it is farthest from Jesus.

Perhaps we may never become famous Christian heroes or heroines but, we too may have to accept the challenge of power. There may be local injustices which we need to fight even though the prospect terrifies us. When that happens we can remember Paul standing alone before the magnificence of Rome and be sure that the same Lord who stood with him also stands with us.

✳ *Lord, when I feel the odds against me are overwhelming, remind me that you have the real power.*

Tuesday July 16   *Acts 26.1-32*

The challenge of failure

The situation looks very promising. Agrippa, no stranger to Jewish beliefs, is giving Paul a careful hearing. Even the ironical remark, 'In this short time do you think you will make me a Christian?' (verse 28) must make Paul think that, given time, there is a chance of converting Agrippa. The next moment, however, Agrippa rises from his seat, walks out of the hall and out of Paul's life. Paul fails to make a convert after all.

The challenge of failure hits sincere Christians especially hard because they really want to live for Christ and are ashamed when they fail him. There is, however, a special pain that comes when, although they have witnessed faithfully, they have failed to win converts. They feel failure so deeply because, like Paul, they care so much. They ask, 'Where did I go wrong?' 'What more could I have done?' In our quest to win others for Christ, we need to remember that people cannot be compelled to love him. Love is a voluntary emotion. Even when the Holy Spirit has done all that he can through us to win a person, that person still has a God-given right to say 'No'.

✳ *Lord, people are always saying 'No' to you.*
You live with failure all the time.
When I get depressed by failure, help me to remember that it is faithfulness not success which counts.

Wednesday July 17   *Acts 27.1-26*

The challenge of fear

Having faced so many different challenges, Paul is on his way to Rome at last! But his problems are not over. Anyone who has watched waves breaking upon a shore and knows the immense power of the sea can understand why ancient people thought the sea was a monster whose moods could change with terrifying rapidity. Those who have actually experienced a storm at sea know just how small and helpless sailors feel at the mercy of the 'North-easter'.

The Bible, poets, artists and musicians liken life itself to the sea. It is calm one moment and, the next, churned up into a raging storm. When that happens, we experience the fear those sailors must have felt, and we know what it means not to be in control. Paul and the sailors are literally 'in the same boat', so why are their reactions so different? Being human, Paul feels fear but he is not overcome by it. He knows that he may not be in control but God is! (verse 23)

✳ *Lord, sometimes I get scared.*
When that happens, remind me that you are not scared and that you are in control.

Thursday July 18   Acts 27.27-44. *
The challenge of panic
As every attempt to save the ship fails and it is driven helplessly towards the shore, the level of panic rises. It is strange how often, when calm and common-sense are most needed, people lose the ability to keep calm and to act sensibly. The word 'panic' is very appropriate for such a reaction because it comes from the name of the Greek god Pan who was believed to drive people mad.

We need to learn from Paul who is like the eye in the calm of the storm. He breathes common-sense into the madness, and everyone 'takes heart'. It is right that 'panic' should be named after a pagan god because it has no place in the life of a Christian. It stems from that fear which either paralyzes us or makes us react stupidly. Faith accepts the challenge of panic and defeats it. Faith injects calm into the most frightening situations by reminding us that God is still in control.

There is another lesson here. There are times when, like Paul, Christians have to inject their faith into crises for the sake of those who, having no faith of their own, are gripped by panic. This requires spiritual maturity. We cannot hold other people firm, if we ourselves are not held firm by God.

✳ *Lord, when I have to face crises for myself or others save me from panic.*

The challenge of success

'He is a god!' That is the verdict of those who see Paul delivered from the snake (verse 6). For once, everything is going well. Paul's reputation is high and he is surrounded by friends. After all the fierce challenges he has faced, he deserves some success and, doubtless, he enjoys it. Yet, in a strange way, this passage highlights another challenge – the challenge of success.

We all like to succeed and there is no harm in that as long as we remember that it can make us proud. Paul is not deceived when the people hail him as 'a god' because he remembers that, just a few moments earlier, they were condemning him as a murderer and were eagerly waiting for him to drop dead! Success and popular opinion are very unreliable.

As Christians, we thank God when life goes well, when we are successful and fulfilled, but we must never forget that true success is not measured by human applause but by how perfectly we are in tune with God's plans for us. If we remember that even this success is due to God's grace and not to our cleverness, we need never fear the challenge of success.

✳ *Lord, when everyone thinks that I am wonderful,*
keep me humble.
When nobody thinks that I am wonderful,
keep me faithful.

The challenge of a dream fulfilled

Paul's dream has come true. He is living in reasonable comfort and freedom in Rome. Whatever eventually happens to Paul, as far as the Acts is concerned, the story has a happy and triumphant ending.

Yet Paul faces a subtle challenge – the challenge of a dream fulfilled. He can relax now that his travels are over and embrace the fulfilment of his dream as a reward for his faithfulness. But instead of relaxing, he seems intent upon evangelizing with even greater enthusiasm than before. For him, a dream fulfilled is just the beginning of a new adventure. Perhaps he can convert the Emperor himself!

We all have dreams for ourselves, our families and our churches, and we are ready to work and pray for the fulfilment of those dreams – but what do we do when our prayers are answered and our dreams come true? There is always a temptation to relax thankfully when a goal is achieved. Like Paul, we need to see that achievement as a God-given opportunity for greater service – a launching-pad for the next adventure that Christ has waiting for us.

✳ *Lord, keep me dreaming and working for you.*

Thuma Mina

(Leader) Thu - ma mi - na.
Send me __ Lord.

South Africa

(Chorus) Thu - ma mi - na, Thu - ma
Send me Je - sus, send me

mi - na. Thu - ma mi - na, So - man -
Je - sus. Send me Je - sus, send me

(Leader) Thu - ma mi - na.
Send me __ Lord.

dla. Thu - ma dla.
Lord. (Chorus) Send me Lord.

For personal reflection or group discussion

What are my dreams for myself as a Christian and for my church at this time?

ACTION

Plan thoughtfully and practically for the fulfilment of those dreams. What is the next step to be taken?

BREAD OF LIFE

Notes based on the New English Bible by

Alec Gilmore

Alec Gilmore is a Baptist minister who spent 20 years in pastorates in Northampton and West Worthing after which he exercised a literature ministry for the benefit of the Third World and Eastern Europe as Director of FEED THE MINDS. He is presently Associate Baptist Chaplain in Brighton and Sussex Universities, and lectures on the Old Testament.

These two weeks lead us from the very practical (bread when you are hungry) to the essentially spiritual (life in Christ) – from a people for whom life is bread to a people for whom Bread is life. Yet the distinction is false. Even in the wilderness bread was a spiritual matter, and even today among the most spiritual the Bread of Life carries material implications. For two weeks allow your mind to pivot on the Bread of Life, swinging to and fro every day from the centre to the material, from the material to the spiritual, and then back to the centre.

---

1. The bread we break

8th Sunday after Pentecost, July 21 Exodus 16.1-15

Hunger pains

It is strange how quickly public mood can change. The previous four chapters saw the death of the first-born, the exodus, the Red Sea crossing and the Triumph Song of Moses. And now, within a matter of weeks, we are plunged into murmurings against the leadership. How could any people have such short memories? But perhaps it says something to us about the power of hunger to warp the mind (the longing to die), to gnaw at the emotions (they idealize even the flesh pots of Egypt, are completely out of touch with what Moses has already achieved and question his motives) and to freeze the will (there seems little attempt to find food for themselves and they are not even very good at recognizing it when it is 'put on a plate' in front of them). This story helps us to appreciate the power of hunger and to begin to understand why desperate people often do strange things. The response of Moses and the Almighty is neither to react to the complaint nor to try to 'understand the problem'. It is to meet the basic need.

✳ *Father, when I meet a hungry person,*
  touch my will to respond before anything else.

Use and abuse

Don't ask 'how much is an omer?' (about half-a-gallon) or about the conflicting instructions (a precise measure but also 'as much as he can eat') or indeed what manna was (probably a form of honey-dew, the secretion of two kinds of insect, rich in three basic sugars and pectin). What matters is that at the end of the day they had all had enough. Measures and agreements, policies and theories, trade and tariffs all come second compared to meeting basic human need. Concentrate more on the point that, even when their hunger is being met, people who have gone through their experience are still frightened and suspicious – it takes a lot of trust not to 'take thought for tomorrow' especially when sometimes (before the Sabbath) they are told that is exactly what they ought to do. Distinguishing between use and abuse is not always easy in crisis, either for 'purchasers' or for 'providers'. Fortunately, life has its own built-in system of checks and balances. Take too much and it will rot! And always keep one omer special – just as a reminder.

✳ *Father if my first duty is to respond,*
  help me next to distinguish between
  'help' which helps and 'help' which hinders.

Purchasers and providers

In the context of bread and hunger, reflect on the tensions of the sheep rather than the comfort offered by the shepherd. Crucial to the sheep are food and water. In Palestine both are in short supply but what the sheep must find hard is why, when they are at least nibbling at something, they constantly have to be moved by a powerful person with a rod and a staff who always seems to know best. But then sheep are sometimes less aware than they might be of dangers from drinking from a raging torrent, or the enemies that lie in wait in the valleys, or the dangers of getting too close to the edge and falling over. On occasions it is re-assuring to have a kindly hand helping you to water, or pouring oil on a few scars. And you can't have one without the other, so it is largely a matter of settling for a good shepherd whom you can trust, taking the rough with the smooth and trying to understand your provider when things go wrong.

✳ *Lord, the source and giver of life,*
help me to seek you in the tension,
in the light of human suffering and not apart from it.

Wednesday July 24   1 Kings 17.8-16 *

Enough for all

When the story begins there is not sufficient food for the widow and her son. When it ends there is enough for the whole household 'for many days'. Why? Because of Elijah? Yes – because it was his need that brought her need to light. If he had turned up in the village complete with flask and sandwiches, like many tourists in Third World countries, none of it would ever have come to light. Hunger and deprivation often need gentle encouragement to come to the surface.

Because of a miracle? Yes – because humanly speaking there was nothing else that could bring change for these two desperate people. Any solution just had to be a miracle.

But (more than either), there was enough food because of sharing – and not really the sharing of the rich with the poor or the 'haves' with the 'have-nots', but the sharing of those who have little with those who have even less.

✳ *Father, take away the pride*
that prevents me from admitting my need
and lead me to the person who has a similar need
so that together we may find in you the Bread of Life.

Thursday July 25   Proverbs 9.1-11 *

A call to live

Proverbs bridges the gap between provision of basic necessities and a different quality of living.

Imagine a wise woman (Wisdom) inviting her friends to a

banquet. She is rich – her house has seven pillars, she has beasts to slaughter, wine to drink, maids to deliver the invitations. Truly a 'provider', a shepherd with some potential and perhaps not too many needs to worry about. Notice whom she invites – 'the simple' (verse 4). The word is variously translated as 'fool', 'simpleton', 'ignorant' or even 'open-minded' but usually has a tendency to the bad rather than the good. Whether they are her normal clientele may be left to the imagination but the impression we are left with is that they are the sort of people who are normally avoided (Cf. Luke 14.15-24).

Notice what she offers. 'Live' (verse 6) suggests participation in 'true life' rather than continuity of physical existence and verses 7-11 fill out the detail, focusing on insight, understanding and respect for God.

✶ *Father, when I am busy sharing my needs*
and responding to the needs of others
help me never to take my eye off my need for eternal life,
and always keep me aware
that the two could be the same.

Friday July 26   *Isaiah 55.1-13*

True worth

Think of these verses as being addressed to a people who are desperate. They have been living in exile for years and have little prospect of return. They have no money and when they get any they spend it on all the wrong things. Isaiah is less concerned with their current plight than with their future possibilities. He wants to give them hope based on the fact that God loves them – he has chosen them and glorified them.

How can they achieve their true worth? It must begin with repentance, both negative ('forsake') and positive ('seek' and 'return'), because of the gap between the life they are leading and the life God has for them. After that it is not so much a matter of effort as of trust and patience. God's word has its own power, even if it is often slow to bring change, like snow and rain effecting change on the earth. But for those who trust there is a new future – out of exile into a different world – and for those in every generation who find themselves in the same situation.

✶ *Father, give me this bread of life*
that I may hunger no more.

All things common

Once the early Christians discover what it is that holds them together (their common life in Christ) it is but a short step to fulfil some of the ancient prophecies. The breaking of bread in the Old Testament, as a sign of God's will that his people should be one, now manifests itself as an expression of the unity already achieved. The breaking of bread in the Old Testament as the first obligation of charity, and as a way of making peace with the person with whom it was shared, now finds fulfilment in the sharing of all things, because all members of the community are at peace with one another. For one brief moment in church history the material and the spiritual go hand-in-hand. The new life creates the sharing and the sharing is the life. Too readily we dismiss it as an early and failed attempt at 'communism' instead of seeing it as an indictment in the past and a pointing forward to what one day might be.

✳ *Lord, when I even so much as glimpse your ideal,*
  give me the courage to go for it, and make my ears deaf
  to those who would hold me back.

For personal reflection or group discussion

1. Identify one or two groups of people who are in desperate straits (not necessarily the result of hunger or poverty) and ask yourself how much allowance you can make for the peculiar and often stupid things they do. If you know someone who works with such people ask them to help you understand their unusual behaviour.

2. A mark of good people is that they share their bread with the stranger (Isaiah 58.7) and even with the enemy (Proverbs 25.21 and Romans 12.20). Reflect on how much time you spend eating and drinking with strangers or with people you find it difficult to get on with.

3. Try reading *How The Other Half Dies, The Real Reasons for World Hunger*, Susan George (Penguin Books, 1976) or *Rural Development. Putting the Last First*, Robert Chambers (Longman, Scientific and Technical, 1983). Ask yourself all the time how far charity really helps, and make a list of those qualities which demonstrate the true worth of people struggling in Third World countries.

---

2. Bread broken for us

This week we move from the provision of food and water as evidence of God's power and concern and from the sharing of bread as an expression of our common humanity to a fuller exploration of the new life in Christ – not the 'bread we break' but the 'bread broken for us'. We explore the divisions that exist even in a caring and sharing society (Romans and Corinthians). We discover that there is more to life than material things (food) and that sometimes that 'something more' has to do with attitude and feeling rather than theory and action.

9th Sunday after Pentecost, July 28   *1 Corinthians 11.23-29 **

Class division

For the church at Corinth, the division had less to do with the hungry and the satisfied and more with social and class division. If we relate these words to our local church they may not seem relevant. But on the world stage, not only are some churches richer than others but even the same Church will be rich in one continent and poor in another as Christians help themselves instead of 'sharing bread'. Paul sees this as a denial of the life in Christ.

For him, first, the regular 'sharing of bread' is a symbol which began literally with the 'breaking of the body' and recognition of this is the first step to healing.

Second, never must they share the bread without remembering it – and not only 'as often as we celebrate the sacrament' but every time we partake of our daily bread.

Third, even to remember is to take a step in the healing process. So a spiritual act brings about a material result and a material result brings about a spiritual healing.

* *Father, may I never eat without remembering*
  those from whom I am separated
  and, as I remember, show me what to do
  so that I may begin the process of healing.

173

Race division

In Rome the division was between Jew and Gentile and one unpleasant aspect of it was judgmental attitudes as between the 'strong' and the 'weak'. The strong were those who could eat anything, handle anything, cope with anything, had all the answers, and lacked nothing in confidence. The 'weak' were those who felt all kinds of limitations and endeavoured to live within them. You might say the strong were those who were proud of their culture and had taken steps to convince others of their superiority. The weak were embarrassed by theirs and had always been made to feel inferior, like fish constantly being told by birds that there is something superior about flying!

Paul pleads with the strong not to be critical of the weak on the grounds that such behaviour is hurtful and offensive. More important than what is right and wrong is what helps (or hinders) our brother growing up in love. But then is it not that which makes something right or wrong? And is not true strength (15.1) fulfilling our obligation to support the weak rather than condemning them?

✳ *Lord, when I feel weak give me strength,*
   and when I feel strong keep me humble.

Not by bread alone

Verses 22-24 are somewhat confusing but the details are not important. Three things stand out.

First, on the day after Jesus fed the five thousand, the people are determined to stay with him. Confused they may be and their motives questionable but this man has something and they have no intention of missing it. Their enthusiasm, determination and single-mindedness all indicate their hunger.

Second, Jesus is not confused. What he had done the day before was to give them food because they were hungry – no more and no less! But today they are not pursuing him because they are hungry but because they believe (or hope) he has superhuman powers. But they must not imagine that his provision of food in the wilderness is going to herald the arrival of the Kingdom of God.

Third, Jesus wants them to see that there is something else they ought not to miss. His Kingdom may include food provision but that is not what it is about.

＊ **Lord, when I am obsessed with the material**
help me to perceive the spiritual within,
and when I am carried away by the spiritual
put my feet back on the ground.

Wednesday July 31   *John 6.28-40*

What else?

People who are activity-driven (as the Jews in these verses
were) find it hard in a world where 'doing' may not be what
matters. So instinctively, their response to the suggestion that
there is a spiritual equivalent to 'earning your bread' is 'what do
we have to do to get it?'(verse 27). For Jesus the answer is
simple. Believe in him and his way of life. 'Being' may be more
important than 'doing'; attitude and feelings come before actions
and theories.

But can he do what Moses did? The manna made people
believe. Jesus says it wasn't Moses who provided it. It was his
Father. And just as his Father had given them physical bread in
the wilderness to satisfy physical hunger so now his Father is
giving spiritual food to meet a spiritual need in the person of
Jesus. (Notice the careful change of tense in verse 32: 'gave'
becomes 'gives'.) But it is too much for them. They cannot
recognize him. They are missing out on what God is giving
because they are too tied to something he gave once before.

＊ **Lord, prevent me from being so committed to the past**
that I am unable to recognize you in the present.

Thursday August 1   *John 6.41-51 ＊*

Jesus 'on the ropes'

Objection! This time Jesus has gone too far with his claim to be
the Bread of Life. They know him. They know where he came
from. How dare he? Under pressure to defend his claims, the
arguments Jesus puts forward are not exactly the clearest. He
reminds them that according to their own teaching a man can
only believe if God instructs him (verses 44-45), which seems
something of a circular argument (almost a 'Catch 22 situation').
He then goes further, and suggests that it is not his business
simply to engage in short-term solutions that will stay a person's

hunger for a day, but to provide Bread (i.e. his flesh and blood) for the life of the world. And so a new dimension is added. No longer are we talking about emergency rations – short-term solutions or acts of love and charity – but about nothing less than a totally different way of life. In short, a revolution! And like many other revolutions, it begins to look as if it could start with an assassination.

✳ *Lord, sometimes I find it difficult*
to see where you are going
but please give me grace to keep following.

Friday August 2   John 6.52-59 *

No other way

The idea of 'eating his flesh' was probably no more readily understood by his hearers then than by his readers now, whilst the further suggestion of 'drinking his blood' would be outrageous to every Jew. Jesus, having stuck his neck out, now proceeds to lay it down upon a block! They may find what he says puzzling and what he advocates offensive, but there is no other way to the sort of life he is putting before them. Providing food is not the answer. A different life-style is. In these verses we have moved from the charitable to the sacramental – from one who is prepared to provide bread to one who is prepared to give his life. And if everyone knows that without bread a person dies – and many would say that if we are unwilling to provide bread something of the 'human' in us dies also – Jesus goes further when he says that without sharing fully in the life he offers, the fully human is not even born.

✳ *Lord, forgive me*
if I find it easier to see you in material things
than in the spiritual,
and please help me to move more easily
through one to the other and back again, as you did.

Saturday August 3   Luke 24.28-35

Our daily bread

Jesus had told them that whenever they passed round the bread and cup they were to remember him. And they were remembering. They had been remembering all the way along the road. But they were not seeing. 'Bread to eat' and 'the Bread of Life' were still in separate compartments – material and spiritual – until the familiar act of breaking the bread, and 'the penny dropped'. Discovering the spiritual in the material is learning to recognize the significance of the ordinary, to remove a layer and penetrate a depth, rather like noticing and learning to appreciate something you have lived with for years and never even noticed, like paint on walls, a tree on the highway, or the ground you walk on. Or suddenly recognizing human need that you have lived with for years and never seen, perhaps because you have met one or two people personally who are committed to meeting it, perhaps because you have actually met one or two of their clients, or maybe because you have felt that same need yourself. On the surface, and to others, it may all look just as material as it ever did, but to you it is different. Your attitude has changed. This is our 'daily bread' – not just food, but life, and vision.

✳ *Lord, open my eyes today, that I may see.*

For personal reflection or group discussion

1. Make a list of the things in your home that you rarely notice, and write alongside each something that strikes you when you stop to look at it. You have removed a layer and become alive in a new way.

2. Choose something in your home that is precious. In a fire you would want to grab it. Why? Reflect on its associations: people, places, memories, emotions and attitudes. As it moves you to thanksgiving, intercession or confession the material becomes the vehicle of the spiritual.

ACTION

Choose someone whom you scarcely know and / or someone whom you find it difficult to get on with and invite him / her to a meal at home or take him / her out to coffee.

THE POWER AND WISDOM OF GOD

Notes based on the New English Bible by

Alec Gilmore

1. The power of God

In first century Judaism the Power of God was not in question. The argument was not whether he existed, nor what he could or could not do. The question was, did Jesus have it? And was what he said and did a manifestation of it? Some people saw the hand of God in everything he touched. Others, for various reasons, didn't.

The question is still with us. How do we recognize God when he comes in flesh (in the form of a man)? How do you decide whether what you read and hear is of God or simply human thinking?

10th Sunday after Pentecost, August 4   *John 6.16-21* *

Recognizing the Master

Many readers will have no difficulty with the idea of Jesus walking on the sea. Those who do may prefer the equally possible (if less satisfactory) English translation which gives 'walking by the sea'. More important is the interpretation of the incident as a whole and it has a triple impact:

- For a group of frightened people the very presence of Jesus brings calm and reassurance.

- Further reflection suggests that this man has something very much in common with the God of the Jews (Yahweh) who is regularly presented as one with power to control the ocean (e.g. Psalm 77.16ff).

- For John, writing 50 to 60 years later, Jesus' use of the words, 'It is I', would recall Exodus 3.13-14, and so reinforce the idea that Jesus is to be taken as God's man, in direct line with Moses the deliverer, the creator of a new nation and the harbinger of a new day.

* *Father God, help me today to identify those qualities*
  and characteristics in the people I meet
  which remind me of you.

Monday August 5   *John 7.1-13 **

Knowing the time

The brothers of Jesus have a touching trust and confidence in
him such as you might expect in a family but they appear to
have little understanding of what he is trying to do. Perhaps they
are too close! The attempts to push him to 'grab the headlines',
like the pressure from his mother (John 2.4) or when he was
tempted in the wilderness (Matthew 4.1-11), have to be
resisted, because in order to fulfil his mission he is driven not by
family pressure, nor by popular opinion but by his own 'internal
sense of timing'. Very definitely his own man, and with a deep
sense of obedience to God! His readiness to go a few days
later, should not be interpreted as a change of mind nor an act
of 'cussedness', and need not even have been simply to avoid
the crowds. He knew when it was right, and that was when he
went.

* *Father, help me to listen to others and take advice,*
  and help me to hear your voice in what they say to me –
  but most of all teach me, like a migratory bird,
  to know my time.

Tuesday August 6   *John 7.14-24*

An unfamiliar package without a label

The mutterings that started when Jesus did not arrive for the
Festival (verses 10-13) continued after he came. There were
two problems. Among the masses, there was a division of
opinion as to whether he was a good man or not. A prophet or a
messenger of darkness? Among the leaders ('the Jews' of
verse 15), there was a problem as to how he could produce
such teaching without formal rabbinical education. Jewish
rabbis survived by quoting their authorities. You could see
where they had come from, whose pupils they were. With
Jesus, you couldn't. It was just him! Both experiences highlight
the problem of recognizing truth (the Word of God) when the
packaging is unfamiliar and there is no label. If it comes from

Rome, Canterbury or Geneva we know what to make of it. But what if 'the Word' suddenly hits us in a drama, a poem or a tabloid journalist? The problem is not that his listeners don't hear or recognize it. It is the difficulty of receiving truth for its own sake without the usual credits and credentials.

In verse 18 Jesus provides one useful clue: does it glorify the messenger or does it point to God?

✳ *Father, when I hear something*
that strikes me as inherently right and good,
help me to receive it as a word from you,
and especially to be open to truth
when it comes in an unfamiliar or unexpected form.

Wednesday August 7   *John 7.25-31*

The known and the unknown

What we have here are confused reactions, made worse by the fact that even if the package is unfamiliar and the label missing they do actually know where he has come from. Whereas in Jewish teaching the origins of the Messiah were to be unknown, and are confused further by the unwillingness of the authorities to arrest him, thus raising the question in the minds of the crowd, 'Do they know something that we don't?' But the confusion has a positive edge. John wrestles regularly with the knowness and the unknowness of the Messiah, and Christian history has continued the tradition. Was he fully human? Was he fully divine? And if he was both, how could he be?

The questions still surface as soon as anyone questions the virgin birth! It is right that they should, for it is in the nature of God to be both known and unknown, both remote and near, and those who claim to have found him and to know him are in danger of deceiving themselves and diminishing him.

✳ *Lord, whenever I read the scriptures,*
see your face and hear your voice,
help me always to preserve that true sense of mystery
and never to try too hard to penetrate the veil.

Thursday August 8   *John 7.40-52 ***

Chinks in the armour

By the end of the Feast (verses 37ff) there were chinks in the armour of many in the crowds. Some have no difficulty: 'off with the old, on with the new!' Others find a conflict within themselves between what they now believe (or suspect and want to believe) and what their previous training has always required them to believe. In a world where nothing stands still, beliefs, like everything else, must face adaptation to stay alive. Faith, like many other things, is different in middle life from adolescence and different again in old age. Our perception of God changes many times. Yet the Centrality does not change. Success in believing depends on knowing clearly what we have to cling to and what we can cheerfully abandon.

✳ *O God, help me to come so close to you*
that I can always recognize you as the same
yesterday, today and for ever.
Then help me so to see the world with your eyes
that I shall have no difficulty with all that changes.

Friday August 9   *John 5.37-47*

Blinding belief

Not an easy passage but the over-riding message seems to be that it is possible to believe ardently in the scriptures and yet to miss the voice of God and fail to recognize the work of Christ. Jesus tries to show the Jews the error of their ways. They claim to believe the scriptures. They are diligent in studying them. So how come they are failing to recognize him (verse 39)? Why do they not find in the scriptures divine sanction for what he is doing? To dismiss them as unbelievers or spiritually dead may be going too far, but at least the experience shows how easily a written word may be misunderstood and how blind we can all be when we do not actually want to see something. It's all there in the scriptures. Jesus shows them, spells it out for them, rubs their noses in it – why can't they see it? But if I had been in their shoes, would I?

✳ *Lord, give me not only the wisdom and insight to see*
but also the courage to admit what is in front of me
and to respond to it.
And help me penetrate through
the word
(that is written)
to the Word (that is alive).

Belief, love and obedience

Today we move from the debates leading up to the crucifixion to the world of the early Christian community some years down the road. The Power Debate (is he, is he not, who is he, where does he come from?) is over. The Power of God has been made manifest in him and is at work in the community. No doubt! But that does not mean that all the problems have gone away. The two key words now are 'belief' and 'love' and the end product is 'obedience to commandments' which are no longer burdensome. It is an effective trinity or 'three-fold cord that cannot be broken'. Belief without love can be hard and unyielding. Consider the Jewish authorities in relation to Jesus or the hurt caused by powerful ideologies in more recent times. But then love without belief can be sloppy and sentimental. Think of weak parents or ill-considered 'do-goodery'. And both without obedience to the commandments (or commitment) can be sterile whereas true love based on right belief can lead to positive action.

✳ *Father, help me this and every day to see things straight,*
to channel my love for you through those I meet,
and so to fulfil your commandments.

For personal reflection or group discussion

1. Choose one or two major decisions or turning points in your life. In how many cases did you get the timing right? What led you to get it right and why in other cases did it go wrong? What is it finally that enables you to determine whether an idea or an action is inherently right or wrong?

2. Reflect on one or two news stories of the week and ask yourself, 'Is this the power of God working in our world or is it not?' Listen to one or two international leaders whom you respect and ask, 'Is this a prophet from God – or is he in fact just like the rest?'

---

2. The wisdom of God

This week we must ask a prior question: do we know what we are looking for? Phrases abound and fashions change. 'Spiritual truth', says one. 'The knowledge of God', says another. But one phrase which runs through the Old Testament is 'the Wisdom of God'. We shall try to 'unpack' the phrase by looking at its usage in the Old Testament, in John and in Paul. Always in our mind will be the question – do we reflect it?

11th Sunday after Pentecost, August 11　　　　　　*Job 28.12-28 **

Wisdom and mountains

Old Testament Wisdom is not to be confused with technical skill or knowledge, of which there was plenty then and infinitely more now. Human beings cannot appreciate it. It is inaccessible – invaluable – something God keeps for himself. This is not the whole story (as we shall see) but it is an important emphasis, focusing on the uniqueness and 'otherness' of God whilst at the same time encouraging and inspiring us to grow in his likeness. Think of a mountain range with inaccessible crags and peaks. You can never scale them – and even if you did you can never re-create them or control them or become one of them. Yet something constantly 'draws you' – you want to explore the foothills, climb the lower ledges and see it from as many angles as you can. The Wisdom of God is something like that. Isaiah's vision of God (Isaiah 6.1-3) is a good example of what happened to one man when he tried to do just that.

❋ *Reflect on Isaiah's vision, use your imagination, and see what it might do to you.*

Monday August 12　　　　　　　　　　　　　　　*Proverbs 3.13-20*

Wisdom with a human face

Wisdom in Proverbs has more of a human face. Like the Beatitudes (Matthew 5.1-12), Proverbs describes the person who reflects it. Today, therefore, without detracting from the uniqueness of the Wisdom of God, we may explore and appreciate some of the ways that wisdom finds expression in human beings.

If we explore the Wisdom of God and covet it for ourselves,

what will it look like? In Hebrew terms it is more understanding and discernment than technical ability, more a sense of judgment and sensitivity than a philosophical idea. It is also practical in its application, as God's Wisdom was turned to practical account in the creation and maintenance of the world, issuing in balance and the avoidance of extremes coupled with respect for people and property. One writer describes it as the skill of the mariner or the ability of a general – possibly craftsmanship. So how do we find it and cultivate it? By a nearness to God which enables something of his Wisdom to 'rub off' on us.

✳ *Father, help me to see*
and appreciate where I am wise without knowing it
and then show me how to acquire more wisdom.

Tuesday August 13   *John 10.20-30*

Try a mirror

With the Feast of Dedication we have moved on two to three months. The questions are the same. The setting is different. This Feast celebrates the cleansing of the Temple under Judas Maccabaeus (165 BCE) when he removed the heathen altar put there by the Greeks and re-dedicated the Temple to Yahweh. By raising these questions in this setting (the portico of Solomon) and at this time, they are virtually asking Jesus whether he is going to do the same. Is he going to be another Judas Maccabaeus?

As often, Jesus throws the question back in a new way. First, they are asking him to tell them – they are authority seekers. Jesus wants them to make up their own minds and take responsibility for their own actions. Second, they are looking to him for action – Judas Maccabaeus! Jesus is looking to them for a change of attitude. Some people ('my sheep') don't seem to have a problem, he says. If you do, perhaps you should ask yourself why? Try looking in a mirror!

✳ *Father, forgive me for asking the wrong questions*
and seeking the wrong things.
Tune my life so that it shares your rhythms.

Beliefs and works

In response to the charge of blasphemy, Jesus applies the pragmatic test. He draws attention to the good things he has done and reminds them that by their own teaching (Psalm 82.6) those who receive the Word of God are regarded as divine. Why can they not accept what he does and judge him by it? The argument is sound, but it raises the difficult question of the conflict within some hearers when what looked every bit like the work of God was in conflict with some of their more fundamental beliefs. Healing, yes! Healing on the Sabbath or by touching the untouchable, no! And so on. Do they accept the works or do they stick to their principles?

Is this perhaps the point where they lack the wisdom we prayed about earlier this week? What they are looking for is a yardstick which will be always, everywhere and for ever the same, whereas true wisdom is exercising judgment, developing skills, making mistakes, accepting responsibility and living with the consequences.

✳ *Father, when your works get in the way of my beliefs,*
may I first recognize and acknowledge your works
and then sort out my beliefs afterwards.

Wisdom and folly

Paul sounds pretty fed up with Wisdom. Might folly be more attractive? But what is the Wisdom of which he is weary and the folly he commends? We cannot be certain. It might be simply local ideas, based on Greek philosophy, working their way into the church as Christians at Corinth inter-act with local culture (i.e. false teaching). Or it might be a new theological system based on a false spirituality related to early forms of Gnosticism, a heresy which develops later. It is certainly not the Wisdom of God as Paul has inherited it and beside which it looks like folly.

At the same time he sees that what he regards as Wisdom (i.e. the death and resurrection of Jesus and his power to change lives) many locals regard as folly. So he turns the tables upside down. Since the world seems unable to aspire to God's Wisdom, perhaps God decides to settle for folly, and even then the folly of God proves wiser than any wisdom human beings can produce.

* *Father, teach me to find something good and wholesome*
  even in the stupidity of the world I live in.

Friday August 16   *1 Corinthians 2.11-16* *
Life in the Spirit
Paul's quest is a penetration to the heart of the true God
(Wisdom) as found in the Old Testament and revealed to those
who are closest to him (i.e. possess his Spirit), for just as
nobody knows a person's thoughts better than the person
himself so nobody really knows God except those who have
received his Spirit, and you cannot expect those who have not
made that journey to understand.

That's fine as long as we don't then go on 'to play God' by
deciding who is and who is not spiritual. For all of us our
closeness to God is partial, and there are times in life, as well as
whole areas of our existence, when we are nearer than others.
So instead of dividing the world into two it is better to see these
antitheses as different moments in our experience. That way the
question is not whether I am part of the wisdom or the folly, but
to what extent in every situation I reflect God's character and
walk in his way.

* *Father, of all the gifts of the Spirit,*
  give me the gift of discernment,
  that I may recognize your presence wherever you are
  and be obedient to your will.

Saturday August 17   *Romans 11.33-36*
Hymn to Wisdom
Good hymns, like the best poetry, defy rational explanation, yet
have the capacity to evoke feelings rich and rare. These verses
are like that. They might be an early Christian hymn, and just as
we often conclude a service with a hymn that sums up the whole
theme so you could use this hymn to reflect on some of the
thoughts of the week.

But at other times it is good to have a hymn which counter-
balances what has been said and this hymn could be used like
that too. A world where there is so much emphasis on 'wisdom'
and 'knowing' reminds us that ultimately the Wisdom of God
and the truth about God for ever elude us. We are back to those
mountains we can never conquer! Always seekers – always

potential finders – occasionally genuine finders – but never fully finders of that Wisdom. That much he retains for himself.

✳ *Father, grant me that constant quest which leads to you. Make me thankful when I glimpse only the outskirts of your ways. And, above all, keep me humble.*

For personal reflection or group discussion

1. Write down a dozen quite ordinary things you do in the course of a day. How many require technical knowledge and how many require Wisdom in the Old Testament sense of skill or sensitivity? Are you satisfied with the proportion? Then ask how much energy you put into increasing knowledge and how much into enhancing wisdom.

2. Try to think of one or two examples during this week (in your own life or in the life of a friend, in social or political life as reflected in the press or on TV, or in TV discussions, drama or 'Soap') where what everyone would regard as folly turned out to be wisdom and what everyone would regard as weakness turned out to be strength.

ACTION

Choose a topic from the week's news, local or national, and write a letter to the press (even if you don't actually send it) saying what you think about it or what you believe should be done about it, and why. State clearly the authority on which your judgment is based.

SOME PASTORAL CONCERNS

1 and 2 Timothy

Notes based on the New Jerusalem Bible by

John Atkinson

John Atkinson is a Methodist minister in Leicester. He has been a circuit minister, a college tutor in the Caribbean, a District Chairman and General Secretary of the Methodist Division of Social Responsibility (UK).

Pastoral care is the loving ministry of looking after one another within the fellowship of the church. It must spill over in active, sensitive concern for all. Every Christian is called to this ministry. In the letters addressed to him, Timothy is offered personal advice and guidance about how to be a pastor to others. These letters help us to understand our own needs and our pastoral ministry.

Good Shepherd, guide and feed me,
and show me how to be a pastor to others.

12th Sunday after Pentecost, August 18   1 Timothy 1.1-11

A firm faith and a clear conscience

What qualities make an ideal pastor? Stop a minute and answer that question in your own mind. Then look at verse 5. Would you expect a pastor who helped you to have 'a pure heart, a clear conscience and a sincere faith' (verse 5)? Can you say why you might find such a pastor helpful?

Now think about what kind of Christian you must be in order to help someone else. Unless your own faith is real, you will never help anyone else's faith to grow. Unless your life is straight enough to stand up to scrutiny, your words will fall on deaf ears. The fact is that we often fall far short of these standards. Can we still help others? Yes, if our hearts are full of love for them. For love matters most (see the opening words of verse 5).

✳ *Lead me, Lord, to firmer faith;*
forgive and change me till my life is pure.
Most of all, increase my love for you
and for all who seek my help.

Monday August 19   *1 Timothy 1.12-20*

Accentuate the positive

The first thing we must give to those we try to help is a listening ear. To put their troubles into words, they need to feel that they are being heard attentively and sympathetically. Can you think of ways in which you could make it easier for others to come and share with you their problems? How can you become a better listener?

Many pastoral counsellors suggest that our priority is not to give direct advice but to help people to see for themselves ways in which their problem could be tackled and then to work with them to choose the best option. What is the wisdom of that approach? If we do offer pastoral guidance, it needs to be positive like that in verses 18 and 19. That advice stresses basics ('faith and a good conscience') is hopeful (it assumes that Timothy will be 'a good soldier') and is not directly critical (other people may wreck their faith, but the assumption is that Timothy won't). This kind of positive pastoral guidance can be a great blessing.

✳ *Lord, show me how to listen to others,*
and when I do,
help us to think through their problems together.
When I speak, make my words positive and loving.

Tuesday August 20   *1 Timothy 2.1-15*

Quietly does it

There is an essential quietness and serenity about the life of the Christian. The word 'quiet' occurs four times in this chapter (verses 2, 9, 11 and 12). Noise is often a sign of 'anger or argument' (verse 8) – not often Christlike characteristics.

Twentieth century readers question the quiet acceptance of secular authorities (verse 2) and the command that women must be quiet (verse 12). Such advice belongs to the cultural and political background of the first century in which the infant church had to work.

But quietness should have a place in public worship and – even more, perhaps – in private prayer. There should be a poise and stillness about our inner lives, and a calm, unhurried, peacefulness in the way in which we care for others. Take time now to consider how we could bring more quietness to all these parts of our lives.

✴ *Drop thy still dews of quietness,*
   Till all our strivings cease;
   Take from our souls the strain and stress,
   And let our ordered lives confess
   The beauty of thy peace.   J G Whittier (1807-92)

Wednesday August 21   1 Timothy 3.1-16

The pattern of the perfect pastor

It is often claimed that the private lives of rulers, politicians, pop stars and sporting personalities do not matter as long as they are 'good at their job'. Do you think that is true? Certainly the private lives of Christians matter if they are to help others and win them in Christ's name. A woman who was helped through a crisis of faith and emotional distress said of the Christian friend who helped her, 'It was not what she said so much as what she was that helped me.' A man who dismissed every argument a Christian had put up for his faith was nevertheless won over by his example, saying, 'You can knock down an argument, but you cannot deny the quality of a good life.' If as Christians we are all to be pastors and evangelists, what qualities do we need? Some are listed in verses 2-4, 8, 11-12. Which do you think are the most important? Which do you most need to cultivate? What other qualities matter? Take time now to think about these questions.

✴ *Pray for grace to live nearer to the perfect pattern.*

Thursday August 22   1 Timothy 4.1-16

Try a little encouragement

People who need pastoral help often lack hope and self-confidence – and are probably finding it very hard to believe in God. Criticism or glib advice will not help. Like children learning to walk, they need someone beside them to encourage and inspire confidence. This chapter talks about thankfulness for God's gifts (verse 3) and trust in God (verse 10). Individuals in trouble need steady, gentle encouragement to rediscover these responses to God. First, they need to know that someone is willing to be alongside them, listening to them. Two strangers came to my door with a difficult problem. At the end of their visit, it still was not obvious what should be done next. 'Whichever way it goes,' they said, 'thanks for taking us seriously.' They reminded me that the first encouragement we are to give others is our acceptance of them and attentiveness to their need.

✳ *Lord, make me an encourager of others,*
  sensitive to their anguish and attentive to their words.
  Show me how to help them out of their darkness
  into the light of your love.

Friday August 23   *Timothy 5.1-16*

Priorities

Among many other pieces of advice, Timothy is told that he will need to recognize priorities in pastoral care. Older widows unlikely to remarry are to be given precedence over younger ones. Where possible, relatives are to be looked after by their own families, thus releasing the pastoral resources of the church for those without family support.

We may question some of the advice Timothy is given. Is it right, for example, that we should concentrate our help on those who are worthy of it (see, for instance, verse 10)? Can we not think of some who may not seem to deserve our help but desperately need it? Sadly we cannot help every needy person who comes our way. Determining priorities is inevitable. Jesus often gave friendship and help deliberately to those who were – in most people's eyes – unpopular, unattractive, unimportant and even downright unpleasant. Our priorities must be determined by how much those who are near us need us. Whoever we are, there are people wanting our friendship, our understanding and – poor though it often is – our sense of Christ's presence.

✳ *Guide us, Lord,*
  that we may go, not only to those who want us,
  but to those who need us most.
                                         After John Wesley

191

There's good and bad in everyone ...

and therefore in us. Before we can help anyone else, we must first seek forgiveness for our own sins and the grace of Christ so that we may grow in goodness. In our dealings with others, we must be impartial (verse 21), not glossing over faults (verse 20) but looking for the goodness which is not always immediately apparent (verse 25). How can we encourage people to overcome their faults without seeming smug or coldly critical? How can we help without hurting? How can we build the close relationships essential in this sort of pastoral care? It is just as important to help people with their goodness – encouraging them in the use of the gifts we see they have. Football teams, for example, use 'talent scouts' to find future stars among school children. How can we be 'talent scouts' for Christ, looking for the gifts and goodness which lie buried in all age groups?

✳ *Lord, make me more aware of my own sin*
that I may help others also to find forgiveness.
Help me to grow in goodness
that I may help others to respond and come to you.

For personal reflection or group discussion

Imagine real-life situations where individuals

- feel defeated, alone or broken-hearted,
- have personal failings which are spoiling their lives,
- cannot see their own potential for goodness.

Take each situation and work out how you would try to help them.

13th Sunday after Pentecost August 25   *1 Timothy 6.1-10*

Keep it simple

As far as we can, we should help people who have honest intellectual doubts about Christianity. But sometimes people ask us questions they do not really want answered, using words as a verbal smoke screen.

The result is much like that described in verses 3b-5a. Real communication is impossible. An agnostic friend of mine once started a conversation in which he used philosophy, mathematics and a good deal of contemporary jargon to justify his lack of interest in Christianity. At first, I tried (perhaps foolishly) to respond in the same terms. For half an hour we got nowhere. Then I decided that my best plan was to talk simply about Jesus. Are there times when the 'simple gospel' is the only thing we really have to talk about (see verse 3)?

Similarly, is a simple lifestyle (see verses 6-10) an essential part of Christian witness? Can sophisticated words and lifestyle be serious handicaps in our caring for others? If so, in what ways ought we to change?

✳ *May I grow firmer, simpler, quieter, warmer.*
Based on a saying of Dag Hammarskjold

Monday August 26   1 Timothy 6.11-21
Encourage generosity

Can people be rich and true Christians? Timothy is advised to say, 'Yes, if they are generous and always ready to share what they have' (verse 18). Maybe – but should we expect generosity to be rewarded (verse 19)? Should we not be generous because it is the loving thing to be? It has its own joy and richness. I knew a man who decided to give a tithe (a tenth of all he received) to the church and the needy. He was just an ordinary working man, but he told me, 'Since I started tithing, I have felt like a rich man. It must be because I could give that money away and still have enough for all my real needs.'

When we are trying to help people pastorally, we may find that their money and possessions are getting in the way of their real happiness. Helping them to be generous can be a way of liberating them. It will liberate us, too.

✳ *Help us who have received so freely from you*
to give as freely in our turn,
and so have the pleasure of giving
as well as the happiness of receiving.
From Contemporary Prayers for Public Worship,
Edit. Caryl Micklem (SCM 1967)

Resist prejudice

Paul and Timothy differed from one another in many ways. There was a generation gap between them. Paul had known much suffering (see verses 8 and 12); Timothy had yet to be put to the test. Paul had come to Christ through the dramatic experience of the Damascus Road; Timothy came from a Christian home and was a third generation Christian (verse 5). Their journeys to faith and their experience of Christ were so different that they might seem to have had little in common. Yet the letter to Timothy 'dear son of mine' (verse 2) is full of deep affection.

The love we are called to offer one another knows no barriers: age, denomination, experience and theological emphasis, styles of worship, social backgrounds, nation, tribe and race. That calls for real commitment and we ought to pause and ask whether or not we can honestly claim as a church to live like this. If not, then it is time we did something about it!

✳ *Pastoral care is love in action.*
  Help us, dear Lord, to fulfil love's first action –
  to break down all barriers.

When the way is hard

Life can be hard in many ways. We may have to work very hard at the jobs we do – including those God gives us (verses 3-7). Life is harder still when we face suffering (verses 9-10). Some early Christians, condemned to death for their faith, shouted, 'We give God thanks!' It takes great courage to regard suffering as a cause for rejoicing, but perhaps we can regard it as a challenge. I had a friend, who was injured in a road accident. He never walked normally again. One day I expressed my sympathy. 'Well', he said, 'I was downhearted at first. Then it seemed that God was saying to me, 'You haven't had much to put up with in your life, Wilfred. See what you can do with this.'

As far as other people's hardships are concerned, our first response will be of caring – trying to understand what they feel, helping if we can with practical problems, and offering emotional support – then, later perhaps, encouraging them to see it as a challenge.

* **Think of two or three people you know who are having a hard time. Pray for them, and then decide what you can do to help and encourage them.**

Thursday August 29   *2 Timothy 2.14-26*

Be gentle

I once saw an elephant pick up a small child in its trunk and lift him high in the air, safely and comfortably. Gentleness is often a sign of strength, as Christians who would help others must learn (see verses 24-25). That is true even when we have to correct them. John Wesley was once greatly wronged by someone. Instead of criticizing the man, Wesley quietly invited him to ask his forgiveness. The man was stubborn and would not. 'Then,' said Wesley, 'I must ask yours.' It was said of a Christian teacher that she corrected her students when it was necessary, 'But always,' they said, 'later, it was as if she had her arm around your shoulders.' We must not only be gentle with people we find attractive and worthy, but also with those whom we so easily reject as unlovely and disreputable.

* **Father, my Father, stretch my heart that it may take in all those who are not lovely in my eyes, and whose hands I do not want to touch; through Jesus Christ my Saviour.**
From the prayer of an African Christian
Morning Noon and Night, edit. John Carden (CMS)

Friday August 30   *2 Timothy 3.1-17*

Face the truth

Timothy is given a long list of people of whom he must be wary (verses 1-9). The advice he is given is to 'keep away from people like that' (verse 5). But can Christians really write off others in that way? Wouldn't it be mere priggishness? And how will they ever sort out their lives if we are not prepared to help them? Some people are, of course, very difficult to help. Their basic trouble is that they have closed their minds to the truth (see, for example, verses 7-8). This is a common problem. Sometimes the truth is too painful or too shameful to face. We shall feel a strong sympathy for them as we help them to cope with the truth. Others will be harder to help because they are wilfully distorting the truth for selfish ends. These are the kind of people Timothy is warned about. Obviously, we cannot go along with their delusions and hypocrisy, but we must find ways of persuading them to have the courage and honesty to live in the real world.

✳ *Healing God, we bless you that, in Jesus,*
   your concern was shown
   in your complete attention to the sufferer
   in your touch and words of challenge.

'Ephphatha – be opened!'
Say those words to us –
   to closed ears, closed eyes,
   closed minds, closed hearts;
ask to come in and make us whole.

Enable us to open ourselves up
to all the resources you offer us:
– to the supportiveness of family and friends
and all who have the grace-full gift of listening ...
– to the touch of caring hands
and the unseen power of the Spirit ...
– to the wonders of medical science
and the skill and dedication
of all who practise the healing arts.

Use especially those who suffer, we pray,
as agents of your wholeness ...

© *1987 Kate Compston, from Encounters, the Prayer Handbook for 1988, United Reformed Church (UK).*

Saturday August 31   2 Timothy 4.1-22

Keep steady

A group of deaconesses had completed their college training and were about to go to pastoral appointments in the church. Their tutor prayed for them: 'Lord, grant to these your servants, the placidity of a cow, the hide of a rhinoceros and the playfulness of little kittens.' The last phrase was meant to save them from the dull unattractiveness of life which never commends Christianity. The earlier part of the prayer for steady serenity and a refusal to be discouraged finds echoes in 2 Timothy 4. The first five verses urge Timothy to 'keep steady' (verse 5). Later (verses 10 and 14), there are examples from Paul's experience of disappointments which Christians may receive.

Caring for people can be deeply rewarding, but we must be prepared for rejection when it comes. We shall have experiences which shake our faith in people – and even in God. So we must 'fight the good fight' to the end (verse 7). It is a fight not only to hold fast to Christ, but also to share his love with others in caring service.

✳ *Lord, I am weak in the faith; strengthen me.*
I am cold in love, warm me, that my love may go out
to my neighbour. Martin Luther

✳ *Lord,*
make us realise that our Christianity is like a rice field:
when it is newly planted the paddies are prominent,
but as the plants take root and grow taller
these divided paddies gradually vanish
and soon there appears only one vast continuous field.

So give us roots that love
and help us grow in Christian fellowship and service
that thy will be done in our lives
through our Saviour, Jesus Christ. The Philippines
From Your Will be Done (Christian Conference of Asia)
Also included in Living Prayers for Today (a new IBRA book
of prayers – see page 49)

For personal reflection or group discussion

How can we build the kind of relationships which will make it possible for us to offer pastoral care to others? How can we preserve this relationship even when we have to help them to face unpleasant truths? Think of situations where this is the crucial problem and imagine a pastoral conversation in which it is tackled.

ACTION

Discuss with your minister or leader how you could help in the pastoral work of the church and explore ways of developing the skills of a good counsellor.

RESPECT FOR PEOPLE

Notes based on the New International Version by

Brian Haymes

Brian Haymes, Principal of the Bristol Baptist College, is the author of the 'Looking at' series published by IBRA. He has served as President of the Baptist Union of Great Britain.

Respect for others often appears to be in short supply. All kinds of prejudice exist. There are too many stories of abuse and of trust being broken. People are treated as things, as means to an end, rather than as the human beings God created. Christians believe that every person is made in the image of God and has a dignity and worth underlined by the fact that Jesus Christ gave his life for us all. To show respect for others is to follow Christ. Such a way of life is bound to challenge present attitudes and responses to other people.

Loving God, help us to look on everyone we meet with your eyes and to love them as you love us all in Jesus Christ our Saviour.

---

*14th Sunday after Pentecost, September 1   Exodus 34.4-9 ***

God shows respect

When people treat us without respect how should we respond? The Hebrews behaved badly towards God. They showed they did not trust and honour him by making a 'do-it-yourself' god. That was like spitting in the face of God, acting as if he were nothing. They were ready to give their loyalty to another in hope that he would give them more. They took what God had given and dismissed the giver.

How does God respond? The two stones remind the people of the basic covenant promises of loyalty God made at Sinai. Here he makes the promises again. Both promises and people matter to him. He comes again to Moses, names himself and promises that, while he cannot overlook their apostasy, he will not be untrue to himself.

So Moses is given confidence to ask for the gifts of God's presence, forgiveness and strong hold upon his people. The story of the Bible is of a God who does these things. He respects his promises, his laws, and his people. In return for their disrespectful disloyalty he gives them his endlessly compassionate care.

✳ *Thank you, loving God, for treating us not as we deserve*
but as you love us.

Monday September 2   Romans 7.1-6 *

Respect is not enough!

There is a kind of respect that is cold and formal. We behave properly, according to good manners, and that is what we show to others. At one level it appears to respect people. At a deeper level it may never move beyond responding to others out of mere duty.

Then there is a great temptation to self-righteousness. At least **we** know how to behave! But a life of legalistic good manners can be empty of love and full of negative goodness. The priest and the Levite who 'passed by on the other side' (Luke 10.30-35) doubtless had great respect for their religious duty. What they lacked was imaginative love that went beyond the proper.

Paul argues that in Christ we are enabled to live not by the law of good manners but in the power of the Spirit. Earlier he has spoken of baptism with its symbolism of dying and being raised. In Christ we died to a way of life that concentrated on respect for ancient traditions which sometimes kept us from living deeds of love. In Christ we are free to show respect, not for good form, but for people.

✳ *Help us, Lord, not to love out of cold duty*
but in grateful joy.

Tuesday September 3   Ephesians 5.11-20 *

Taking good care

Sensible people take care of their health, their families, their friendships. They are attentive to their work, their education, their responsibilities. It is because these things – and even more the people involved – matter that care is taken. To say 'I couldn't care less' is to dismiss someone utterly. By contrast, have you noticed how, when people are kind to us, it really does make a difference? We feel better, affirmed, valued. In an impersonal world like ours, to respond to someone with kindness is almost subversive of modern values. It is living differently, sending out signals of the alternative society of the Kingdom of God. When that happens then the Christian response of caring respect for people is light in a dark world.

Ephesians 5 deals with contrasting ways of life. Read verses 1 and 2. They set the direction, the call to imitate God. The apostle clearly looks for the lives of Christians to be light. When we know the respect and care God has given us in Jesus then thankfulness will characterize everything we do, including the care we give to others.

✳ *Caring God, help me to imitate you,*
   so that your light shines through my care for others.

Wednesday September 4   *Ephesians 5.21-33*
Respectfully yours!

This is a 'touchy' text. The idea of submission is not popular and the suggestion that one person should submit to another in marriage on the grounds of gender is capable of causing explosions in the most mild mannered of people.

Christians do have different views about this. For some, Paul is spelling out a God-given order of life. Others say that he is reflecting the culture of his day and, in fact, giving a more positive affirmation of women than we realize. What do you think?

What is beyond doubt is that Paul does not think that submission demeans anyone. Verse 21 is the controlling text for the passage. To submit does not mean to give in feebly to another's demands. The text talks about submission to one another out of reverence to Christ. Such submission, thinking of the other person's interest and not merely your own, is an act of respect. It is recognizing your proper claim as a human being in Christ. Marriage in Paul's eyes has the characteristic of the relationship of Christ and the Church. Did not Christ give himself for the Church? Is that submission or the sacrifice of love?

✳ *Thank you, Lord, for feeding and caring for your*
   Church.

Honour your parents and children

The problem with the fifth commandment is that some parents are not worth honouring! Some children are physically and sexually abused. Others are left bearing the pain of their parents' broken promises.

But this is a perversion of parenting and family relationships. Notice the phrase 'in the Lord'. Children are to respect parents, those who have responsibility for them, in the light of the fact that God's provision of guidance and care comes through parents. For all their human frailty that has been true for many of us and we give thanks to God for those who made God's love real through their love.

There are few responsibilities more precious than the care of a child. Not to respect a young life is to fail to discern the gift and image of God. It is tough being a parent. But where the parents live in and share the 'training and instruction of the Lord' there is good family life, built on the respectful way God looks on us all. Through such faithful care we all have a future to which we may look forward.

✶ *O God, help us grow in respect and love*
  for all the members of your family.

Relationships and risk

Attempting to rebuild a relationship is to take a risk. Suppose you are rejected, then the pain will increase. Attitudes may harden making hope or reconciliation harder.

Jacob was a rogue and a cheat. There is nothing admirable about sending the women and children first in the meeting with his brother. But he comes home in hope of reconciliation.

In Genesis 32.22-32, there is the story of another meeting. Jacob met a stranger with whom he wrestled all night. He was wounded but hung on for a blessing. The experience was an encounter with God.

Then comes the meeting with Esau. Reading the two stories together leaves the impression that these incidents cannot be separated. Is it that in being forgiven by his brother Jacob is blessed by God? What is the relationship between the face of Esau and the face of God?

The two meetings are not the same. Yet both acts of reconciliation have crippling and blessing. Respect for others is learned best when we see the face of God, especially in the crippled figure of the cross. But was Esau wise to trust Jacob? And is God wise to trust us with the love of the cross? There is no respect without risk.

✳ *Loving God, give us courage to take the respectful risks of reconciling love.*

Saturday September 7   *John 8.3-11 **

Guilty, of disrespect!

The narrative is so vivid. We can almost see the gloating faces of the accusers. They are eager to embarrass this young teacher who seems soft on sin. Their trap is set.

The woman is guilty. Jesus accepts that. The issue of the story is that neither the accusers nor the accused are innocent. All are guilty. Those who want the woman punished are even more guilty, for the worst sins are not sexual but spiritual, like assuming a righteousness you do not have and condemning others on the strength of it.

A human being's life is at stake here. How easy it is to condemn the sinner by concentrating everything on the sin. But this woman is a person, no less than the Scribes and Pharisees. What will her death accomplish except to secure them in their righteousness? Yet in such lovelessness they declare their guilt. If the woman deserves death so do they. So do we. Jesus did not come to condemn. That is too easy. He came to save. That is difficult and costly because it involves love. And there is no love without respect.

✳ *Gracious God, have mercy on me, sinner that I am.*

For personal reflection or group discussion

What do you think is at the heart of having respect for others? Why do some people lose all self-respect? What has struck you as being particularly significant, for yourself, and for others, in the Bible passages for this week?

ACTION

Write your own 'Charter of respect'. Say why people are worthy of respect. Then identify what respect means in practice. Be positive and specific.

RESPECT FOR TRUTH

Notes based on the Revised Standard Version by

Lesley G Anderson

Lesley Anderson, a Panamanian, is Chairman of the Belize District of the Methodist Church in the Caribbean and the Americas. From 1987 to 1995, he served with the Methodist Church Overseas Division (UK) as Secretary for the Caribbean, the Americas and Europe.

For centuries the question has been asked: 'What is truth?' Do we all respect truth? Why do some people tell untruths? Is it right sometimes to tell a lie? Do people freely put their trust in you? Do you regard yourself as a trustworthy person? Why do some governments, businesses, organizations and individuals present distorted facts to the public? To have respect for truth necessitates living by the truth. The people I admire are those who live with integrity, who avoid deception, dishonesty, falseness and fabrication. This study will enable us to distinguish between the 'spirit of truth' and the 'spirit of error', and we will see how through Jesus, 'the truth will make us free'.

15th Sunday after Pentecost, September 8   Genesis 32.22-32

Learning a truth about God

When we arrive at our own 'ford of the Jabbok' (verse 22), that shallow place in a stream which may be crossed on foot or by wading, may we not like Jacob have to wrestle with God?

Was the writer of this passage thinking of a physical wrestling (verse 24)? Jacob had a profound spiritual experience at a critical moment in his life. It convinced him that he could not wrest the blessing from God's hand. A blessing is a gift of grace. Let us learn not to rush God. The truth is that God needs time with us, day by day, to influence our lives with his presence.

A significant moral change took place in Jacob's life. He was no longer Jacob, the 'crafty one', but Israel, 'the one who perseveres with God'. Let us persevere in the truth and wait on God's blessings to come.

✳ *O Lord, my God, teach us how to wait on you*

and experience your presence in our lives.

Monday September 9   *Jeremiah 28.1-17 ***

Put your trust in the Spirit of truth

Hananiah boldly but foolishly spoke of peace. Blatantly opposing his predecessors, he incited Zedekiah and his people to resistance. This act was certain to increase servitude, and so he was reprimanded and punished.

We can avoid making Hananiah's mistake and suffering the same consequences. We need to live by the Spirit of truth. John gives us some encouraging words: John 14.17; 15.26; 16.13, and 1 John 5.7. How are we further challenged by these words of Jesus: 'He who is of God hears the words of God; the reason why you do not hear them is that you are not of God' (John 8.47)?

God challenges us to have respect for truth. Let us live as children of the Spirit of truth.

✳ *Lord, forgive us for not placing our trust in the truth.*
   Help us to live in the truth,
   that our lives may be a blessing to others.

Tuesday September 10   *John 8.31-36 ***

Find freedom in the truth

Only the truth will give us that ultimate freedom from slavery to sin. Jesus addressed certain Pharisees who were prepared to believe he might be Messiah and acknowledge the power of his message. They turned against him when they found he demanded:

● an entire change of life (they thought themselves perfect);

● that they accept saving truth (they thought they already possessed it);

● spiritual freedom – *cheruth* – freedom from sin (they thought Jesus was referring to political bondage).

Does a genuine concern for morality free us from sin? What is your attitude to a legalistic religion?

When we groan under the weight of sin, let us remember that Jesus died on Calvary's cross to set us free. Let us make his words our own: 'the truth will make you free' (verse 32).

✱ *Lord, we believe your words.*
Give us the joy of knowing
that you are able to make us truly free.

Wednesday September 11   *John 8.37-47* *

Jesus is the truth, believe in him

The Jews claimed they were the spiritual as well as the natural descendants of Abraham. They were the inheritors of his sacred covenant and faith. This being so, how would you account for the fact that Jews in the first century wanted to kill Jesus (the promised seed of Abraham)? Did they misunderstand his message? Did they not believe him? Do we not as Christians crucify Jesus afresh by the things we say and do? Sometimes we speak evil and falsely accuse each other. We formulate xenophobic immigration laws; we set barriers between ourselves and others – the poor and the oppressed, and they become 'marginalized', 'outcasts'. The cross of Jesus challenges us to be open to the truth of Jesus, who calls us all to forgiveness and reconciliation.

Jesus the sinless Son of God speaks the truth. His message to you and me is true. Believe in him and he will make you free.

✱ *Lord, you only will we follow:*
show us the way,
reveal to us the truth,
that we have the life you offer.

Thursday September 12   *Matthew 12.33-37*

Always speak the truth

What is meant by this popular saying, 'the tree is known by its fruit' (verse 33)? Can the fruit (result) of the tree be good if the tree (Jesus) is, as they accuse him, corrupt, rotten or evil? Why did religious people in Jesus' day make these accusations?

Jesus charges them with using venomous words, and refers to them as 'a brood of vipers' (verse 34). Jesus emphasized that our words will

● either justify (vindicate, defend) us,

● or condemn (decry, denounce) us.

To speak the truth is not always easy. Nevertheless, Jesus challenges us to express truth in our lives. Let us stop speaking evil by doing good, exercising justice and showing kindness to the marginalized, and oppressed.

✳ *Lord, help us to live with your integrity*
that we may always speak the truth, do good,
and bear the good fruit you ask of us.

Friday September 13　　　　　　　　　　　　*1 John 4.1-6*

Choose and live in the spirit of truth

In these verses, we are confronted with a challenge: to choose between the 'spirit of truth' and the 'spirit of error' (verse 6). How would you distinguish them apart? Which would you choose? Why?

Show in your life that you are a bearer of the 'spirit of truth'. Let your life glow with the flame of love for the unlovely; be merciful to the marginalized in your society; pray for those who despitefully use you; exemplify in your life the light and goodness that shine from Jesus, with the spirit of truth.

Be strong in the Lord that you may overcome the 'spirit of error'. He will give you strength to gain victory. For those who know and love the Lord, the Lord listens to you.

✳ *Lord, we turn to you that we may be guided*
to know the spirit of truth.

Saturday September 14　　　　　　　　　　　*1 John 5.10-21* ✳

Keep faith in Jesus

I know a woman whose life is spiritually fulfilled through prayer. She endeavours to live in accordance with the will and purpose of the Lord. She trusts him completely and accepts that he knows best. She gives herself unreservedly to him, and is steadfast in faith. Why do we marvel when me meet such a person? Do we not also have a grasp of the truth?

In this passage I am reminded that we are possessors of great Christian beliefs:

● we have eternal life (verse 11);

● our prayers are answered (verses 14 and 15);

● we can achieve righteousness (verse 17);

● we can experience new birth (verse 18);

- we can participate in Christ's mission)verse 20).

Embraced by Christ and being possessed of the great Christian truths, evil cannot really touch us.

* *Lord, draw us closer to you*
and keep us in your safe embrace.
You have assured us of the truth of your word.

For personal reflection or group discussion

1. What are some of the reasons people tell untruths? Is it ever right to tell a lie? What practical steps can we take in helping others to appreciate the truth?

2. Read again John 8.31-36. Is it really possible that 'the truth will make you free'?

ACTION

Always speak the truth. Discipline yourself to reflect on occasions when you have not done so, and strengthen your resolve to stand by the truth.

THE GOOD SHEPHERD

Notes based on the Good News Bible by

Rosemary Wass

Rosemary Wass – Local Preacher and former Vice President of the Methodist Conference (UK) – and Howard her husband farm in partnership. Their stock includes sheep, so lambing and the care of sheep are everyday experiences!

Perhaps the most well known and universally loved Bible passage is Psalm 23. It has given strength, courage and consolation to so many, and though many things have changed over the centuries, the overarching message and image of the Shepherd have remained meaningful and solid.

The vocation to be a shepherd is all consuming, similar to our call to follow Christ. These readings encourage us to continue to enter the gate to the fold and care for others.

16th Sunday after Pentecost, September 15

Jeremiah 50.4-7 *

I once was lost ...

People in high office are not always good leaders. They are 'bad shepherds', not caring for the welfare of those they are appointed to serve. A truth learnt from hard experience is that 'Power corrupts'. As a result, the people are lost and vulnerable. Today, we can think of issues like the Arms Trade, imbalances in World Trade, reduced Aid from 'developed' countries and International Debt. We recognize injustices that occur because of selfish deals and the power that one country holds over another.

Although he doesn't say it, Jeremiah was a true shepherd to the people of Judah, but his caring, prophetic words fell on deaf ears. Yet all was not lost: the flock he had shepherded for so long would come to their senses. They would find their way back from their exile in Babylon to Jerusalem. Sheep who wander from their pasture do not always find what is best for them. They are vulnerable to other animals and food that may be attractive but unsuitable. The shepherd may limit their choice of pasture, but s/he knows what will bring long-term nourishment to them. It may take a long time for the sheep to appreciate the wisdom, patience and faithfulness of the shepherd, and it may be even longer before they express that new level of understanding.

Are there times when we have gone our own way, rather than listen to the words of those who have offered uninvited advice? What has it taken to appreciate their care and genuine concern with hindsight?

✴ **Through many dangers, toils and snares**
   I have already come;
   God's grace has brought me safe thus far,
   And he will lead me home.   John Newton (1725-1807)

Monday September 16   *John 10.1-6* ✴

... but now I'm found

Shepherds and sheep develop special relationships with one another. The shepherd is sensitive to the sheep, keeping a careful eye for telltale signs of trouble. Leaning on a crook is time well spent ... observing the habits of the flock. If one ewe is separated from the rest, she may be unwell and deserve further scrutiny. Movements are smooth and steady so as not to alarm sheep who may be in some distress. The shepherd develops a pattern the sheep recognize and trust. The sight of a person carrying a sack may alert them to the fact that it's feed time! There is one acceptable way into the sheepfold – one recognizable pattern. Any other way is seen as false and unacceptable. Only when the shepherd has gained the trust of the flock will the sheep follow.

Jesus told the parable, but it fell on ears that were unable to understand. The images are powerful but not enough to lead listeners to the real truth about the authenticity and the mission of Jesus. *Does this say something about how long it takes to build relationships?*

✴ **Good Shepherd of the sheep,**
   Grant me this day a place to rest and feed.
   I feel secure in your abiding presence
   Knowing that you offer me your care.
   Remind me of those who need to know your peace
   this day, and grant them new pasture tomorrow. Amen

Fear not little flock

A local mission carried out by Jesus is an overwhelming success. He knows there are unplumbed depths of need in the crowds. They lack direction and confidence – like sheep without a shepherd. He is in the business of training shepherds who will recognize need and be able to offer relevant help. He knows that one man alone cannot meet this scale of need, and recognizes his own physical limitations! Mission begins where you are, recognizing the context, and the strength of being part of a team. The disciples are to put into practice what they have seen and heard from their Shepherd, and become shepherds to the villages in their locality. Jesus knows his disciples by name. He knows them well. He is aware of their gifts and graces, and their shortcomings. He equips them with knowledge and company, and then awaits their return to see if their confidence in one another, and the message they have to share, have grown as well as the size of the flock. *How does our confidence grow as we share in Christ's mission?*

✳ *Enlarge my faith and my willingness to share it. Amen*

What matters most?

Jesus' ministry set out a new guide for living, freeing people from rigid rules and traditions. His natural response to a person in need of healing was to heal! A shepherd's natural response is to look after the flock. In lambing time, it is an all consuming responsibility ensuring that all is well as the flicker of life is given in the birth of lambs. All else is forgotten in the task. The pursuance of wholeness and healing is part of our calling as Christians, and there are times when these must take priority over what is expected or assumed of us in our 'church life'.

Are there times when you feel the Church is the safest place to be? Is your involvement with the Church sometimes a reason for not doing something else – visiting, joining another grouping, actively working for justice – locally or internationally?

Do not let the Church be your cocoon. Be a shepherd and think about where your Christian care is most urgently required!

✳ *Great Shepherd, show me the sheep who need support.*
  Feed me and lead me to their pasture,
  that I may be your sign of care to them.

True commitment

There were no lengths to which Jesus was not willing to go to express his Father's love for humanity. God is our supreme authority and this is exemplified in the whole life and death of Christ. In his ministry too, there were times of suffering and rejection for Jesus.

There are no lengths to which the shepherd will not go, to do what is best for the sheep, separating one sheep from the rest to give individual treatment. There are no time frames around these jobs; they are done whatever the cost.

The complete giving of Jesus on the cross reminds us of the need for complete commitment to our calling. We are part of the flock. What we are and how we are, may be the example that others are looking to.

✳ *We are not worthy to be members of your flock.*
We recognize the greatness of your example
against the poverty of our meagre efforts.
But in your great giving is our calling.
Help us to follow in your footsteps.

A time is coming

One of the noisiest days on the farm is the time of weaning offspring from their mothers. It is a distressing time. The sound of high pitched bleating can be heard from quite a distance. Jesus talks of separating sheep from goats – this time perhaps ready for shearing since goats lose their coats naturally, but sheep need a little help with a pair of shears!

Jesus is preparing for what is beginning to look inevitable. He is warning his disciples that commitment demands more than simply talking about it! He says there will be a 'sorting out day' when the evidence will be seen and decisions made as a consequence.

✳ *When I am hungry, Lord give me people to feed,*
When I am weary, Lord show me people with energy,
When I am downcast, Lord give me someone to love,
When I am happy, Lord give me someone who needs
sparking with joy,
When I am quiet, Lord nourish me from your pasture.

I am the good shepherd

Shepherding is a vocation ... it goes beyond hire and money. It is a vocation which puts whole caring beyond self preservation or safety. It goes beyond the realm of duty and beyond those who are considered safe. Parallels can be drawn to the example of Jesus and the costly commitment required of those who respond to the call to follow him.

The emphasis is on the personal 'I'. It is sure and confident. The sheep need to be sure of their Shepherd. Then they can also recognize those who make false statements and impressions.

✱ *God has raised from death our Lord Jesus, who is the Great Shepherd of the sheep as the result of his sacrificial death, by which the eternal covenant is sealed. May the God of peace provide you with every good thing you need in order to do his will, and may he, through Jesus Christ, do in us what pleases him. And to Christ be the glory for ever and ever! Amen*

Hebrews 13.20-21

For personal reflection or group discussion

Can we think of ways in which governments have been bad shepherds? What can we do about it?

What do you know of groups in your local community or nation who care for the marginalized? What can we learn from them, and what challenges do they make to us?

ACTION

Focus on one person you know who could benefit from some encouragement, and think of ways to help him or her towards feeling part of something bigger.

INTERNATIONAL BIBLE READING ASSOCIATION
1020 Bristol Road, Selly Oak, Birmingham, Great Britain B29 6LB

ORDER FORM – For 1997 Books

Please send me the following books:　　　　　　*Office Ref: 96101*

Name: _____

Address: _____

_____

_____

_____ Post Code: _____

*To qualify for 1997 books at the prices shown, this order form must be used (photocopies not accepted). Your order will be dispatched when **all** books are available.*

Code	Title of Book	Quantity	Unit Price	Total
ZYN0866	Words For Today 1997		£3.65	
ZYL0867	Light For Our Path 1997		£3.65	
ZYL0870	Light For Our Path 1997 (Large Print)		£8.50	
ZYB0868	Finding Our Way Together 1997		£4.50	
ZYP0869	Preachers' Handbook 1997		£4.50	
ZYE0213	Everyday Prayers		£4.95	
ZYM0325	More Everyday Prayers		£4.95	
ZYF0495	Further Everyday Prayers		£4.95	
ZYL0575	Looking At The Cross		£4.50	
ZYL0684	Looking At Advent		£4.50	
ZYL0762	Looking At Pentecost		£4.50	
ZYL0762	Looking At Easter & Ascension		£4.50	
ZYL0871	Living Prayers For Today		£10.95	

I enclose cheque/PO (Payable to IBRA)	**Total cost of books**	
Please charge my ACCESS/MASTERCARD/VISA Card No:	**Post – UK free** Overseas – add £1.50 per book surface	
☐☐☐☐☐☐☐☐☐☐☐☐☐☐☐☐	**Donation to International Fund**	
Expiry Date: _____	**TOTAL DUE**	

Signature: _____　　　　　*Payments in Pounds Sterling, please*

The INTERNATIONAL BIBLE READING ASSOCIATION is a Registered Charity

213

Scheme of readings for 1997

1. God of the nations
2. Called to serve
3. Called to unity – Jubilee of the Church of South India
4. Jacob – flawed yet blessed *(Genesis 25-33)*
5. Life or death?
6. Good or evil?
7. Why do the innocent suffer? *(Job)*
8. Mountain-top experiences
9. Were you there? *(Matthew 21-27)*
10. We die and rise with Christ
11. Work of the Spirit *(Acts 1-5)*
12. Threads of creation – earth, fire, wind and water
13. Cries for help *(Psalms)*
14. Standards for today?
15. Lord, hear our prayer
16. One God – Justice for all *(Deuteronomy)*
17. In every place
18. An extended family
19. A prophet for all *(Isaiah)*
20. The Kingdom of heaven is ...
21. Work
22. How much faith?
23. Living in God's world
24. Holiness
25. Practical faith *(James)*
26. Advent and Christmas

Themes continue to be based on the Joint Lectionary (JLG2), and an attempt has been made to respond to some readers who requested that we study more books of the Bible: many of the themes are drawn almost entirely from **St Matthew**, the longest of the four Gospels.

- For links with Sunday worship, use our *Preachers' Handbook* (see page 14)

- Form a group and reflect together on these themes, using our booklet for house fellowships – *Finding our Way Together* (see page 31)

- Order your copies now using the form provided overleaf.

- Encourage others to read the Bible daily (see page 125)

PRAY FOR THE PEACE OF JERUSALEM

Notes based on the New Revised Standard Version by

Harry Hagopian

Harry Hagopian is an Armenian Christian from Jerusalem and Assistant General Secretary of the Middle East Council of Churches (MECC) – an ecumenical organization which represents the region's 14 million local Christians. He has been particularly involved in the Council's humanitarian work with refugees, human rights advocacy, interpretation and the communication ministry.

Jerusalem out-ranks all other cities of the Bible in prominence and wealth of sacred associations. It appears in nearly two-thirds of the books of the Old Testament and in nearly half of the books of the New Testament.

1996 is destined to be a special year for Jerusalem. It has been earmarked for political discussions by Palestinians and Israelis over the future status of the Holy City – following the PLO-Israel Declaration of Principles in September 1993.

All three monotheistic faiths have an historic claim to the city. For Jews, Jerusalem is home to their holiest site, the Western Wall, the only remaining Wall of the Second Temple. For Christians, it is the place of Christ's crucifixion and resurrection, and birthplace of Christianity. For Muslims, it is the third holiest city of Islam whence the prophet Mohammed ascended into heaven.

Religious passions are matched by political ones. The Israeli government is determined to keep Jerusalem its 'united and eternal capital'. To that end, the city is now ringed with densely populated Jewish settlements, and the traditional Arab majority in East Jerusalem has recently been reversed. The Palestinian National Authority insists that East Jerusalem will be the capital of a new Palestine. Now, more than ever before, prayers for the peace of Jerusalem are needed. If there can be religious and political co-existence in this 'faithful city' as Zechariah calls it (8.3), there can surely be peace in the Middle East.

Recommended Reading

Whose Promised Land? Colin Chapman (Lion Publishing)
Jerusalem, A Shared Trust? (MECC July 1990, issue #8)

---

*17th Sunday after Pentecost, September 22   1 Chronicles
11.1-8 and 17.1-15*

Jerusalem and the desire for a temple

We find an account here of the building of the famous city walls that greet every visitor to the Old City. The walls remain intact, but both Temples built in Jerusalem were destroyed by the Romans in 70CE and 135CE respectively. All that remains of the second Temple is the Western Wall, where Jews gather every day to pray. Nowadays, there is even a service that accepts prayer requests by fax and then places them in the cracks of the ancient wall!

Built on the site of the ancient Jewish Temple, at right angles to the Western Wall, is Al Aqsa Mosque and the Dome of the Rock. Its recently restored golden dome dominates the Jerusalem skyline and is a constant reminder of the presence of Islam in the Holy City. However, some religious Jews, called the Temple Mount Faithful, want to destroy the Muslim complex and build the third temple.

The issue of the Temple today should not be one of confrontation. Surely, a religious site holy to Muslims in an area also holy to Jews, should be a sign of how both faiths, related by their common father Abraham, are intertwined in this city. And just a few minutes' walk away is the Church of the Holy Sepulchre, a Christian holy place where tradition says Christ was crucified. Shouldn't the peaceful sharing of such Holy Land then be symbolic of the mutual tolerance and respect that needs to infuse current political dialogue and underpin any real political progress toward peace?

✳ *Pray that all those who have played a part in making Jerusalem into a theatre of division and conflict turn afresh to God, the God of Abraham and Isaac, the God of Mohammed and the God and Father of our Lord Jesus Christ. Pray for the increased sensitivity of Jewish, Christian and Muslim leaders in Jerusalem towards each other and their different traditions and beliefs.*

Belief that God is present there

This psalm expresses the belief that God, whose majesty stretches over Israel, is not only present there, but is all powerful, awesome – and in control. Some Palestinian Christians have been wrestling with such verses which refer to God as the 'God of Israel'. Surely, God is also the God of Palestinian Christians? Are we to believe, they ask, that this God of Israel is now causing Palestinians to be dispersed? How does God allow Christians to face persecution, torture and hardship, to be treated as second class citizens in the land of Jesus – and be forced to forsake their ancestral property for foreign climes? N.B. Today it would take only four jumbo jets to remove all Christians from the Holy Land.

An ecumenical Palestinian Liberation Theology Group was recently formed at St George's Anglican Cathedral in Jerusalem to biblically explore and pray about these issues. Its members say their faith in a God who loves all those created in his image – whether Jewish, Christian or Muslim – has been restored. After all, they too are God's children and God's people. Colin Chapman, author of *Whose Promised Land?* goes further. He quotes Paul in one of his earliest letters, describing all followers of Jesus, both Jews and Gentiles, as 'Abraham's seed' and therefore inheritors of the promise given to Abraham (Galatians 3.26-29; Ephesians 2.14-20 and 3.6).

So, Palestinian Christians can also put their trust in the Lord of verse 5 as 'the father of orphans and protector of widows' who will give 'the desolate a home to live in' and who will lead out the prisoners to prosperity and provide for the needy. Palestinian refugees, prisoners and those who are oppressed can truly sing praises to God's name (verse 4). God is non-exclusive and non-tribal.

But with that must come belief in the sanctuary of God in his Holy City. Is our behaviour today in Jerusalem – whether Palestinian or Jew – fit for the presence of God?

✸ *Pray for the Liberation Theology Group at St George's Cathedral as it attempts to discover an all-inclusive understanding of our selective attitudes as 'Children of God', as well as for a renewed sense of awe in the presence of God in Jerusalem today.*

A vision of God's banquet for all the nations

This is the Palestinian Liberation Theology Group's inclusive God at work – describing the feast he will prepare for all peoples and assuring us of the Salvation he will bring.

It is the day anticipated by many who have suffered in Jerusalem, who have seen political processes falter or fail, promises broken, and self-interest rule.

'Then the Lord God will wipe away the tears from all faces' (verse 8). It is surely this vision of the future that must keep bigotry, intolerance and hatred at bay. It does not, however, mean Christians can abdicate responsibility for the present. Human rights' workers, staff of non-governmental organizations, church workers organizing rehabilitation for the suffering, and encounter groups between those of different faiths, must all continue in their uphill struggle for peace in Jerusalem. They too, in the midst of their busy and at times frustrating lives, must not lose sight of the day of salvation.

✳ *Pray for the Israelis and Palestinians who are weary and exhausted through their peacemaking efforts.*

Written after the Babylonian exile, believing that Jerusalem will become an international Centre

Many Jews dream of their people coming to Jerusalem from all the nations of the world – an in-gathering after centuries of exile. Indeed, thousands of Jews do arrive in Israel each month to settle. They are guaranteed citizenship.

But if the people of God are not only Jews, but all followers of Christ who seek righteousness and peace, what a magnet their presence would be to the city of Jerusalem! This city would indeed become transformed into a shining symbol of peace. However, the prospect of an end to violence and destruction, the prospect of 'calling the walls of Jerusalem Salvation and its gates Praise' is one that still seems far off.

In recent years, the walls of Jerusalem have witnessed frequent bloody clashes between Palestinian stone-throwers and the Israeli army, with tear gas and gunfire spewing from its gates. Chilling fear often stalks the old city's narrow winding streets and colourful souks: Israeli settlers, Palestinian militants and tourists rub shoulders, one wary of the other. Violence is never far from the surface: in minutes it can transform a bustling scene. Shutters are pulled down on the Arab shop fronts in the old city whose windows display Bethlehem olive wood carvings of the Holy Family, Armenian pottery, mother-of-pearl and hand-woven rugs.

The vision for Jerusalem here in Isaiah is the peacemakers' dream. But such peace comes with the statement that the people shall all be righteous. What does that say to us today about where the quest for peace should start?

✳ *Pray for the righteousness of church leaders, politicians and individuals in many countries as they discuss the future of Jerusalem this year.*

Thursday September 26   *Isaiah 65.17-25*

Vision of peace – and the innocent

Many Palestinian Christians today draw comfort from this passage. After the creation of the state of Israel in 1948, between 60 and 70 per cent of Palestinian Christians fled or were driven out of their ancestral homes. My own family home still stands in West Jerusalem: it was occupied by a Jewish family hours after my family, dispossessed, fled in the mistaken belief they would soon return home. Over the years, many other families have seen their land, with the crops and the vineyards their families tended for centuries, taken from them by force and now worked by others.

One of the greatest tragedies of the last half century of conflict is how women – of all faiths – have 'borne children for calamity'. Palestinian mothers see their sons gaoled, beaten, maimed or killed; Jewish mothers see their sons hated and reviled, injured or brutalized as they carry out their compulsory military service patrolling the unwelcoming streets of Jerusalem and the West Bank.

A group of Jewish women, called 'Women in Black', held a vigil every Friday in downtown Jerusalem calling for an end to Israeli military occupation. Their dress changed to white when the PLO-Israel Declaration was signed, in the hope that this was indeed the beginning of a peace where their sons and daughters would no longer face death, where 'no more shall there be an infant that lives but for a few days, or an old person who does not live out a lifetime.'

Equally, a crucial principle of forging true peace is spelt out here in verse 17: 'The former things shall not be remembered or come to mind.' How often have peace proposals been scuppered because one side hurls accusations of past atrocities at the other? How often have politicians whipped up opposition to peace by reminding their people what the enemy has done and how it cannot be trusted in the future. True forgiveness is painful and often unpopular – working to wipe out the past in order to move to a time when 'no more shall the sound of weeping be heard' in Jerusalem' (verse 19).

✳ *Pray for a sense of true forgiveness among all sides involved in the Palestinian-Israeli conflict and for those organizations working today to promote subsequent reconciliation.*

Friday September 27   *Luke 19.41-44 and 23.27-31*

Jesus' tears over the future of his people

Jesus' words seem as relevant today as in Biblical times. As opportunities for peace in Jerusalem have come and gone in recent times, it appears that 'the things that make for peace' are hidden from peoples' eyes (verse 42).

The consequences of missing the opportunity for peace are equally relevant. As in yesterday's passage, here is a prediction that mothers will say 'Blessed are the barren, and the wombs that never bore, and the breasts that never nursed.' Given the importance placed on having children in the Middle East (remember Sarah's plight of barrenness or Elizabeth's joy at being pregnant after so long), it is a prediction that strikes at the very fabric of oriental society. The family is the collective unit around which that society operates, unlike the individualism often cherished in the West. A woman's identity is still largely centred around her children. Great joy comes from their birth and great pain from the inability to conceive, emotions shared by Palestinians and Jews alike. In addition, for Jews, the emphasis placed on having children comes in the wake of the brutal death of six million Jews in the Holocaust. Today, in an attempt to replace those killed, it is said that Israel has the highest rate of *in vitro* fertilization (IVF) in the world. It is a powerful image therefore for mothers to see the childless as blessed.

Jesus' weeping over the city of Jerusalem was not a one-off occasion. There has been little cause for him to cease weeping as people have continued to reject him and his teachings and failed to see him as the Prince of peace.

**✳ *Pray for the acceptance of Jesus as prime peacemaker in
the Holy City.***

Saturday September 28   *Psalm 122*

Pray for the peace of Jerusalem

This is an appeal to all nations to pray for the peace of the Holy
City. David wishes prosperity to those who work and pray for its
peace – a peace 'for the sake of relatives and friends' who live
there (verse 8). But to what end should people seek the good of
Jerusalem? 'For the sake of the house of the LORD our God',
says David (verse 9).

Peace is often concluded for pragmatic, political self-
interest, or because of the strategic importance and the
resources a country can offer. In its history, Jerusalem has often
been a pawn between nations, kings and governments. Today
Jerusalem is still being fought over. Since 1993, political
controversy has raged around whose capital it should be:
Palestinians claiming East Jerusalem as theirs; Jews claiming
the whole city as theirs!

Claims over religious ownership or guardianship of the holy
sites are equally contentious. Muslims hold the key to the
Church of the Holy Sepulchre because Christians have often
bitterly disagreed how it should be denominationally divided and
managed. Even who should clean a windowsill or sweep the
floor has been under dispute! Jordan wants to retain
custodianship of the Dome of the Rock complex, while the
Palestinian National Authority claim it as their duty. Even Saudi
Arabia wants to enter the fray!

Few people work for the good of Jerusalem as a symbol of
the healing power – the reconciliation and forgiveness – of the
Lord our God; a place where all God's people can come in
peace to 'give thanks to the name of the Lord'.

Christians have a duty to pray for the peace of the earthly city
of Jerusalem – remembering at the same time that the true
worship of God can never again be localized either there or at
any other place on earth (John 4.21). The new Jerusalem of
Revelation is no earthly city but one that will come down 'out of
heaven from God' (21.10).

✳ *Pray for the peace of Jerusalem.*

For personal reflection or group discussion

What do you know about 'the Forgotten Faithful' – the indigenous Christians of the Holy Land who have been witnessing to their faith since the Church of the Pentecost?

Do you tend to forget their stake in Jerusalem and see the conflict in terms of a stark Muslim/Jewish confrontation?

Does striving towards mutual respect and accommodation of all three faiths, as much as different denominations, have anything to say to your own situation at home? Does it question any intolerance or prejudice you may harbour?

ACTION

- When visiting the Holy Land, make sure you meet with some of its 'living stones' – local Christians – as well as visiting sites of historic and religious importance.

- Consider inviting someone from a church in the Holy Land to speak to your group/congregation, or develop a prayer link between a local church/group and your own.

- Perhaps your church can 'twin' with a church in the Holy City – providing Arab Christians much-needed spiritual comfort and moral support.

- In conversations with friends and acquaintances, do not shy away from taking a stand that might be politically unpopular: Jesus himself never courted popularity and acceptance, but spoke out strongly against the injustices and oppression of the establishment.

PROCESSES

Learn to love, help to heal.

Remember not to judge a light by the size of its container. Even a small oil lamp can give light to a big room.

USEFUL ADDRESSES

Middle East Council of Churches   Christian Aid
P O Box 1248   PO Box 100
Jerusalem   London SE1 7RL

HOPE IN THE VALLEY

Notes based on the Revised English Bible by

Bernard Thorogood

From 1953 to 1970 Bernard Thorogood served as a minister in the islands of the South Pacific and later became the General Secretary of the Council for World Mission. From 1980 to 1992 he was General Secretary of the United Reformed Church in the UK, and since retirement has settled in Sydney, Australia.

Is life nasty, brutal and short? Is the darkness overwhelming? Is death the final switch-off? These are the testing questions we meet in the passages for the next two weeks. We start at an early period when sudden death was commonplace and we move through the Gospels to the apostolic certainty that a greater glory lies beyond our sight. We can all find ourselves somewhere in this human story, for the shadow of loss and sorrow touches us all.

18th Sunday after Pentecost, September 29 Judges 11.29-40 *

A promise and a death

Here is a strange story, which has some echoes of Abraham and Isaac in Genesis 22. Both are about devotion to God and a beloved child. But in the case of Abraham it was God who created the test of faith and then saved the child's life. Here Jephthah takes a vow and nothing intervenes to save his daughter. It is as though folly and stubbornness triumph over mercy.

Yet there are some very human touches here. The child rushes out of the house to greet the returning warrior, full of excitement. There are the broken heart and torn clothes of the dismayed father, and then the two months of companionship on the hills before the tragic end. This feels like reality. With few words the writer sketches the tragedy, almost as though it is the outline for a film.

The heart of the story is the vow. Jephthah may have been foolish to make the vow, but having made it he believed that it had to be kept even at this cost. I find it impossible to hold that

God would wish the death of a child, for in Jesus we know God's heart of love. But for the warriors of that early period a vow made to God was an absolute duty. The story stands to remind us that any promise we make to God is a solemn commitment.

✳ *Help us to keep our promises, Lord God,*
  as you keep your promises
  from the world's beginning to the very end.

Monday September 30   *2 Samuel 1.17-27*

A song of sorrow

With the death of Saul and his sons in battle with the Philistines, the fortunes of Israel came very close to disaster. David was mourning both for that defeat and for the loss of those who were dear to him. The hand of God had not saved them. God is not mentioned in the lament; God is absent. But can that be so?

God weeps for wars and grieves for all who are killed in battle. It is as though God is speaking through this poem, every verse a cry for his children. We also live in a century of wars, and the lament could be translated many times in many lands: Flanders, Gallipoli, Stalingrad, Cambodia, Bosnia – there the bodies of the warriors lie broken. Sudan, Rwanda, Liberia, upon your soil your beauty lies slain. We too can chant the lament.

The miracle of God's grace is that Israel was not forsaken; David was to rule with a touch of greatness. Out of the hopelessness of war some new initiatives for peace may grow, some new ways of healing wounds, or some fresh attack on injustice.

✳ *We pray for those who mourn.*
  May they be touched by healing friendship,
  by hope for tomorrow,
  by the nearness of God the Holy Spirit.

Tuesday October 1   *Job 10.1-22*

In deep darkness

For this good, faithful person everything goes wrong, with the loss of family, disease and poverty, and he reaches the point of despair. It is as though God has turned against him and has poured one anguish after another on him. All he can see ahead is 'a land of gloom, a land of deepest darkness' (verse 21) where death will be oblivion.

Our word for it is 'acute depression'. We know people who have suffered like this, who find the whole world is against them, that one sorrow leads to another and life has no value. At such a time the 'comforters', who are the other speakers in this drama, may only talk of God's justice, of human sin and the reality of punishment. That was no help to Job. He was in the grip of darkness and could only be touched by the hand of God.

So we pray for all gripped by depression that the Holy Spirit may be the true Comforter, bringing fresh light to the mind and heart. Medicine and psychiatry may help too, and are surely not to be discounted, but the Spirit of God touching the human spirit is our central hope.

✳ *We name, with love, any who are known to us*
  who live in such darkness ...

Wednesday October 2   *Job 19.21-29*

In court

This is a passage which has proved difficult to translate from Hebrew, with the result that English versions differ considerably. Verses 25 and 26 are familiar to many people in the King James' version because Handel used them so beautifully in *Messiah*. 'I know that my redeemer liveth, and that he shall stand at the latter day upon the earth: And though ... worms destroy this body, yet in my flesh shall I see God' – a great affirmation which points to Christ and to resurrection. The Revised English Bible is equally dramatic but sets the whole scene in the court of judgment. The friends of Job have only nagged at him and brought him low. So Job depends on the one who truly knows the heart, the 'defending counsel' who will make the final speech.

The ultimate test of our lives does not lie with what people say about us, but with God who has given us life and knows what we have done with that gift. This brings a new dimension to the Last Judgment, for the Lord who is judge becomes the prisoner's friend. So Job does point forward to the grace of God.

✳ *Stand beside us, companion God,*
  when all goes wrong and we need a friend;
  you alone know all our hopes and fears.
  Give us the strength to meet this day's challenge.

Final curtain

This passage brings the drama to an end. In chapters 38 to 41 the Lord answers Job's complaint. It is a tremendous speech which lifts the debate to a different level. How can a man judge the justice of God? God is infinite and eternal, holding the whole cosmos in being. The vision that a suffering human being has is very limited and often very distorted. So Job submits. He acknowledges the majesty of God. Therefore, he says, I yield, repenting in dust and ashes. This was one way for the people of Israel to handle the ageless question of human suffering. Argue as much as you like. Complain to God. But at the end submit, for the answer is far beyond you. We have another perspective, that of the suffering God who is with us in the tragic events of life and who meets us face to face in the agony of Christ. It is not the great gap between God and humanity which says to us 'Submit' but the closeness of God to each one of us which says 'I am with you'. Both the gap and the closeness are part of the mystery.

✳ ***Eternal God, you are beyond us as the star is from the ship.***
Eternal God, you are beside us as the wind is to the sail.
You are supporting us as the ocean is to the hull.

What lies beyond?

In the last part of the book of Daniel we find a vision of judgment. It was probably written about 164BCE during the reign of Antiochus IV who tried to suppress the Jewish faith. He destroyed the Temple scrolls, banned Sabbath observance and put his own idol on the holy altar. The prophet glimpsed the authority of God triumphing over the power of a wicked dictator. He saw Michael, the angel, leading his righteous people (verse 1), guiding them in that other world where justice is done by God. Those whose names were written in the book, the faithful ones, will be set free and wise leaders will shine for ever like stars.

There is a beyond: beyond the present suffering and injustice, beyond the present weakness and pain. The writer of Daniel had a glimpse of this reality. He wrote to comfort and strengthen his people. So in the period before the coming of

Christ there was a preparation, a developing belief that death was not finality. This was to be fulfilled in the good news of the gospel.

✳ *Beyond our sight, you are Righteousness;*
Beyond our years, you are Creating;
Beyond our knowledge, you are Saving,
God for all and for ever.

Saturday October 5   *Psalm 116*

Rescued

This psalm does not need explaining, for its message is very clear. We hear the gratitude of the singer who has been very near death, destined for torment, yet has come through to be part of the joyful crowd in the Temple. We hear many Christian echoes. We apply verses 12 and 13 directly to the service of Holy Communion.

Yet the words were written long before that act of salvation which came in Jesus Christ. There were, and are, other experiences of deliverance. Those who have lived through a period of terror and come out of it sane and hopeful, or those who have lost everything and yet have rebuilt their homes, they can sing a song of deliverance.

The Creator of the human family rejoices at every rescue from sorrow and pain and despair – that is the nature of the loving Father. Whatever language people use to sing of their rescue, we can share their joy and praise the Lord. Christians and Jews can hold hands. There is no exclusive right to the song of deliverance.

✳ *We praise you and thank you, God of all,*
for every human life rescued from disaster,
and every home healed from bitterness.

For personal reflection or group discussion

Can all humanity, of whatever faith, join in praising God when a person is rescued from pain or injustice or despair? In all this week's readings there was only a faint hope of eternal life. Many people are still in that position. Does it make suffering harder to bear?

Lazarus

We take four days to study this action of Jesus. It is a tremendous story, selected by John the Evangelist as the last of the seven signs in his Gospel. By these signs Jesus was displaying who he was; the disciples were being led into the full truth. The Synoptics do not mention Lazarus. They tell of the raising of the widow's son at Nain (Luke 7.11-17) and of the daughter of Jairus (Mark 5.21-24, 35-43), so there is a common theme, 'the dead are raised to life' (Matthew 11.4). In Luke 16.19-31 the poor man in the parable is named Lazarus, maybe because at the end of the parable we read, 'they will pay no heed even if someone should rise from the dead' (16.31). So the actual event gave a name which was added to the parable.

In this passage John's themes of light and life are brought together. Jesus does not fear death in Judaea because it is still God's daytime, when God's work is to be done (verses 8-10). Only when that work is finished will Jesus enter the darkness of night. Jesus will call Lazarus into the light from the sleep of death (verse 11).

✴ *We are grateful, Lord Christ, for light and life.*
  May we so live that your light may shine more brightly
  in our homes and throughout our world.

Monday October 7   *John 11.17-27 **

Faith is born

Luke 10.40 tells of Martha the busy housekeeper, too practical to dream of holy things. Here she is still very direct, ready to complain about the slowness of Jesus to reach Bethany. 'I am the resurrection and the life,' says Jesus. 'You do not have to look to a distant, doubtful future when the saints of God will rise up. It is here and now. Where I am, there is resurrection; death is being defeated. Renewing power touches you in my presence.'

Martha responds to the challenge with a confession of faith (verse 27), one of the great statements about Jesus. The Synoptics tell of Peter's confession at Caesarea Philippi, which became a foundation of the Church. John lifts up the memory of a housewife who proclaimed the faith in almost identical words. In ways the church has not always noticed, the Gospels challenge a male-dominated church. Thank God for Martha.

✻ Awaken in us, dear Lord, a living faith.
May we know your resurrection power
and give our confession of faith with confidence and
joy.

Tuesday October 8   John 11.28-37 *

A friend's tears

We see Martha running back to call her sister from the home
where the mourners were gathered. Mary hurries out and meets
Jesus on the road, the company following her. So the little
conversation is not private. Why was Jesus so 'moved with
indignation and deeply distressed'? (verse 33) I think it was
because his close friends had been through such a depth of
sorrow. He knew his mission was to bring life, but in the very
exercise of God's purpose, there were still the mourners' tears
to meet. Jesus himself was moved to tears. What a precious
revelation this is. The way of the healer, the liberator, the way of
the God of peace and hope, is not a road of easy victories,
where people are healed at no cost. There is sorrow along the
way, for it is the way of the cross that runs through Bethany.

In 1824 John Smith, a missionary in Guyana, was imprisoned
by the British governor for encouraging the slaves to stand up
for their rights. His last letter before he died in Demerara prison
ended:

'The Lord's hand is heavy upon me; still, I can praise his
name, that though outward afflictions abound towards me,
yet the consolations of the Gospel abound also, and I believe
he will do all things well. I am, dear sirs, in much affliction,
your useless but devoted servant, John Smith.'

✻ May the tears, dear Jesus,
be but one step from the joy that follows.

Wednesday October 9   John 11.38-44 *

With a great cry

The climax of the story is packed with emotion. Jesus knows the
critical moment has come. Martha is still the practical woman.
The company of mourners is quietened as Jesus prays. That
prayer tells us a lot. In total confidence Jesus is with the Father
and the Father is at work in his Son. The miracle that follows is
not in order that Jesus should be adored as a great divine

magician, but that 'they may believe it was you who sent me' (verse 42), that it is God's power at work and God who is to be worshipped.

With a great cry Jesus awakens Lazarus and calls him out. The shock is overwhelming, the joy is not described, but the result is increased opposition to Jesus. Did it really happen? You will make up your own mind. I believe this is genuine reporting of real events. God, in Jesus, was preparing the disciples to trust in the reality of resurrection. Christ is the wine at the wedding, the bread from heaven, the light for the blind, the resurrection and the life, the Saviour for us all. A household at Bethany was the sign.

✳ *In your eternal power and grace, Father,*
  call from the tomb those who are dead in spirit,
  that they may begin life anew.

Thursday October 10   *Hebrews 9.11-15 ***

Self-offering

Although with our minds we may understand this chapter about sacrifices, we can never feel it with our hearts as the first readers did. For them animal sacrifice was the great traditional way of drawing close to the holiness of God. It was the essential core of worship under the old covenant. So to read that it was replaced by the death of Jesus was a revolution in religion.

It is not helpful to press the parallel too far and treat the death of Jesus as a sacrifice to God, to please God and persuade God to forgive us. That makes too great a division between Jesus and God. The value for us is to see the cross as a self-offering by God in Christ, an offering for us all. It was not just an unholy mess caused by jealousy and a corrupt system. It was a pouring out of life and love; it was a burden willingly carried. Through it we are brought directly into the holy place, the presence of God – new life for you and for me, joined by faith to the love of God. The cross fulfils all that the old system had hoped for.

✳ *Never was love, dear king,*
  Never was grief like Thine.
  This is my friend,
  In whose sweet praise
  I all my days
  Could gladly spend.   *Samuel Crossman 1624-84*

A life in Christ

It was a tough life. Paul knew the hardships of travel, violent opposition and ill-health. He was not surprised, for Jesus had told his followers, 'You will be handed over to the courts ... summoned before governors ... Everyone will hate you for your allegiance to me' (Mark 13.9,13). The way of the cross was for the disciple as well as the Lord.

In 1870 James Gilmour was a pioneer missionary in the vast plains of Mongolia. In a letter he wrote:

'Today I felt like Elijah in the wilderness. He prayed that he might die. I wonder if I am telling the truth when I say that I felt drawn towards suicide. On all occasions two missionaries should go together. I was not of that opinion a few weeks back but I had no idea how weak an individual I am. O the intense loneliness of Christ's life, not a single one understood him. He bore it. O Jesus, let me follow in your steps.'

The triumphant note in Paul's letter is a song of faith. Verses 14 and 15 call the reader to see through all these hardships to the resurrection life. Through suffering to glory, is the apostolic song.

* *We pray for all who, in obedience to God's call, follow a hard way.*

Confident hope

Paul was writing to a small, confused church at Corinth, giving them the confidence he knew in his own life. However battered we are now, we are not, as the ancient Jews thought, heading for oblivion. Ahead is something more wonderful, a new being, a life in God and with God for ever. Faith makes possible what hope longs for.

Today we realize that this teaching carries a risk – to discount human suffering as but a temporary pain on the road to everlasting joy. But suffering is terrible, cruel and persistent. Jesus did not make light of it. He was moved by compassion to heal the sick, and was in agony at the end. The valley of the shadow is a universal human experience, never to be minimized. That is precisely where the gospel meets us. In the depths, in the darkness, 'in this present body we groan' (verse 2). Jesus is there. A criminal's death and a stranger's grave, that is where eternal hope begins.

✳ *Loving God, help us to care for those who suffer,*
to bring hope to the sorrowing
and share the burdens of the oppressed,
as Christ who entered the valley of the shadow for us
all.

For personal reflection or group discussion

'New life the dead receive', says a hymn of Charles Wesley. In what ways is it true? Is the resurrection of Jesus our only evidence for life beyond death?

ACTION

Collect information about groups in your area which are active to bring light and love to those who suffer. Is there anything you feel called to do to support them? Simple forms of help are often the most urgent.

PEOPLE MATTER

1. The weak and defenceless

Notes based on the Revised English Bible by

Stephen Allott

Stephen Allott, born in Madagascar, the son of Quaker missionaries, has taught Classics and Religious Education in Britain and Ireland, and since 1977 has contributed commentaries on Bible passages in the Quaker weekly, THE FRIEND.

October 13-19 – WEEK OF PRAYER FOR WORLD PEACE

Leviticus, the Levites' book, is not only a book of rules and rituals for priests: its message of holiness is for everyone. The ideal set in the covenant at the time of the exodus from Egypt – that Israel was to be 'a kingdom of priests, a holy nation' (Exodus 19.6) – is the theme of the book: 'You must be holy, because I, the Lord your God am holy' (Leviticus 19.2).

Holiness meant 'separateness'. God was present especially in separate places – the tabernacle, the Temple and the burning bush which were on holy ground, and priests were 'separated'. But it was the separateness of commitment which is for everyone – and its inner nature, the nature of the God to whom we are committed, – which is made clear by his commandments. He is present wherever he is obeyed (Leviticus 26.12), and all who obey him are his holy ones, his saints, as the New Testament puts it.

20th Sunday after Pentecost, October 13   Leviticus 19.9-18 *

Living justly

The Ten Commandments of Exodus 20 have a mountain-top starkness – do not murder, do not steal, do not commit adultery. And in this chapter they are set in the context of a farming community – rich and poor, kinsfolk, neighbours, fellow-countrymen, and especially the disadvantaged who had no land: the resident aliens, the hired workers, the blind, the lame. No false witness, said the Commandments: here the dangers of slander are noted and even-handed justice between rich and poor is demanded, with especial concern for cases where a life was at stake. Do not murder, certainly: but we must also learn how to handle the anger from which murder may arise.

Various ways in which the strong can rob the weak are particularized and condemned, anticipating in spirit the mission of Jesus to the oppressed. The protection of gleaners' interests is reminiscent of the concern of Boaz for his reapers to be generous to Ruth. And the underlying principle is identified as love for our neighbour; for it is the Lord who is behind it all.

✽ *Loving Lord, help us to care for those around us,*
   open our hearts to those with greater needs,
   and show us that our neighbours throughout the world
   are your children as we are;
   help us to work for peace for them.

Monday October 14   *Leviticus 19.32-37*
Showing practical love
God's laws are to be kept in all the diverse activities of life, whether through fair trading practice, or by consideration by the young for the old (not only by children for their parents) or by extending the law of love to foreigners who have come to live among us. The Israelites knew from their history what it was like to be aliens; so we too, if we think what it's like to be 'the other person', can be helped to feel their need and to love them as ourselves. It was the Lord who brought them from bondage in Egypt, and they are bound by the covenant which they made in the desert to be faithful to his laws which teach how the love – which is his nature – is to be expressed in all the practicalities of life, great and small. It is because the Lord is as he has shown himself to be that his teachings must be obeyed; love draws us to comply with them, and practical love is the basis of peace.

✽ *God of strangers,*
   help us to make strangers welcome,
   Teach us as a people to seek justice for others
   rather than advantage for ourselves,
   that we may be at peace with them.

Tuesday October 15 *Leviticus 25.1-7*

At peace with the earth

We begin with a reference to Exodus 23.10-11, where the law of the sabbatical year was first laid down. After six years of sowing and reaping, the land was to be left fallow for a year. As the law of the Sabbath, with its weekly rhythm of six days' work and then a day of rest, gave relief to ox and donkey and allowed slaves and foreign labourers to refresh themselves, so the sabbatical year is set in a context of relief for the poor and the alien, who were to share with native families in the natural produce of the land; there was to be no sowing or pruning. Fallowing of course allowed the soil to recover the fertility lost in six years' continuous cropping; but the purpose of the year was to serve as a reminder that it was the Lord who was the giver of the land and its produce, and that all people, no matter what their status, were equal in their basic needs.

✳ *God of all growth,*
teach us to respect the land and its gifts,
to share its resources with all other living things,
to live at peace with the earth.

Wednesday October 16, World Food Day *Leviticus 25.8-22*

Sharing our food

The word 'jubilee' comes from the Hebrew *yobel*, probably meaning 'a ram's horn'. But the Septuagint, the early Greek version of the Old Testament, renders it *aphesis*, 'release', which accurately describes the purpose of Jubilee – to free the land from the burden of mortgage. The poor could raise money on their land by going through a form of sale, the price being proportionate to the number of years to the next Jubilee, for it represented the number of years' use which the purchaser would get. But every 49 years, at Jubilee, all land was to return to the original owners; this ensured that capital in land could not be accumulated indefinitely – the poor were given a fresh start.

The passage also explains how people lived through the sabbatical year: the sixth year's harvest would be enough to live on until the harvest of the first year of the next seven year period. Under the law of the Lord everyone would have enough to eat; whenever people go hungry, God's will is being denied.

✳ *Lord of all riches,*
we know that what we own is not ours in perpetuity;

free us from the sin of possessiveness;
show us how the food which the earth produces
may be shared fairly.

Thursday October 17   *Leviticus 25.23-34*

The spirit of jubilee

The land belonged to God, who had brought Israel to settle in it; each tribe and each family had been allotted a portion, which they held as God's tenants. It did not belong to the individual occupant; hence Naboth's refusal to exchange his vineyard for a better – it had always belonged to his family (1 Kings 21.3). He could have sold it, if he needed to raise the money; but any relative who could afford it had the duty and right to buy it back for him. It would return to him in any case at Jubilee. He also had the right to buy it back himself, if at any time he could afford to compensate the purchaser for the number of years' use still outstanding.

The law was to ensure that every family had land to live on; so it did not apply to town houses, except for the houses of Levites who had no land but depended on the common land around their towns for pasture. 'To the Lord belong the earth and everything in it ...' (Psalm 24.1); it is not owned by its occupants, but is for their use; it can be bought and sold, but always under conditions which protect the poor.

✳ *Lord of every land, and people,*
show us how the poor can be restored
to their inheritance,
and the spirit of jubilee can root out
the seeds of war and division.

Friday October 18   *Leviticus 25.35-38*

Seeking justice for the deprived

The deliverance of the Israelites from Egypt not only established them as a free people in their own fertile land, but revealed the nature of God as the love which saves the oppressed and meets the need of the poor. It is because this is what God is like that the Israelites were to help the foreigners amongst them, and if any of their own people could not support themselves, they were to share their homes with them. If they lent them money, they were not to take advantage of the situation by charging interest, which would enrich themselves but make the plight of the poor even worse. The law against usury was based on the law of love. Here the spirit of Christ is foreshadowed in the practice of daily life, dealing with homelessness and poverty: 'If God thus loved us ... we also must love one another' (1 John 4.11).

✳ *God of the oppressed,*
show us that our comfort may mean others' hardship,
and that seeking justice for the deprived
is part of our work for peace.

Saturday October 19   *Leviticus 25.39-55*

Serving rather than being served

The institution of slavery is accepted, as it is also in the New Testament; but in the case of fellow Israelites at least there was the prospect of release at Jubilee. Slaves lived and worked as hired labourers; they could not be sold to other owners and must not be overworked. The right of redemption remained, if the slave himself or a relation could afford it. Conditions were no doubt more humane than in many a modern prison; slaves at least lived in society till their debt was paid off.

In a sense all Israelites were God's slaves and eternally in his debt, for he had saved them from Egypt. So too Christians being freed from sin are 'slaves of righteousness' (Romans 6.18); in our service we belong to the God of love, and we look forward to 'the year of the Lord's favour' of which Jesus read at Nazareth (Luke 4.18-19), the Jubilee for all the oppressed; but we are committed to living already by its principles.

✳ *God of love,*
whom we have seen in the form of a servant,
teach us to serve rather than demand to be served,
to love rather than seek to be loved,
and to work for a world at peace.

For personal reflection or group discussion

1. Can the structures of our society be improved to provide food and homes more fairly?

2. What are we doing personally to help the disadvantaged in our community?

3. Do we all need regular sabbaticals from work?

ACT

Take a positive step towards peace and justice in the world, perhaps by joining an organization which works to build up the institutions of peace, or, if you live in a wealthy country, by writing to your government for an increase in its contribution to overseas aid.

Use the following prayer with people of all faiths at midday every day:

Universal prayer for peace

✳ *Lead me from Death to Life*
from Falsehood to Truth
Lead me from Despair to Hope
from Fear to Trust
Lead me from Hate to Love
from War to Peace
Let Peace fill our Heart
our World, our Universe
Peace – Peace – Peace

PEOPLE MATTER

2. Those who care

Notes based on the Revised English Bible by

Michael J Townsend

Michael Townsend, Chairman of the Leeds District of the Methodist Church (UK), is author of The Epistle of James (Epworth Press), and a book review editor.

Christians do not have a monopoly of caring, and should rejoice in it wherever it is found. Important insights into the nature and motivation of caring, however, are found in biblical writings. This week's theme explores some of these, and we shall see how our caring for one another is rooted and grounded in the care and love God shows to us.

21st Sunday after Pentecost, October 20   2 Samuel 23.13-17 *

Affirming the carers

When the 'heroic three' heard David's wish and fetched the water from the well, it was not that water from this well had greater thirst-quenching properties. It was on the other side of Philistine enemy lines. David's hope for the success of the military campaign was so that he and his people could again drink freely from the well. By their action, David's companions affirmed his leadership and their confidence that his aims could be achieved.

A second act of caring was David's action in offering the water to the Lord. It had been obtained at great risk. To offer it to God in this way was a sign that David recognized their sacrifice and valued their loyalty.

In this way, they affirmed one another's goals and quality of service. Affirming one another within the community of faith is an important way to show that we care.

✻ *Think of a leader in your church. In prayer, affirm his or her hopes and dreams before God.*

Caring about the future

Jeremiah lived at a time when God's people could see no reason for hope. The conquest of their land by Nebuchadnezzar, and deportation of the strongest and fittest of their population, marked the greatest single disaster which had ever befallen them. It was made worse by their belief that, because God had given them the 'promised land', they were invulnerable. It seemed that their faith had been destroyed along with their homes, and there was little room for hope.

Yet God had a message for them, and it came through Jeremiah's letter to those in exile. They were to look to the future in all things: build, plant, marry, raise families, and seek the welfare of the cities to which they had been exiled (verse 7). Above all they were to remain faithful to God, and wait in hope for God's future. Jeremiah's message was that God cares even in the darkest moments. God sent it through a prophet who himself cared passionately for the welfare of his people.

✳ *God of hope, we pray for those without hope,*
that some measure of your care
may reach them through us.

Unknown carers

Western societies are becoming increasingly individualistic. It is a considered mark of personal maturity that we can 'stand on our own feet' and cope with life by ourselves. From a Christian perspective, this culture of individualism is unhealthy, and untrue. It will not take much reflection to realize that we do in fact depend on the work and support of others. In an increasingly complex world we may not know who they are but we can't do without them.

Today's reading shows us how Jesus set about his God-given work of proclaiming the Kingdom, supported by a group of women who provided for him and the disciples. Is it too much to say that without their support Jesus could not have continued his preaching ministry? Yet only a few of them are named and there were 'many others' (verse 3).

Today's reading reminds us of the gratitude we owe to those closest to us, especially family and friends, and prompts us to give thanks for the way they care. It reminds us that there are 'many others', and if we cannot thank them personally, we can thank God for them.

* **Give thanks for those, known and unknown, who care for you.**

Wednesday October 23   Acts 6.1-7 *

Organized caring

From the earliest days of the Church, it was recognized that feeding the hungry complemented evangelism. Today's reading indicates that the Greek speaking widows had not been treated fairly, and a grievance arose from this minority group. Busy though they were, the apostles did not dismiss the complaint, but brought the issue before the whole Christian community. The result was the setting up of a way to care for the poor justly and efficiently.

Christian caring cannot be left to individuals only. It requires organization and funding, and the setting apart of people with particular gifts to ensure that it is done properly. This is the thinking that lies behind national and international charities like Christian Aid, as well as the work of church and community groups at local level. Even where it is voluntary, the church's caring needs to be well organized and thought through, because justice is an integral part of true caring.

* **Give us good Lord,
the will to care, the skills to care well
and the commitment to care justly.**

United Nations Day, October 24   Luke 11.5-8

God's care for the world

Today's reading has some strange features. According to Luke, the story is told by Jesus in response to a request for teaching on prayer (Luke 11.1). Yet it is about someone who responds reluctantly to a request for help, perhaps to rid himself of a nuisance rather than because he wants to help. Is Jesus saying that God will care for us only if we persist in asking him long enough? Or is he pointing to the amount of sharing that goes on in communities, however imperfect the motives may be?

We can read this story alongside a similar one in Luke 18.1-8. There the conclusion is more explicit: God's way of caring and giving always exceeds that of human beings. If a reluctant friend and a corrupt judge can eventually be persuaded to respond to human need, how much more will God do so, especially when, by our persistence, we show how much we need such care?

It is not always easy to effect right relationships between nations or individuals. Trust in God, who wants only the best for all his children, is a key to making it happen.

✻ *On this United Nations Day, pray for a greater sense of caring throughout the human family.*

Friday October 25   *Romans 12.9-21* ✻

Spontaneous caring

Someone once said that for Paul, 'religion is grace and ethics is gratitude'. So it is in today's reading, with its exhortation to live out the Christian life in community with love, zeal, hope, hospitality, humility, peaceableness and many other desirable qualities. It is worth taking a moment or two to imagine what our world, our local communities (and our churches) would be like if we actually achieved the quality of caring for one another pictured in these verses!

Yet this is only possible if life is lived thankfully. In the preceding chapters of this letter, Paul has written about God's love and care in sending Jesus to be the world's redeemer, and of how human beings enter into a new relationship with God through him. It is those who have first received this great gift of God's love in Christ who can begin, however inadequately, to live the life of gratitude depicted in this reading. We know, to our shame, that we rarely achieve the level of caring Paul commends. But it is there before us as a vision and a challenge. Let us pray that by allowing the living Lord to dwell in us more fully we shall come closer to it.

✻ *Be it my only wisdom here*
To serve the Lord with filial fear,
*   With loving gratitude;*
Superior sense may I display,
By shunning every evil way,
*   And walking in the good.*   *Charles Wesley (1707-88)*

242

A fellowship of caring

The Jerusalem Church was in great material need, and Paul appealed to other churches, like Corinth, to contribute.

Why should Corinthian Christians, mostly Gentiles, care in this way for Jerusalem Christians who were mostly Jews? The insight expressed in verse 12 is significant. Caring for the needy is in itself a good thing, and, as it releases a 'flood of thanksgiving' to God from those who receive, it binds both parties together in a fellowship of giving and receiving.

This insight lies at the heart of Christian caring. In meeting the needs of others we may not seek to bring honour to ourselves. By reflecting God's care for us, we evoke a response from others which gives glory to God.

* May new avenues of service open for us
and may we grow closer to one another
in the love of the Lord.   *Zimbabwe*
From Oceans of Prayer (NCEC)

For personal reflection or group discussion

1. How can we affirm (a) our families and friends (b) those with whom we work and (c) others within our church? Is it possible to affirm those with whom we disagree? How far does 2 Samuel 23.13-17 help us find the answer?

2. What does 2 Corinthians 9.6-15 teach us about Christian giving? In what ways would we benefit from applying the insights of this passage to our giving, both to our local church and to the World Church?

ACTION

In the light of Acts 6.1-7, think about how the local church organizes caring. Are any groups neglected? If so, prepare some plans for putting this right.

PEOPLE MATTER

3. Individuals and communities

Notes by

P Victor Premasagar

Bishop Premasagar – former Moderator of the Church of South India, writer and well-known teacher of theology – has served as pastor in rural and industrial congregations.

God comes to establish his Kingdom, strengthening the weak and the poor, the deprived and the disabled, bringing joy to people as individuals, communities and nations. He guides human destinies and history calling human beings to be responsible towards each other and the whole creation.

God became human to redeem creation, including men and women whom he created in his image. He cares for the smallest creature and human beings both as individuals and in communities. He desires justice and righteousness in our relationships. The poor and oppressed, the weak and handicapped matter in God's Kingdom. Prophetic visions speak of the deaf hearing, the dumb speaking, the lame leaping with joy, and the whole created order rejoicing at the reversal and transformation of all things. The hungry will be fed and the rich sent away empty.

9th Sunday before Christmas, October 27   *Psalm 8*

Human dignity and stewardship

Human beings are infinitesimally small in creation. The psalmist is probably meditating on God's glory at night time – the heavens which God has made, the moon and stars in that vast expanse. He sees that God has crowned men and women with glory and honour – the divine image in them – and given them responsibility over the whole creation. In verse 6 he does not use the Hebrew word for 'dominion' as in Genesis 1.26, but a word which means 'to rule over', emphasizing responsibility which has nothing to do with oppressive subjugation or the exploitation of nature for human greed. People, the crown of creation, are given responsibility to act as stewards. Our whole ecological responsibility is reflected in this psalm. Irresponsible use destroys the balance of nature and its usefulness.

'Man' in this psalm implies women and men: the way we organize ourselves in communities. We are responsible to God for our development and culture.

✳ *Almighty God, we praise you for your creation*
and its preservation,
and for the renewal of the world and its communities.
Make us aware of the awful responsibility
you have placed upon us in nurturing, protecting and
conserving its resources.
Let your image be perfected in us through Jesus Christ.

Monday October 28   *Proverbs 8.1, 22-31* ✳

Wisdom for life

Wisdom is God's gift to us to enable us to use God's other gifts for the well-being of all. Found in every nation and every culture, it has inspired the development of science, medicine, technical skills, the organization of social, economic and political structures, art, music, sculpture, painting and other fine-arts.

Wisdom is described here as created by God before the universe, being present with God in creating, assisting him as his darling child. Wisdom is personified as a woman, offering the gift of wisdom and well-being to human beings, who out of all creation, are in a relationship of dialogue with God. In the story of the Fall, God converses with Adam and Eve but not with the serpent. Human beings have that unique gift to respond to God. But wisdom and knowledge have to be used for good and not for evil, and it is 'the fear of the Lord' which gives direction to use God-given resources for life and not death. Creative ideas are given to us for the growth and development of our community and the whole creation. Wisdom has to be practical, not just theoretical; it has to be imaginative and inspiring.

✳ *The fear of the Lord is the beginning of wisdom:*
Grant us obedient hearts to perceive your will
and use your gift of wisdom for the good of all.

Confessing Christ before the world

Paul is an elder of a village congregation, a poor labourer on the land of rich Indians. A government official who was distributing land to the landless came and asked him to become a Hindu to avail himself of privileges given to scheduled caste Hindus. Christians are not listed in the Constitution of India and therefore do not qualify for privileges given to outcast communities known as *daliths.*

He replied, 'I will not deny my master even if I do not get these privileges.' Paul confessed his faith in Christ despite what it cost him and his family.

Often Christian witness is confined to sharing information about Jesus Christ. But confession involves facing loss and persecution and openly standing on the side of the crucified master, willing to share suffering for his sake.

Confession also involves positive action on behalf of the Kingdom against oppression and injustice, resulting in suffering, persecution and degradation. The Kingdom demands from the disciple more than the sharing of information. The Greek word for 'witness', *martureo*, implies martyrdom. And that is why Jesus says, 'Fear not' (verse 31). Responsible discipleship involves positive action. Such decisiveness and engagement ushers in the Kingdom, overcoming evil and injustice in the world. Even more than the sparrows, disciples are loved by God, for they are to proclaim the message of the Kingdom, and confess God's reign before a hostile world.

✳ *Lord, make us bold to challenge oppressive systems*
   and confess your name and the gospel
   in the face of these life-negating structures,
   for the coming of your Kingdom in our midst,
   through Christ our Lord.

Women are liberated

In many cultures, women are oppressed in the community, and this is still so in India. Dowry is such an enormous burden for the parents of a bride that they dread the birth of a girl. Developments in medical technology can terminate the pregnancies of female children. The girl-child is not wanted and is often neglected in Indian families. Even after marriage, the bride may be harassed and tortured by the bridegroom and his family to extract the unpaid dowry and other benefits from her family.

Jesus, in healing this woman and going into the house of Jairus to raise his daughter, gives new status to these neglected, oppressed members of the community. In the Kingdom, those who are neglected or exploited by their own community receive priority. They are released, strengthened and their situation is transformed. Women and girls, who assure a future for the community, matter to Jesus. He puts aside other matters and makes time to speak with them.

✳ *Lord, who made time for unimportant people and children,*
we pray for the removal of oppressive traditions
that enslave and subordinate women
whom you created in your image.

Thursday October 31　　　　　　　　　　　　*Luke 18.15-17*

Children are important

Children are rarely given their due place in the community. In poor homes in India, children are sold into bonded labour, and, from an early age, many work in industries – making, for example, carpets, match-sticks, and sandalwood scented sticks – working for long hours in unhealthy and harmful places for meagre wages. This drudgery prevents them from developing their human potential.

In blessing the children, Jesus brought their rights to the forefront of the attention of nations and society.

Free elementary and secondary education in many countries has been inspired by these words of Jesus. In India several laws have been passed in recent years, liberating children from bonded labour and inhuman conditions. But these are only on paper and need to be fully implemented. Many individuals and families, through charitable organizations from other parts of the world, sponsor and support children from poor, destitute families.

Children come as God's gift to parents, the nation and the world, and we all share the responsibility of nurturing them in the faith, and with sensitivity to all their needs.

✳ *Lord, increase our awareness of children in our midst,*
that we may work for a better future for them
and especially for those who are deprived,
through Jesus Christ, the child of Nazareth.

We are meant to share what we have

In India, we often complain that we are poor and have no mind to give. I tell our congregations that there are three kinds of poor people in the Bible:

- The *anawim* – the poor, oppressed, exploited and destitute. They have nothing, not even the energy or ability to complain. Life is drudgery, full of pain and suffering. These are the poorest of the poor.

- The *ebyonim* – those who are comparatively better off but always poor by increasing their needs. They are always grumbling and complaining, and do not have the mind to give because they are always in need.

- The *hasidim* – those who are poor for the sake of the Kingdom. They have no complaints, but only joy that they are able to serve God and others.

Most of us belong to the second group. St Paul in 2 Corinthians 8.1-15 says that God gives blessings in abundance that we may give, and that his grace will so transform us that we will minimize our needs to contribute to the needs of others. In India we have a tradition that God is poverty-stricken – *Daridra Narayana* – not because he does not have, but because he gives all that he has to his creation. In Indian translations of the Bible, the word *Daridra* is used to describe Jesus (2 Corinthians 8.9), who became poor for our sakes that we might become rich. The grace of God gives us self-reliance, so that, like the widow, we may be able to set aside our needs and give for others.

✳ *Lord Jesus Christ,*
who became poor for our sakes,
grant that we may be transformed to follow your lifestyle
and give to meet the needs of others.
Give us your grace, that,
following in your way,
we may serve instead of expecting to be served,
and accept the challenge of your life
given as a ransom for all.

A new heaven and a new earth

At times when all seemed lost, the people of God looked forward to a future when God would transform all things and comfort them, turning around world events to redress the wrongs done to his people and assure them of peace and joy. This hope sustained the Church in times of persecution.

The vision here is of a new creation, God dwelling with his people, wiping away all tears, and death will be no more. This motivates the people of God never to be satisfied with the *status quo*, but always to work for a new order. The present order which is politically oppressive – causing pain and suffering to many – is not sacrosanct. Even people's understanding of God is conditioned by those in power and serves the interests of the powerful. All this will have to change. People and their state of affairs matter to God, and he is working to bring about a new heaven and earth. There must also be a new understanding of God to avert exploitation, pain and death and bring in an everlasting age of joy and peace for all people and all nature. God is engaged in this work, and we should co-operate with him and work for it.

✳ *Almighty God,*
Creator and Lord of the whole universe,
we join with countless disciples in praying,
'Let your Kingdom come
and your will be done on earth'
and may this world be renewed by your Spirit,
through Jesus Christ our Lord. Amen

For personal reflection or group discussion

How much do we as Christians continue to support the powerful and neglect the poorest and weakest, both in the community and in the fellowship of the Church?

ACTION

Think of another practical way to support those in need in your community.

MARKS OF TRUE RELIGION

1. No humbug!

Notes based on the Revised English Bible by

Donald Hilton

Donald Hilton, Moderator of the Yorkshire Province of the United Reformed Church (UK), has compiled several anthologies of material for Christian education and worship, and has written a number of resource books for all-age worship, all published by the NCEC.

'Religion is full of humbug, and they are all hypocrites!' We can't ignore the jibe if we want to show the marks of true religion.

- A 'humbug' proclaims strong ideas that have not been thought through; everyone else's opinion is dismissed.

- A hypocrite is someone who fails to live up to professed beliefs and doesn't 'practise what s/he preaches'.

Humility is one antidote to both problems. Our most deeply held beliefs must be open to the comments of others, and we need to recognize that the higher our ideals are, the more likely we are to fall short of them.

For three weeks we are to think about the marks of true religion. 'Humbug' cannot be one of them so we will try to define it better so as to grow out of it. The final two weeks will look at two of the positive marks of genuine religion.

---

*8th Sunday before Christmas, November 3   Isaiah 44.6-17 ***

Think about it!

The sheer nonsense of it angered Isaiah. A tree trunk was cut into three pieces. Any piece might end up either as fuel to be burnt or a god to be worshipped. Such silly religion is humbug. No sensible person can believe in it.

The twentieth century has as many idols as Isaiah's time. What or who are they? Millionaire T.V. and football stars?

Success? The world of fashion that seduces people into spending more money than clothes deserve? Have right wing politicians turned the market-place into a god just as surely as Communists turned the state into a god?

Christians are not exempt from idol worship. Isaiah would be equally scathing of:

- the Sunday-only-god we ignore the rest of the week;

- the do-it-all-for-us god who expects no effort from us;

- the I-look-after-my favourites god with special gifts to the few (including me, of course!) and punishment for everyone else.

These verses, however, do not only condemn idol worship. They are a plea to put faith on a sound rational basis. If that wood-cutter with his three pieces of wood had thought for one minute about what he was doing he would have seen the nonsense of it all. But he didn't think! A religion that doesn't think so easily becomes sheer humbug.

✵ *Lord, give me that penetrating thought*
that cuts through my superstitions
to reach the very ground of true faith.

Monday November 4   *Matthew 23.1-12*

Get off your pedestal

Hypocrisy we call it. Humbug, too: to 'say one thing and do another'. Note two points:

- If we are whole people then our words and lives must be integrated; neither denying the other. If we advocate generosity in others we must be generous ourselves. If we say that the world should be one community, there can be no petty bickering in church.

- Reflect on the suggestion that in fact all good Christians 'say one thing and do another' because we have deliberately accepted ideals that we know we cannot fully live up to. We are reaching for the skies whilst our feet are earthbound. We are delivered from hypocrisy only if our lives are moving ever closer to our ideals.

Read verses 8-12 again. They seem to turn our usual thinking upside down. Of course we call some people 'rabbi'; it means 'teacher'. Thank God for Christian teachers! We call our male parent 'father'; it is natural and right. The meaning of the verses lies deeper. They exhort us not to put anyone on a pedestal, not even beloved parents and honoured teachers. Only those who sacrificially serve others deserve pedestals – and they would run a mile if you showed them a pedestal! It is interesting that in Matthew's Gospel only Judas calls Jesus 'Rabbi'.

> ✳ *He that is down needs fear no fall,*
> *He that is low, no pride;*
> *He that is humble ever shall*
> *have God to be his guide.* John Bunyan

Tuesday November 5   Matthew 23.13-15

Mission for what?

Here's a double humbug! 'Dog in the manger' is the first. There's an old fable of a dog that stood guard in the straw growling. The dog didn't want the straw but attacked the hungry cows if they got near. The Pharisees wouldn't accept the good news of God's love themselves and then tried to stop people hungry for the gospel from receiving it.

Simon enjoys the church but doesn't like to get too serious. The social life is fine, the church youth club is a must, and the chance to meet friends is very welcome But let it stop there. Peter, a newcomer to the church, wants Bible study and time for prayer. But he always gets the same response from Simon. 'Don't be so serious,' he says. 'Keep it light.'

Distorted mission is the second humbug. You can travel the world as an evangelist but it you offer a distorted gospel – what's the point? Ask some penetrating questions:

● *Does the gospel you preach give people a real sense of joy or just pile guilt onto converts?*

● *Is your own knowledge of the Bible so scant that children will have to 're-learn' its message when they study for themselves?*

● *What is your motive in sharing the good news? Is it to win people for Christ or to fill the church pews?*

● *If new converts wanted to change your church, would you listen?*

> ✳ *Open the doors, Lord!*
> *The doors of your Kingdom*
> *and the doors of my heart and mind.*

Get your priorities right

The word 'Alas' was used twice in yesterday's reading to introduce a comment and twice today. In the original it has a double meaning. It expresses sadness. The Pharisees' intention was to honour God but they based their relationship with him on law, not love. How sad to have the right intention and then build it on a false foundation.

'Alas' is also 'a warning'. Such a misunderstanding of God can lead to sin and divine judgment. It can shut people out of the Kingdom (verse 13).

The same two meanings can be seen in today's verses. Is a solemn promise more binding because you swear by the gold on the altar rather than the altar itself? Of course not! To think it so is not only sad but could lead to the sin of putting money before the Presence of God which the altar symbolizes. Tithing is important but you can spend so much time worrying about whether you've tithed the last penny that you miss God's greater call to work for justice and faith. Get your priorities right. A young child wrote a prayer:

'God, what kind of a world is this that the adult people are going to leave for us children?'

The answer to her prayer will depend on our priorities.

✳ *Reflect: in the place where you live, what kind of a world will you hand on to your children and grandchildren?*

Judgment

These verses are dynamite and can't be ignored. Whitewashed tombs! Vipers! Snakes! Is this 'gentle Jesus, meek and mild'? Even our politicians are polite to each other in comparison. But the message is clear: what is hidden within our lives and what people see from the outside must be the same; otherwise it is humbug and hypocrisy.

Scholars see the seven 'Alas's' or 'Woes' of Matthew 23 as a counter-balance to the eight Beatitudes or blessings of Matthew 5.3-10. The Beatitudes describe the life of Christian disciples, and the woes point to lives moving away from Christ. Can these woes of sadness and warning speak to our time? Would Jesus say to us:

Woe to you when houses stand empty and young people live in cardboard boxes in inner cities.

Woe to you when you prepare for a family Christmas and ignore the lonely.

Woe to you when you deplore reducing congregations but refuse to change your church life to attract others.

Woe to you when you complain that few children come to church and then ignore the ones who do.

Woe to *you* ... What humbug in you saddens God?

✳ *Holy Spirit of God, cleanse and renew us*
within and without.

Friday November 8   *James 2.1-13*

Discrimination

The service had begun. It was a respectable English congregation; well-dressed and a little formal. As the congregation sat down after the first hymn the church door swung open clumsily and three young men entered. They had long hair and wore tattered jeans. One had his nose pierced and a ring through it; another kept on his very large hat. The minister later acknowledged that he saw what a wonderful opportunity the church had for witness; he began automatically to simplify his language because he thought they might not understand; he quickly looked to see whether the cash box on the bookstall was safe.

After ten minutes the three young people left. Do you think the congregation felt sad or relieved at their departure? How welcoming is your church? Think carefully before you answer. For example:

● How many people under-25 serve on your elders or deacons or stewards meeting?

● Could someone in a wheelchair enter your church as easily as a fully able person?

● Are the opinions of newcomers treated as seriously as those of long-standing members?

● Would a homosexual be allowed to become a member?

✳ *Father God, your family is broken and divided.*
Let your love heal and unite us
into a community of care and peace.

Root causes

In explaining the gospel Paul also throws light on some of the root causes of humbug and hypocrisy.

The first root is human pride and selfishness. We are too tied up with ourselves. Our life-style is the best! If people don't see things our way then they must have got it wrong. Thus we draw a circle around our little lives and exclude those who don't conform. Humbug and hypocrisy!

A second root is our preference for law rather than grace. We draw up rules about how people should think, behave, and believe. Those who break them are excluded. God is much more generous. He leaves no-one outside his circle.

The most serious root is our failure to love. Jesus has shown that our response to God is not that of a subject to a ruler, or servant to a law-giver. Above all, it is that of a lover to a Lover.

'Tis mercy all, immense and free;
For, O my God, it found out me.'   *Charles Wesley*

If God so loved us then love is the root of our relationships with others. Once that happens, humbug flies out of the window and hypocrisy disappears. Few achieve it fully. The vision of Jesus is both a challenge and an encouragement to fulfil it.

✳ *Lord Jesus Christ, as you have accepted me,*
help me to accept others.

For personal reflection and group discussion

Decide three or four principles you think ought to be followed for the world to become a more loving and accepting community. Then go through them one by one and ask if your local church is living by the same principles.

Scholars compare the 'Alas's' (or Woes) of Matthew 23 with the Beatitudes of Matthew 5 but suggest that they are in reverse order: that the first Beatitude is a counterbalance to the last 'Alas' and so on. Judge for yourself if you think they have hit on Matthew's intention. As there are eight Beatitudes and only seven 'Alas's' you will have to decide if one 'Alas' is missing or if two Beatitudes can be coupled.

ACTION

What action has to be taken in your own life to decrease humbug and increase love? Is some action also needed in your local church?

MARKS OF TRUE RELIGION

2. Integrity

Notes based on the Good News Bible by

Mary Cotes

Formerly chaplain to a community centre in Exeter, Mary Cotes now serves as minister of the United Church, Pontypridd, South Wales.

The Scriptures frequently remind us of the necessity of making the all-important connection between what we say we believe and what we do. 'If you have love for one another,' Jesus says, 'then everyone will know that you are my disciples' (John 13.35) – not by your beautiful prayers or your knowledge of the Bible. But in a world as complex and ambiguous as ours, and as culturally different from that of the Biblical writers, making the connection is not easy. This week's readings challenge us to think again about the demands of practising what we preach.

7th Sunday before Christmas, November 10

Genesis 13.1-18 *

A costly business

Pilgrimage seems a lovely metaphor for our life's journey of faith. We are inspired by the idea of striding into the future under the protection of the God we follow, the road strewn with light. But the reality is different. The pathway of a true pilgrim is often dark, ambiguous and hard going.

Abraham, one of the first pilgrims in the Scriptures, does not have an easy time. He is called by God to make a journey and given a great promise. Yet because of this calling, his life is full of darkness and testing: his child's life is threatened (Genesis 22.1-19); there are times when, as Lot does here, even his close relatives exploit his good will and leave him 'the short straw'. What makes Abraham special is his conviction that he must hold firm to his calling, even if that entails being stripped of comfort and material advantage and being left with the raw deal.

> * **Unless thou lead me, Lord,**
> **the road I journey is all too hard.**
> **Through trust in thee alone can I go on.**   T Kagawa,
> Japan

Monday November 11   *Matthew 3.7-12 **

Faith and fruit

My friend Juanita is living in England now. You only have to talk to her for a matter of minutes before she starts to recount the ways her people are oppressed and the atrocities and injustices committed against them. Probably she will not tell you of the five years she herself spent in prison in her country, or the torture she endured for daring to speak against the regime. And as best she can, she will disguise the psychological and physical scars she bears. I tell you about her not because she's brave but simply because of who she is. So profoundly does she believe in her right as a human being to speak her mind that already she acts as though she was free to do so. Despite continuing threats, she can't keep her mouth shut.

John rails against the Pharisees and Sadducees who come for baptism to escape punishment. True religion, he says, does not look for the safe option. God demands a coherence between belief and acts, faith and fruit. Such integrity does not always come cheap.

> * **Father, hear the prayer we offer:**
> **not for ease that prayer shall be.**   L M Willis 1824-1908

Tuesday November 12   *Galatians 3.1-9 **

Not by Law but by Spirit.

In his late twenties, Richard is a virtuosic organist who has played for services at his local church since he was seven. A profoundly spiritual person, he considers it part of his Christian commitment. But recently his priest discovered that Richard has a homosexual relationship, and has banned him from playing. Richard has received abusive phone-calls from church members whom he used to count as friends. In tears, he says he cannot face going there again.

The idea that Gentiles could be part of the Church without first becoming Jews was anathema to Jewish Christians of the Early Church. After all, Scripture made it clear: uncircumcised folk just could not be counted among God's people. But in the light of the gospel and in face of the genuine faith of Gentile believers, Paul asks the Galatians to rethink all their views. He dares them to live openly by the Spirit and leave behind the legalism of their childhood.

✻ *But we make his love too narrow*
   By false limits of our own;
   And we magnify His strictness
   With a zeal He will not own.

F W Faber 1814-63

Wednesday November 13   *Galatians 3.10-14 ✻*
Shedding the armour

It's not easy to change your mind, especially about something you have believed deeply. It hurts even more to admit to it in public. Our beliefs and opinions provide a coat of armour, and when we are asked to change our minds it's like being invited to remove our greatest layer of protection and stand before others naked and vulnerable. We risk being accused of inconsistency or disloyalty or, worse, of losing our friends. It is easier to stick to the rule-book we've inherited and not worry about questioning its authority.

Of all people Paul knows the cost of changing his mind. Once a persecutor of Christians, he is now persecuted as one of them. Here he challenges the Galatian Church to do the same. Living by faith is not, as we may mistakenly think, a question of assenting to the right creeds concerning Jesus. That only turns the act of correct believing into a law. Rather, it means daring to live provisionally, knowing that at any moment, in the light of new circumstances, God may call us to reassess what we hold dear.

✻ *From the cowardice that dare not face new truth,*
   From the laziness that is contented with half truth,
   From the arrogance that thinks it knows all truth,
   Good Lord, deliver me.

Kenya

Feel the pain

I am speaking to a group of members from a local church. They find it a loving fellowship with enthusiastic worship and good sound teaching. There is a good mix of ethnic origins and ages, and the membership is growing steadily. A strong leader, the new priest is quickly becoming a favourite, encouraging his flock to stand firm on what they believe. This is the church Richard used to attend. He cannot face going there again. He is too hurt. But his absence allows the congregation to forget that he exists. They return to feeling united in the gospel and to imagining they are standing for Kingdom values. Paul warns us against the dangers of living according to 'human nature.' Until we are ready to hear and feel the pain of those people the church has pushed out, we will never fully understand the damage our legalism does. It is Richard and those like him who must judge us and our reluctance to display the gifts of the Spirit.

✴ *Lord, make me a channel of your peace.*

Same questions, new answers.

Why were verses 9-10 missed out of this reading? Maybe because a passage exhorting slaves to be submissive is thought inappropriate in an age which recognizes slavery as immoral. But I object to this omission! After all, Paul is wrestling with the question, 'What sort of behaviour is proper for the Christian community?' And from his first century standpoint, he suggests that, in order not to arouse the criticism of outsiders, the community should conform to the traditional pattern of the patriarchal household. Within this structure, not only slaves but also women must learn submission to their masters. Meanwhile men, whose status is unquestioned, must make sure their behaviour is exemplary.

It is not just the instructions to slaves that might be thought immoral today, but the whole patriarchal mentality upon which all the instructions are built. Two thousand years on we are still required to wrestle with the question which faced Paul. But we shall need to come up with different answers.

✴ *Questions weigh heavy upon me, Lord.*
Come, share my burden and reveal your will.

Where we are

I have the good fortune to live in a democracy which accords me many basic rights, including that of opposing the party in power. So I am not too horrified when I read that as a Christian I should obey the authorities. But when Juanita reads this passage, she stumbles. For her, 'doing good in every way' is incompatible with submitting to rulers. Undoubtedly she speaks for many who live under oppressive regimes.

Appropriate Christian conduct is something which has to be worked out where we are. Even if Paul's advice to Christians in first century Crete may not be universally applicable today, his method of thinking holds good. Reasons for acting in a particular way must take into account both culture and circumstances, and assess them against the central truths of the gospel. It is a precarious process, and we always run the risk of being wrong. We pray for grace to wrestle honestly and lovingly with the questions and for courage to live humbly and provisionally with the answers.

✳ *Thanks be to thee, O Lord Jesus Christ,*
  for all the benefits which thou given us;
  for all the pains and insults
  which thou hast borne for us.

  O most merciful redeemer, friend and brother,
  may we know thee more clearly,
  love thee more dearly,
  and follow thee more nearly; for thine own sake.
                        St Richard of Chichester 1197-1253

For personal reflection or group discussion

Look again at notes for November 14. Which people are being judged, ignored or pushed out by your church?

Over the last year, which were the hardest decisions you had to make in your personal and your church life? Which Christian truths did you draw on to help you make the decision? If you didn't draw on any, why didn't you?

Think of a person whose integrity you admire and tell his or her story.

ACTION

Read a book on an issue which argues a point of view different from yours. Make a list of the book's good points.

MARKS OF TRUE RELIGION

3. Love

Notes based on the New International Version by

Brother Martin SSF

Brother Martin is a Franciscan Friar and priest of the Church of England living in Scunthorpe (UK), involved in parish work and the chaplaincy of a hospice for cancer patients.

In classical writings of Biblical times different Greek words were used for 'love', distinguishing friendship, brotherly love, kindness and passionate sexual love. In the Bible *agape* represents a love which is entirely devoid of self. It was used in the Greek version of the Old Testament (e.g. Deuteronomy 6.5). In the New Testament, Paul uses it nine times in his well-known hymn of love in 1 Corinthians 13. Older versions translate *agape* in this chapter as 'charity', from the Latin word *caritas*. It includes the idea of caring which is a very important aspect of real love.

6th Sunday before Christmas, November 17

Colossians 3.12-17

Signs of love

Paul addresses Christians at Colossae as 'God's chosen people'. Christ's Church as the new Israel inherits the promises which God had made to his people of old (Deuteronomy 7.6-8). Elsewhere Paul writes: 'the Gentiles are heirs together with Israel ... and sharers together in the promise in Christ Jesus' (Ephesians 3.6). This is the reason why he can confidently call them 'dearly loved', for they are loved by God. God's love for us calls us to respond with love: 'compassion, kindness, humility, gentleness and patience', in forgiving one another and the quest for unity. Do others recognize these signs of love in us?

Soon after the days of Jesus, even his enemies remarked, 'See how these Christians love one another!' How sad it is that today these words may be used with sarcasm.

✱ *Pour into our hearts that most excellent gift of love,*
the true bond of peace and of all virtues,
without which whoever lives is counted dead before you.
Anglican Alternative Service Book
© Hodder and Stoughton. Permission sought

Monday November 18   Matthew 5.38-42 *

Love has no limits

Jesus quoted the Old Testament saying 'eye for eye, and tooth
for tooth' (Leviticus 24.20). This had been intended to teach
earlier generations to set a limit to revenge.

Jesus said that there must be no revenge at all. There must
be forgiveness, which springs out of love for one another.
Elsewhere he taught us to pray, 'Forgive us our trespasses as
we forgive those who trespass against us.'

We pray for peace, and acknowledge that war is evil, but are
we always so good at practising personal forgiveness? A faithful
church member who had committed an immoral act turned to
Christ and repented but said that she would find it difficult to
return to church because 'Church people can be so unkind'.
Would this be true of your congregation?

✱ *'Forgive our sins as we forgive'*
You taught us, Lord, to pray;
But you alone can grant us grace
To live the words we say.   Rosamond Herklots 1905-87
© Oxford University Press

Tuesday November 19   Matthew 5. 43-48 *

Love bears no grudges

The *Torah* defined the duty of loving others:– 'Do not seek
revenge or bear a grudge against one of your people, but love
your neighbour as yourself' (Leviticus 19.18). Jesus had this
text in mind. The words 'and hate your enemy' are not in
Leviticus. But people persuaded themselves that the idea was
implied, since they assumed that love of neighbour was
confined to those of their own nation.

When Robert Runcie preached in London at the service to
commemorate the end of the Falklands War in 1982 he asked
people to remember in prayer and compassion the relatives of
the young Argentinean soldiers who were killed. Many criticized

him for saying this, but it came from our Lord's teaching. Indeed, Jesus told us to pray for those who persecute us (verse 44). When a lawyer asked the question, 'Who is my neighbour?' Jesus told of the good Samaritan (Luke 10.29-37). We are slow to lay aside old hurts, and yet if we could banish hatred and bitterness from our hearts, we could begin to demonstrate the power of love in a world which certainly needs it.

> ✳ *In Christ there is no East or West*
> *In him no South or North,*
> *But one great fellowship of love*
> *Throughout the whole wide earth.*   *John Oxenham*

Wednesday November 20   *Matthew 10.34-39*

Love is not possessive

This is one of the most difficult passages in the Gospels. Jesus had said, 'Blessed are the peacemakers' (Matthew 5.9). Now he is saying that he had not come to bring peace but to divide families. Is this a contradiction?

Simeon in the Temple had prophesied that Jesus would be 'a sign that will be spoken against' (Luke 2.34). Jesus did not set out to provoke division, but it became inevitable as people rejected him. In today's reading, Jesus was stressing in the strongest possible terms the duty of complete loyalty to the demands of God; this even transcends family ties. Jesus loved his mother dearly (John 19.26-27) but filial love never got in the way of God's mission (Luke 8.20-21).

Genuine love within our families is wonderful, and it can be a beautiful reflection of the love of God. But in determining our priorities, our love for God must always come before possessive relationships.

> ✳ *Grant, Lord, that we may hold to you without swerving,*
> *and serve you without failing,*
> *faithfully seek you and happily find you.*
> *From a prayer of Saint Anselm (11th century)*

Thursday November 21   *1 John 3.11-18*

Love knows no hatred

In today's passage a sharp contrast stands out. On the one hand we have love, which is life; on the other there is hatred, which is death. Disciples of Christ have passed from death to life. Lack of love is itself a form of hatred and is the way of death (verse 14). Hatred is tantamount to murder because our inner thoughts are actually part of us. God said to Samuel when he set out to find a king, 'Man looks at the outward appearance, but the Lord looks at the heart' (1 Samuel 16.7). We all need to be reminded that hateful thought is incompatible with eternal life (verse 15).

But love is not just a passive state of mind. It must be translated into action (verses 16-18). In July 1941, Maximilien Kolbe, a Polish Franciscan priest, died in the concentration camp at Auschwitz because he took the place of one who had been condemned to death. Read verse 16 again. How far would you be prepared to go?

✳ *Lord, make me an instrument of your peace.*
Where there is hatred, let me sow love;
Where there is injury, pardon.

From 'a prayer of St Francis'

Friday November 22   1 John 4.7-21

God is love

John is often styled 'the Apostle of love'. According to a beautiful legend, in the early days of the Church, when disputes arose, people used to seek John's advice. He always said, 'Dear friends, let us love one another' (verse 7). In today's reading John reminds us that all love comes from God. It is because he loved us that God sent his Son into the world as our Saviour (verses 10 and 14). Our love is in response to God's love for us (verse 19).

Thomas Aquinas, one of the greatest scholars of the 13th century, said that in this life we come closer to God through love than we do through knowledge or learning.

When I was a school chaplain, the children of our school were invited one year to write down a resolution at the beginning of Lent, to put it in a sealed envelope and place it in a 'letter box'. I was strangely moved by the fact that one child addressed his envelope 'To God, with love'.

✳ *Beloved, let us love: for they who love*
are born of God, his children from above.   H. Bonar

That you may be rooted in love

The Greek word *patria* translated as 'family' in verse 15 comes from the same root as *pater*, 'father', and so emphasizes God's universal parenthood. Some versions render verse 15 as 'from whom every family ...' (e.g. NRSV) and interpret this as referring to all families on earth.

In today's reading, the writer gives us some insight into his own prayers for the families of the Church at Ephesus. He prays that they may be 'rooted and established in love' (verse 17) and that they may know Christ's love 'that surpasses knowledge' (verse 19). He ends his prayer with an ascription of praise to God. Praying for each other is one way Christians express love. There is much value in the old saying 'The family that prays together stays together'.

* *Help us to live as the holy family,*
united in love and obedience,
and bring us at last to our home in heaven.
Anglican Alternative Service Book
© Hodder and Stoughton. Permission sought

For personal thought and group discussion

Read John 3.16. What effect does God's love have on us? Ernest Gordon's book *The Miracle on the River Kwai* tells how prisoners of war, in the midst of suffering, learned to pray. At first they couldn't say 'as we forgive those who trespass against us', but when they realized they could not omit these words, their hatred of those who tortured them began to melt. What can we learn from their example?

ACTION

Think of someone with whom you find relationships difficult. For the love of God, try to perform some act of charity towards that person.

HYMNS OF PRAISE

Notes based on the Hebrew Bible by

Jonathan Magonet

Jonathan Magonet is a Rabbi who has specialized in the teaching of the Hebrew Bible. He is particularly interested in bringing readers back to the Hebrew text of the Bible so that forms of composition and the inner links between words and all their related nuances can be taken into account in trying to understand each individual passage.

The theme of 'praise' is difficult, especially when it comes from a book like the Psalms, so much of which was meant for public worship. While individual prayer is a private matter, public liturgies always have a 'political' dimension, because they also seek to define and educate the particular community. So the task of the interpreter is somehow to be true to the language and spirit of the Psalm as far as we can before remaking it in our own image.

For an introduction to the poetry of the Psalms and the different ways in which the same Psalm can be understood, the reader may like to consult Rabbi Magonet's *A Rabbi Reads the Psalms* (SCM Press 1994).

5th Sunday before Christmas, November 24   Psalm 147

Exile and return

It rarely snows in Jerusalem, yet when it does the city is utterly transformed. Perhaps just such an experience inspired this Psalm, as well as some darker memories. The snow that blankets the city can suddenly melt and the water simply run away. Israel had once 'blanketed' the city with people, and then, also at God's command, been 'poured away' into exile. Now the writer, while celebrating their return, understands how their hold on the city depends upon obedience to the will and word of God.

For God's power is without limit: knowing each star of the sky by its name and summoning it to appear in its place; feeding every single creature on the earth and in the sky; watching over the destiny of every individual and of all nations, raising the lowly and humbling the wicked. It is not military power that determines the fate of nations but their fear and knowledge of God.

The awareness of this lies behind the Psalm, but now it is time to celebrate the restoration and to sing praises to God who punishes yet binds up wounds and heals the heart of those who have suffered.

✳ *Before Your cold who can stand?*
Sustain me with the warmth of Your word.

Monday November 25   *Psalm 19*

Inner and outer

Bible scholars have tended to see this Psalm as two parts that got stuck together: an original pagan hymn to the cosmos and a meditation on the inner life. It is easy to see why. The opening is a magnificent evocation of the sky at night and of the majestic path of the sun across the heavens. But the closing section speaks of our inner life, the forces acting within us, the drives that lead us into error, folly and arrogance. How are they related?

Between the two are six manifestations of God that together underpin the quality of human society. The first is *Torah*, often wrongly translated as 'law'. Rather it means 'teaching', 'direction', the 'way'. In the Hebrew, the six sentences, with their exact parallel structure, are like the rungs of a ladder, uniting the outer and inner worlds, holding together the universe and the individual human soul.

What is our personal ladder that links our inner and outer selves? Our Psalm itself offers no answer but ends with a prayer and a plea for personal integrity.

✳ *May the words that actually come to my lips*
and the inner thought in my heart
together be acceptable to You, my God.

267

The use and abuse of tradition

This Psalm feels like a sampler – 'the best of the Temple Psalms'! With minor variations, you will find these parallels:

verse 1 = Psalm 113.1;
verse 2 = Psalm 134.1;
verse 6 = Psalm 115.3;
verses 15-18 = Psalm 115.4-8;
verses 19-20 = Psalm 115.9-11 and Psalm 118.2-4.

It also quotes variations on other Bible verses:

verse 4 = Deuteronomy 7.6;
verse 7 = Jeremiah 10.13;
verse 9 = Exodus 7.3;
verse 13 = Exodus 3.15;
verse 14 = Deuteronomy 32.36.

God is the ruler of nature (verses 6-7) and of human history (verses 8-12), supreme above all the other imagined gods of the nations (verses 5 and 15-18), and therefore free to choose Israel as God's special people (verses 4, 12 and 14). The traditional quotations reinforce these themes and may be intended to reassure a nation whose self-confidence has been shaken. God is still our God; the ancient covenant is still binding; history is still moving towards the acceptance of God by the nations of the world.

So is the Psalm simply a case of the triumphalism that so often emerges in times of religious doubt? At the heart is still a call for self-criticism and repentance: 'God will judge His people!'

✳ *May I never hide behind my tradition*
from the task I must face today.

When our world falls apart

The Temple contained 'off the peg' Psalms. Someone who went through a difficult experience might vow to bring an offering to God if saved. Now, standing before the community to offer thanks, the person would select a Psalm that most fitted the danger that had overcome him or her.

So what has this writer gone through – a severe illness, a bereavement, a life-threatening event, a fall from office or power? Something shattered the Psalmist's customary feeling of being 'at home' in the world. 'I said in my "safety", "security", I shall never slip!' But when the world fell apart, those certainties went, and only emptiness and terror remained.

Anyone who has seen the bottom drop out of their world can recognize this experience: a love gone sour, a betrayal by someone we trusted, a medical diagnosis that transforms our life. For some, turning to God might seem normal; others may feel it is like cheating, to pray just because 'the chips are down'. The Psalmist seems to know all these feelings, and tells us they are all legitimate, for God is waiting to be found.

✳ *In my joy,*
let me not forget the troubles that once beset me;
in my trouble, give me the help I need.

Thursday November 28 Psalm 40

The enemy within

A highly individual personality emerges in this Psalm, especially if we notice how certain words are used both of God and the Psalmist (though these are not obvious in all translations):

● God's deeds are '*more* than can be *numbered*' (verse 5) – I experience evils beyond *numbering* ... *more* than the hairs of my head (verse 12);

● You do not *desire* sacrifices (verse 6) – I *desire* to do Your will (verse 8);

● I have not *restrained* my lips (verse 9) – do not *restrain* Your mercy from me (verse 11);

● God has *thoughts* for 'us' (verse 5) – have *thoughts* for me! (verse 17)

It is a kind of negotiation. Knowing God's power and our powerlessness, all we can do is cajole, or barter, or plead. We struggle to hold on to our ego, our identity, our self-respect, knowing that we have to let them go. 'I desire to do Your will'. But knowing this and doing it are not the same.

The 'enemies' seem to be internal here rather than external – our own taunting voices, the sins that keep us from God. The 'quaking pit' is still there, and God has to be found again and again.

✳ *You are my help and my deliverer; do not tarry, my God!*

269

The passing of earthly powers

This Psalm seems to speak of certainties – that God's justice
will prevail; that those who set out to conquer others will in the
end be defeated; that their very arrogance will trap them – 'let
the nations know they are but men'.

But is it composed out of personal experience of God's
victory, or does it simply express a hope? The opening is a
hymn of gratitude for God's triumph over enemies, whose very
conquests will be forgotten. But in verse 13* comes the
personal plea for rescue from 'the hands of those who hate me'.
Is this quoting the plea of the 'humble' mentioned in verse 12*?
or is it the actual author, having asserted confidence in God's
power, finally asking for help?

(These verses are numbered differently in the Hebrew Bible in
which the title counts as verse 1).*

The Psalm is also a meditation on Genesis 9.5 – 'God seeks
out' the shedder of blood (the common translation '*avenges*
blood' in verse 12* is misleading). It reflects a Rabbinic
teaching: that God is always on the side of the victim, and the
painful reality that once violence begins it is not easily stopped.
So the Psalmist's prayer can be ours:

✳ *Arise, O Lord, do not let man prevail –
let the nations know they are but men!*

The missing letter

This Psalm is an alphabetical acrostic in the Hebrew. And it has
a very formal structure: the three central verses, 11-13, acclaim
God as King; the previous verses describe how creation praises
God, and the following ones highlight the generosity with which
God sustains creation.

Such formality suggests some kind of religious complacency
– everything is all right in a world ruled by God. But sometimes
formality is a defence against a world where there is actually
very little certainty and no room for complacency. Asserting
God's rule may be a defence against the anarchy without and
our fear of dissolution within.

God provides enough for all but there is one crucial element
missing from the picture. 'You open Your hand and satisfy all
the living with their needs' – but only if we provide the human

hands to ensure this.

One letter is missing from the alphabetic acrostic – perhaps out of ancient fears of perfect formality. But this leaves room for our own contribution, the letter we have to provide. Without it the promise of the psalm, the maintenance of the world under God, would simply fall apart.

✳ *Open our hands,*
   so we can satisfy the needs of the world.

For personal reflection or group discussion

1. How far is my prayer life 'my own' private affair, and how far is it affected by the formal liturgies of my community?

2. How much of my liturgy can I take at face value and how much do I have to 'interpret' for myself?

3. If there is a conflict between what my formal prayers say and what I believe or feel, where do I find the personal strength or authority to find my own way?

4. If my liturgy is intended in part to colour my way of thinking, and help create a 'community' of shared values, what responsibility should I take in its creation and development?

5. If I accept its values and teachings, how far do they actually affect the way I live my life?

ACTION

When reciting the phrase, 'You open Your hands and satisfy the need of every living thing' (Psalm 145.16), there is a Jewish tradition of opening up our hands, palms outwards, to symbolize God's actions in feeding the world. Food is available for all God's creatures, but we have to be the distribution network – 'God's hands'. Some congregations have opened up their building to provide 'hospitality luncheons' once a week for the local unemployed and street people, with a hot meal, bathroom facilities and clothes, friendship and care. This programme can be undertaken by any community that is willing to provide the 'missing letter' in Psalm 145 and make our own small contribution to feeding the world.

ADVENT 1 – Look to the future

Notes based on the Good News Bible by

Simon Barrow

Simon Barrow is an Adult Education and Training Officer in the Anglican Diocese of Southwark. He works with inner-city parishes and has a practical concern for the link between spirituality and social issues.

Advent is a time of preparation for the coming of Christ into the world. It is a moment of hope in the face of change, challenge and transformation.

All readings in the coming week focus attention on the impact which Christ makes or can make to a troubled, anxious world. But they also remind us that the incarnation of God's freedom and love in the person and work of Jesus is an event which calls for response, not just assent. The Gospel is about changed lives, not just changed minds.

1st Sunday in Advent, December 1   *Matthew 24.3-14*

Turmoil or transition?

As we approach the end of the millenium one thing we can guarantee is a huge rise in apocalyptic speculation. Human beings have an endless curiosity about the future, and over the years Christians have not been immune to macabre misinterpretations of passages like this one in Matthew.

The events predicted here are not, in fact, about 'the end' in a global sense. They refer to the circumstances of the fall of Jerusalem in CE 70 (see also verses 1-3). We should bear in mind that the impending collapse of the Temple was seen by Jewish eyes as an event of universal significance. Given that the whole faith was centred on Jerusalem, the distinction between the loss of the Temple and the loss of all hope was much less than we can ever imagine these days, especially with the benefit of hindsight.

Naturally conflict, disorder (verse 7) and deception (verse 4) would increase in the context of historical upheaval on this scale. For good measure the Gospel writer throws in ecological devastation (earthquakes) to emphasize the shock of it all. But these threats are, in Christian eyes, not a counsel of despair but a cause of faith. Turmoil will give birth to God's new dawn (verse 8) and the response called for is an ever more urgent witness to the gospel (verse 13). This draws our eyes, too, to the 'signs of the times' and the need for a renewal of faith. Christ comes to turn us and our world upside down.

✳ *God of power and might, preserve and strengthen us through times of trial and despair.*

Monday December 2   *Matthew 24.15-28*

Contending the faith

For a pious Jew the 'awful horror' referred to here would have called to mind the idolatrous statue of Zeus set up in front of the Temple by Antiochus Epiphanes in 168 BCE (1 Maccabees 1.54), the cryptic warning of Daniel (9.27) and possibly the Roman emperor Caligula's attempt to have a statue of himself placed in the Temple in CE 40.

The meaning is clear (verse 15): the very identity of faith is threatened. The military strength of the invader towards Jerusalem makes retreat inevitable (verse 16) and if it all happens on the Sabbath, when all travel is forbidden (verse 20), the people will face a crisis of religious conscience as well as physical danger.

Meanwhile impostors claiming Messiahship will seek to exploit the confusion of the faithful, gathering followers in the wilderness. But those of discernment will recognize the true Christ just as clearly as a vulture recognizes a dead body (verse 28).

Our age being one of shattering social change and religious uncertainty, we can surely see echoes here of the contemporary attractiveness of esoteric cults and beliefs. They gain a foothold when old hopes are threatened. There is even more reason, then, to fix our eyes on the true Christ – the one who frees rather than enslaves, reveals rather than deceives.

✳ *Grant us wisdom, God of all truth,*
to recognize your Christ in the midst of many faiths
and ideologies.

An eternal promise

To underline the epochal significance of the fall of Jerusalem, Matthew's Gospel uses imagery which is powerfully close to that of the Old Testament prophets as they looked towards the 'Day of the Lord'.

The mourning of the people, the appearance of a sign, a trumpet blast and the preservation of the faithful are pictures found variously in Isaiah, Zechariah and Joel. They also underline Jesus' acceptance of the prophetic mantle.

The picture of the fig tree reminds us to pay attention to the signs of the times. For God is at work through, and not in spite of, the world and its circumstances. Just as Matthew's contemporaries (verse 34) faced the Jerusalem trauma, so we will have our faith sorely tempted by the vicissitudes of earthly turmoil. But the loving purposes of God (verse 35) will survive and flourish nevertheless. Christ himself fleshes out this promise.

✳ *God of wisdom and understanding,*
restrain our wilfulness and help us to rest in your love.

Letting God be God

We have now undoubtedly shifted from events surrounding Jerusalem to the wider Christian hope of all things being brought to fulfilment through Christ.

Here we are reminded that the timing and circumstances of the consummation of God's purposes for the world are not for human beings to play with and speculate about (verse 36). According to most manuscripts even Jesus himself disowns such knowledge. What greater modesty should believers show, therefore!

As in Mark 13.32-37, the key phrase is 'be on your guard'. The God of surprises asks us to be ready to respond to the tasks we have been given just as surely as we would deal with a burglar.

The early Christians certainly imagined 'the end' to be sudden and dramatic. But once again the emphasis is on active obedience rather than on lazy guess-work. Our role is not to be God-like but to be faithful. This is both a warning and, lest we forget it, a relief!

*＊ God who constantly watches over us,
keep our eyes open and our hearts tender.*

Thursday December 5   Matthew 24.45-51

The challenge of Christ

The climax of Matthew's discourse about the up-ending of traditional religion and the advent of Christ is not an abstract theological theory, but a story on the lips of Jesus himself. Even so, there is a surprise in store for the modern reader. For the story of the trustworthy servant is not simply a call for vigilance.

Many estates in the Palestine of Jesus' day were owned by wealthy foreign businessmen. Given that they could not run all their holdings directly, most were managed by agents and by household staff (usually slaves). In this case the landlord's agent was also a slave whose reward for loyalty and efficiency would be greater responsibility rather than higher wages, and whose failure would be met by death rather than dismissal.

In this context, our Gospel reading contrasts the attitudes of true believers and hypocrites. But Jesus' original hearers would also have known that it was their current religious leaders, the scribes and Pharisees, who were running God's household. It was they who should particularly fear the time of reckoning.

Woe to us Christians, then, if we use the Advent of Christ as a stick to beat those of other faith or no faith. For it is we who have been given custody of the gospel and it is we who are primarily accountable to it in the merciful purposes of God. Humility, awe and commitment are what God desires of us. But pride should remain off the agenda.

*＊ Save us, God of justice,
from trusting our own judgments too much.*

Friday December 6   Romans 13.8-14 *＊

Baptized into Christ

Some years ago a Christian congregation in London took part in a public protest against Western governments' denial of aid and fair trade provisions to poorer countries. Seeing this denial as contrary to the gospel, they thought long and hard about how to put across a distinctive Christian message. Finally someone came up with a pointed and amusing banner which read: 'Jesus is coming – and boy, is he fed up!' It is unlikely that the

275

originator of this slogan ever intended it to be a translation of Romans 13.11, but it actually sums up Paul's convictions rather accurately.

In New Testament thinking, ethical demands such as those spelt out in verses 9 and 13 arise not from abstract moral duty but from a practical experience of God's love. It is this personal challenge to which Advent returns us each year.

Here Paul points to the three interlocking foundations of Christian morality: the congruence between love of neighbour and love of self (verse 9); the universal promise that light will triumph over darkness (verse 12); and the imminent fulfilment of human nature as embodied in Jesus, the Christ (verse 14).

The formula in verse 10 sounds oddly close to that classic post-religious ethic: 'do what you like so long as it doesn't hurt anyone.' But whereas this easy phrase usually avoids the tough question about what really harms our neighbour or ourselves, the Christian formulation focuses concern precisely on that issue.

Similarly, Paul's conviction about the coming 'Day of the Lord' is intended to concentrate our minds fully on the central issues of discipleship: Where do we stand? Where are we going? and What do we stand for?

Finally, the injunction to 'clothe yourselves with the Lord Jesus Christ' (verse 14 NIV) directly recalls the language of Christian baptism (see Galatians 3.27) and its deep ethical consequences.

✶ *God of endless love, help us to turn words of faith into deeds of hope and witness.*

Saturday December 7   *Isaiah 2.1-5 ✶*

Hope for all the world

It was once rather cruelly pointed out that Jesus came to announce the Kingdom of God, and what we ended up with was ... the church. Unfair though that caricature may seem, it does correctly alert us to the ever-present danger of the church usurping or substituting itself for the universal scope of the gospel.

Faced with the narrowly nationalistic tendencies of his religious heritage, Isaiah shows himself to be quite clear about God's ultimate purposes: a Temple for all nations and a hope for all the world. In other words, salvation (like judgment) is a promise for the whole earth, not just for a self-selecting minority.

This vision represented a substantial enlarging of religious understanding in its own day. But it had its limits. Note that Israel's Temple remained central (verse 2), with the nations streaming to it. In the New Testament, Christians re-thought that notion. The Gospels suggest that Jesus, not a temporal location, is the focus of our hope in God. And Revelation speaks of a New Jerusalem 'descending from heaven' (that is, originating from God) which symbolizes a new heaven and a new earth.

We should never lose sight of the fact that the Christ event is a sign and promise of God for all the world, demanding both personal (verse 3) and social (verse 4) transformation.

✳ *Spare us, God of all people,*
from the desire to grasp you selfishly in a world of
need.

For personal reflection and group discussion
How and when are we seeking to discern the 'signs of the times' and to respond to God's loving purposes in them?

ACTION
What practical difference has the coming of Christ made recently to our church life and to the options which face us as Christians in the world?

ADVENT 2 – Be prepared for opposition

Notes based on the Good News Bible by

Magali do Nascimento Cunha

Magali do Nascimento Cunha is a young, lay journalist who works for an ecumenical organization in Brazil: Koinonia – Ecumenical Presence and Service. She is involved as a volunteer in projects of Christian Education for poor communities in Baixada Fluminense (on the outskirts of Rio de Janeiro).

'To live is not easy,' is a saying heard from birth by most people in Brazil. As life is not easy, it means that it is full of adversities and challenges, and we need to be prepared for them and get ready to overcome them.

Even God, who gave people freedom to decide the way to follow, had to face opposition and adversities and has taught us how to cope with and overcome them. Courage and strength to continue life's journey come from the Lord. Let us learn from him!

2nd Sunday in Advent, December 8   *Matthew 13.53-58 ***

Facing and practising rejection

It isn't easy to be a (true) prophet! Reading the prophetic testimonies of the Bible, we learn that a prophet was destined to face opposition. The explanation is not difficult: sin is present in human nature, impelling people and groups to oppress each other. So it is not easy to shout against it and show that God's will is different.

One sin is prejudice, which Jesus encountered many times in his journey. 'How could a carpenter's son have such wisdom?' 'Can anything good come from Nazareth?' (John 1.46). For the narrow minds of traditional Israelite society the role of prophet implied status. Of course, those 'false prophets' who worked to sustain tradition and oppression had status ... Jesus was rejected. Being poor, he could never be a prophet!. Think about

Jesus' experience at his home town (Luke 4.16-30). Has your authority been questioned when you thought you were doing right, or working for the benefit of others?

Have you been prejudiced at any time? Have you rejected the challenge of another person as inferior? How can we be true prophets today and defend God's will?

✳ *Dear Lord,*
Help me to understand and accept your will.
Help me to accept and learn from the messages
that come through simple people. Amen.

Monday December 9   *Isaiah 59.12-20 ✳*

'Rowing against the tide'

The years 1964 to 1978 are known in Brazil as 'the age of the darkness'. It was the time when the military dictatorship imprisoned, tortured and killed thousands of people who opposed the regime and fought for democracy. It is a long and sad story of many young people, workers, students, teachers, poor and rich, men and women, who knew the risks but offered their lives for what they believed: freedom and justice for all Brazilians.

They were 'rowing against the tide'; they were opposers of an oppressive system. Perhaps many of them did not know, but they were prophets and martyrs who were – in holy action – defending the will of God.

We learn about that through Isaiah. 'The Lord is displeased that there is no justice ... he will use his own power ... he will wear justice like a coat of armour, he will come like a rushing river, like a strong wind ...' (verses 15-19). Yes. The Lord is ready to oppose injustice and oppression. He gives us strength even if we are 'rowing against the tide'. It is a fight to defend God's will, reinforced with mercy and love. In ordinary situations of life or in something bigger in community or society, let's clothe ourselves with justice, mercy and love.

✳ *Our God, thank you for giving us strength*
and courage to defend your will.
Do not let us to be afraid of serving you.
In Jesus' name. Amen

The wind blows wherever it wishes

Like Jesus, Amos faced prejudice. How could a herdsman come and preach against the king? There was prejudice in that question but there was something more. Kings' actions were sustained by prophets and priests; how could they be contested? The people believed they spoke in the name of God; how could Amos come in the name of the same God and cause agitation? For 'God's people' nothing appeared to be wrong. The structure was there, firm, stable, secure. How could anyone shake it?

The Spirit of the Lord could! God's action through Amos was there to show that God is not imprisoned within structures which can prevent the realization of God's will for their own benefit. The Holy Spirit, like a wind, blows and shakes, changes, and provokes movements that impel simple people like Amos to leave everything behind and preach, defending human rights, against all oppression. Amos was rejected and humiliated, but the Spirit who moved him to act gave him power to face opposition.

How important it is to learn from this experience! Our churches and religious groups need to reflect how pernicious structures can be, if they are not ready to serve. For service is the reason for their existence. We need to reflect how important it is to be ready to move with the wind and leave behind all security and stability. We will then be working for the right of life, the most precious gift we have from God.

✶ *Come Holy Spirit,*
  prepare us to change everything that imprisons
  the life that comes from you. Amen

Do not be afraid

It isn't easy to be a prophet! Jeremiah knew it well, even being so young. He also knew how to listen to the Lord's voice and that happened very early in his life. He felt fear, a very human feeling.

Jeremiah's experience shows to us how the Lord's mission is for all. Old and young, rich or poor, all of us are called to take part. Jeremiah has inspired young people in our churches in Brazil to find ways to serve the Lord. His voice comes to them and to all of us today: 'Do not say you are too young, but go to the people I send you to ...'

When we decide to serve the Lord, adversities and difficulties can come but as he promised to Jeremiah, 'Do not be afraid. I will be with you.' A Latin American song sung at youth gatherings expresses the challenge:

'I need to shout, I need to risk
Woe is me if I do not do it!
How can I escape from you?
How can I silence
if your voice burns inside me?'

✳ *Our God, forgive our fear and incapacity to overcome it.*
We are nothing without you.
Touch our lips and speak through us
to those who need to listen to your voice. Amen

Thursday December 12   Isaiah 49.6-7

Hope is alive

For more than twenty years, the Bible has been rediscovered in Latin America by many Christian communities. Theologians have called this process 'Biblical Spring'. The beauty of this experience is to link the Bible story to our own story today, to discover what we have in common and how we can learn from the experience of God's people in the past.

The fact that the Hebrew people suffered – the humiliation of slavery, oppression by their own kings, exile and loss of dignity – identifies with the sufferings of our people today. There is the humiliation, like slavery, of working for low salaries, of being oppressed by self-interested governors, of losing citizenship and dignity for the sake of big business ...

Going deeper, what is great is to discover that there is a God, who was there in the past and is here in our present. The Lord God is the bearer of all hope that humiliation and suffering will have an end. That is the reason for God being hated and opposed by the nations (verse 7). However, God is greater than all opposers and is faithful. He fulfils his promises to restore the greatness of the people and bring them to life.

God's promises are alive today. We need to listen to them and become as servants, a light to the world, bringing hope to all who need it to survive. The Bible is our instrument for doing that. How can we bring it to life?

✶ *Lord, thank you for your Word through the Bible.*
I praise you for your faithfulness and greatness.
Praise be to you this day!

Friday December 13   *Psalm 17*

Opposing and defeating enemies

'Come Lord, oppose my enemies and defeat them!' How can we pray today, using the words of the psalmist? What are the meanings of this prayer for us? Who are our enemies today?

Sometimes Christians spiritualize this reflection, identifying 'the enemy' as the Devil. By exorcizing the Devil from our lives, our problems would be solved. Isn't that an easy solution? Maybe. But evil is also present in our world to oppose God's justice and peace. What or who is the Devil?

The enemy, most times, is ourselves. Yes! How many times do we opt for attitudes that cause bad consequences, just by using the freedom God gives us? When we fall into temptation sometimes we fall by our own nature and personality which become our enemies. When Jesus was tempted in the desert, the Devil offered him those things that human nature always fights for: power, wealth, political domination. Aren't they? Jesus' faithfulness to the Kingdom's values is a great lesson to us. Sin is more than the immorality to which it is reduced by many Christian groups. It is part of human nature – the enemy within us which is ready to act if we permit it.

If we accept the presence of God in our lives and decide to live for his Kingdom, sin will still be present, as we are human, but it will be a defeated enemy and we will really be new creatures.

✶ *Come, dear Lord, to my life*
and your presence will fill me with joy.

Saturday December 14   *Romans 16.25-27*

The Lord supports and liberates

Many temptations and trials come to us that make us weaker and lose our faith. Paul says that we can praise the Lord because he is able to make us stand firm according to the good news of Jesus Christ and according to God's promises through the prophets.

So, God can make our faith firm, both making us grow in the

knowledge of the truth and helping us to avoid mistakes that break us. That is a great teaching from Paul: if we want to grow in faith we need to learn about the truth through the writings of the prophets.

The knowledge of the Word of God, the testimonies that come from Jesus, from the prophets, and from all those anonymous people who had an experience with God, is a source of strength to us who face all sorts of adversities in our world. What testing times have we faced? In our family ... in our work ... in our community ... in our church ...? Remember again the temptations Jesus faced in the desert. Think again about the values of the Kingdom of God, about Jesus' teachings.

Thanks be to God for his action among us and his support. But let's be ready to act and overcome the adversities and not accept them easily. Be firm and trust the Lord!

✳ *Glory be to you, our Lord, for your mercy and support.*
Do not lead us into temptation
but deliver us from evil. Amen

For personal reflection or group discussion

1. Have you felt called to do something in the name of God? Have you felt afraid or ashamed of acting in God's name? What were the difficulties? Think about the testimonies of Amos and Jeremiah. What can you learn from them and apply to your own experience?

2. What temptations come to you? Can you identify them easily? Compare them with the temptations Jesus faced. What can you learn from Jesus' experience and apply to your life?

ACTION

Identify in your daily life, in family, work or community, situations that require your action as a prophet, both speaking or acting. Ask for God's help, and struggle to do the will of God.

ADVENT 3 – Remain true to your calling

Notes based on the Good News Bible by

Gordon Jones

Gordon Jones is a Supernumerary minister who has served in West Africa and the UK.

Some of this week's readings are about John the Baptist who, like Samson centuries before, was to be the forerunner of one greater than himself.

We too are called to be 'forerunners' and messengers, to prepare people's minds so that they can recognize and commit themselves to the One whose coming we celebrate in Advent – Jesus Christ. That is our vocation as Christians. Our readings remind us of what this calling involves and how we shall try to remain true to it.

3rd Sunday in Advent, December 15   *Judges 13.2-14 **

Called to offer thanks by the way we live

A barren woman was promised a son, one who was to begin freeing Israel from the Philistines, a process to be completed by King David many years later. This son was to be a Nazirite. This meant being consecrated from birth not to cut his hair, drink wine or go near a dead body. Such a vow might be taken to thank God for a specific calling or blessing. And it marked a quality of life that stood apart from the excesses of society. Samson was to be such a person, responding to God's call to be his people's saviour.

The Christian life also involves commitment, a thankful response for the gift of Jesus Christ. And this response is shown by the quality of our lives, our obedience to his way of love. This is our vow. Are we faithful to it?

✴ *We thank you Father, for your gift of life in Jesus.*
You call us to respond by becoming his witnesses.
Forgive us when we fail,
and help us to be true to our calling.

Called to turn others' minds to Christ

The promise to Zechariah was similar to that made to the parents of Samson. A priest was assured that his wife will have a son, called to a special life. Like that of Samson, it would be the beginning of a process, but in this case its consequences would lead to the salvation of all humankind. Zechariah's son was called not to be the Messiah, but to call people to repentance, to prepare their minds, to encourage new attitudes, and make them ready.

As Christians, our task is a wonderful – but humble – one. Ministers and preachers, Junior Church teachers, leaders of small groups, we have failed if we have only set ourselves on a pinnacle. We are to point away from ourselves to the One who is the true Saviour. The test of a good sermon is not in words of praise but when people respond, 'What a wonderful Saviour you have shown us!'

✳ *Behold the servant of the Lord!*
  I wait thy guiding eye to feel,
To hear and keep thy every word,
    To prove and do thy perfect will,
Joyful from my own works to cease,
Glad to fulfil all righteousness.   *Charles Wesley 1707-88*

Called to be a voice

John fulfilled the calling his father had been promised. He simply called himself 'a voice', quoting from Isaiah (40.3).

Think about this: my voice is the gift I have for putting my thoughts into words, opening the minds of those who listen to new understanding, to see new truths and values which they had not grasped before. Sometimes your voice must be stern, as a parent to reprimand a child. Or it may be gentle and encouraging, helping others to overcome fears and to build confidence. Sometimes your voice is vibrant and joyful, helping the depressed to find peace.

John's voice was stern when he spoke to Pharisees and Sadducees whose minds were closed. But usually his voice spoke 'good news'. Your voice too may be a path that leads your neighbours to new life and fulfilment. If so, it is an echo of the loving, forgiving voice of God.

> ❋ *Lord, speak to me, that I may speak*
> *In living echoes of thy tone.* Frances Ridley Havergal

Called to take the humbler part

Our reading suggests that Jesus was baptizing people, though this is doubtful. As far as we know, Christian Baptism began after Jesus' resurrection and ascension, on the day of Pentecost. It may be that some of Jesus' followers were re-enacting John's baptism as a sign of repentance. Some took Jesus to be a rival of John. Not so, says John. John's humility is seen again. This time he describes himself as the 'bridegroom's friend' at a wedding – Israel is the bride and Jesus the bridegroom. The best man steps into the background so that attention is focused on the married couple whose day it is. John's calling was to stand back and let the spotlight fall on Jesus. How does your calling compare? Do not imagine it is greater than God wants it to be!

> ❋ *Lord God, you reminded us through the apostle Paul*
> *that the Church is like a human body*
> *depending equally on each of its members,*
> *including those which seem unattractive*
> *or less important.*
> *Lord, what is my part?*

Called despite the doubts

John the Baptist, imprisoned by Herod – alone, forsaken, tortured – began to doubt. Was Jesus really the Messiah God had called him to proclaim? Nothing really sensational seemed to be happening. And so he sent his question to Jesus. Jesus' answer was straightforward: 'Don't look for a military chief. My work is to serve ordinary people, bringing forgiveness, healing, encouragement, affirming their sense of self-worth as children of God, loved and needed. That is the Kingdom I bring.'

We all have doubts when things go wrong. 'Why does God not save me or my loved one from illness?' 'Why did he let my friend be killed in a car crash?' 'Is he really a loving God?' Doubts or questions are a natural, healthy human response, but they need to be faced so that we come to a deeper understanding of life's purpose. The God we worship is not removed from us, sitting on a heavenly throne, unmoved by our suffering. He is with us, suffers with us, shares our distress. For he is supremely revealed not in spectacular events that hit the headlines, but in the ignominious, unjust execution of his Son on a cross. Ponder on these words of Malcolm Muggeridge: 'The road to faith is paved with doubts.'

✳ Father, I bring my doubts to you,
   as well as my certainties.
   Help me to learn from them.

Friday December 20   *Isaiah 51.7-16*

Called to learn that God is not dead!

Perhaps John the Baptist took comfort in these words of an exiled prophet six centuries earlier (see verses 7-8). His central message is that Israel will be freed to return from exile. The Israelites had always thought of themselves as 'God's Chosen People' – but how could they believe that any more? The prophet, as God's 'mouth-piece', reminded his listeners of God's power, his past triumphs over evil powers (verses 9-11). God is not dead!

This is the central message of our faith. We are just five days from Christmas. What joy we shall share – parties, decorations, cards, new clothes ... But let us not forget that Good Friday is not far away. Immediately after his birth, Jesus becomes a refugee, and in his ministry he is constantly opposed by religious people, tortured and killed. This is part of the Christmas story too – the cost of remaining true to God's call to proclaim what is just and true. And there is hope amid the suffering: the saving love of God is at work. God will win, if we his people stand firm and bear our witness. God is not dead!

✳ Truth of our life,
      Mary's child,
   You tell us God is good;
      Prove it is true,
         Mary's child,
   Go to your cross of wood.   *Geoffrey Ainger*
      Reproduced by permission of Stainer and Bell Ltd. (UK)

Called to witness to experience

The writer claims that his message about Jesus is true because he and others have found it so in their experience. Most of us do not see visions, or hear voices, but time after time Christ's words reveal him to us with wonderful clarity and relevance. I have known so many people who for twenty, thirty, or forty years have known about Jesus, but that was all. Then, suddenly, he has come alive to them in a new way. Some have harboured bitterness against others, and then looking at his cross have realized, with immense relief, that forgiveness is for them, and have gone away to tell others about it.

Our calling is to 'go forth and tell' by our changed lives and in our words what we have come to know in our own experience. The message of Advent is not an intellectual argument, but personal witness to a living faith.

✳ *We have no mission but to serve*
   In full obedience to our Lord:
To care for all, without reserve,
   And spread his liberating Word.   F Pratt Green
      Reproduced by permission of Stainer and Bell Ltd. (UK)

For personal reflection and group discussion

What, in the light of these readings, is your calling? What is God calling you to do, to say, to be? How can you fulfil your call so that people to whom you witness will not be offended or become defensive or think you are being self-righteous? Is it always possible to do this?

ACTION

This Christmas, read one complete Gospel. Talk with another person, in your family or community, about your faith, listening as well as talking!

CHRISTMAS

Notes based on the Revised English Bible by

Pauline Webb

Pauline Webb is a writer, broadcaster and Methodist 'local' (lay) preacher. In her case the locality of her preaching is worldwide. As a former executive officer of the Methodist Overseas Division and subsequently as Organiser of Religious Broadcasting in the BBC World Service, she has travelled extensively. Through offices she has held in the World Council of Churches she is also a well-known personality in the international ecumenical scene.

The theme of this series is the continuity of the coming of Christ with God's whole plan for the world, in which we too have our part to play.

For unto us a child is born

4th Sunday in Advent, December 22   *Isaiah 9.1-7 **

To govern wisely

It is hard to hear these words of Isaiah without hearing Handel's music in the background and linking them immediately with memories of Christmas past. But the prophet was looking forward to an event still to come. He was addressing the people of Israel at a time of immediate crisis, when a beloved king had died and the nation had become a ready prey for its enemies. The moral laxity of the people had weakened their military strength and even the Temple worship was being neglected. But the prophet begged the new king Ahaz not to put his trust in arms nor in neighbouring allies, but to rely on the promises of God that one day a leader would arise who would lead all nations into the way of peace.

One of the tragedies of our time is that many of the younger independent nations still feel the need to imitate their former colonial masters by arming themselves against potential enemies, even when their own nation's children are in desperate need. The message of the Christ child is that truly wise government rests on the shoulders of Him who gave priority to the poor and the vulnerable and was called the Prince

289

of Peace.

✳ *Lord, for the sake of all the world's children*
teach us and those who govern us
how to be peacemakers,
worthy to be called the children of God. Amen.

Monday December 23   *Matthew 1.18-23 ✳*

To set people free

Matthew, the evangelist who wrote his Gospel particularly with
the Jewish people in mind, refers back to the prophet Isaiah as
evidence that this child of Bethlehem is indeed the one who
figured in the prophetic promises. The prophet had said that a
child would be born called 'Emmanuel', a reminder that God
was still with His people. To this name Matthew adds another,
equally evocative in Jewish history – Jesus, another version of
the name Joshua, meaning the one who sets people free and
leads them into the land where God's promise is fulfilled. So the
infant Jesus has come not only to rescue a captive nation from
its captivity but to free us all from enslavement to our sins.

Note that the emphasis in Matthew's account of the nativity is
not so much on the strange circumstances surrounding Christ's
birth as on Joseph's willingness to trust God's promise even
when he cannot fully understand how it will come to pass.

✳ *Lord God, help us to trust your messengers*
even when they tell us of mysteries
beyond our comprehension.
Concentrate our minds,
not so much on the means of your coming into the world
as on the meaning of it for our own lives
and for the life of the nations.

Christmas Eve, December 24   *Isaiah 7.10-17 ✳*

To prove God's confidence in us

The birth of any baby can be said to be a sign of God's
continuing confidence in humanity. The king Ahaz is assured
that he will not have to wait long before knowing that God is still
present among his people. He must simply be as patient as a
young woman awaiting the birth of her child – even before that
child is old enough to know right from wrong, God will have
shown how his purposes are working out for the nation.

Christmas Eve is for all of us a day of expectancy, a day when little children have to learn the art of waiting patiently for the promised gift that will surely come on the morrow. 'I *can't* wait' is often their excited cry, but the waiting is an important part of the preparation for receiving the gift.

✳ *O God, teach us the lessons of expectancy,*
  that through both the patience and the pain of waiting
  you are bringing to birth within us
  the fulfilment of your promise.
  As we prepare to celebrate
  the birth of Your Son among us,
  help us to recognize in every new infant
  the sign of your continuing love for
  and confidence in our human nature,
  For Christ's sake. Amen

Christmas Day, December 25   *Luke 2.1-7; Micah 5.2-4* ✳

To fulfil the promises

How amazing it is that a Roman governor's decree should become the means of the fulfilment of a Hebrew prophecy and set the stage for the coming of the world's Saviour! So God works through the events of secular history to bring about His eternal purposes. Luke, like Matthew, stresses the continuity of the story of Jesus with the vision of those who, centuries before, had longed for the coming of a new leader who, like their past great leader David, would be both shepherd and king. Even the little town of Bethlehem links the story with a foreigner who played a role in Jewish history long ago. It had once been the home of Ruth the Moabitess, who became the great grandmother of David and so wove her own strand into the story of Jesus. And now Mary, like the woman in travail foreseen by the prophet Micah, has in this obscure place given birth to One who shall outlive the decrees of governors and the dynasties of kings.

To ponder: Spend some moments today looking at the cards you have received this Christmas and trace how the people and the places they have come from have woven threads in the tapestry of your own story.

✳ *God and Father of our Lord Jesus Christ,*
  help us to see in close friends and distant acquaintances,
  in places near and far,
  those through whom you break into our own lives

291

and prepare the way for the coming of the Christ child.

To banish our fears

In the biblical stories, angels often begin their message with the words, 'Do not be afraid'. It is like an answering chorus to the first words Adam spoke to God when he was discovered hiding in the Garden of Eden: 'I was afraid.' Now the shepherds on the hillside hear God's response to all people everywhere, 'Do not be afraid'.

In his book *The Gospel of Solentiname*, Ernesto Cardenal records how a group of peasants in Latin America were discussing why it was that Jesus was born in such a poor place rather than a palace. 'If he had been born in a rich house', one of them said, 'the shepherds would probably never have been let in at all.' Another commented that poor people would have been too afraid to go there. Another added, 'What happens in rich houses is never good news for the poor.' But the coming of Jesus was, said the angel, good news for *all* people *everywhere*. So the shepherds decided they were included and went to see for themselves.

✳ *To ponder: Whatever makes you most fearful, lay it aside today and as you listen to the many Christmas songs, remember that you are included among those to whom the good news is addressed and can join confidently in the celebrations of the birth of Jesus.*

To re-create us

Just as Matthew and Luke were eager to set the story of Jesus' birth within the continuity of Hebrew history, so John sets it in the context of a cosmic continuity. The Christ event is linked with the event of Creation itself. The Word which had spoken the world into being, and which had 'happened' (as they expressed it) among the prophets is the same Word which has now itself come into being in the form of Christ. 'Being's source begins to be,' as Charles Wesley puts it in the concise theology of one of his hymns.

God's Word is never only a spoken word. It always makes things happen. How far do our words give birth to events? How far this Christmas has the Christ event become so real to us through the words we have sung and spoken, that our words have become deeds embodying in tangible form what Christ's coming means for us, for those around us and for our world?

'Though Christ our Lord a thousand times in Bethlehem be born
And not in thee, thy soul remains eternally forlorn.'

Scheffler, quoted in Youth at Worship (Methodist Youth Department 1934)

✻ *Christ, the Word of God, re-create us,*
Christ, the Light of the world, illuminate us,
Christ, the Giver of Life, fill our lives with your love.

Saturday December 28   *Matthew 2.1-12* ✻

To warn against evil

Evil as well as good seems to follow the continuity of history, and every generation produces its crafty tyrants who misuse their power. But the wise men fortunately were forewarned against the subtle flattery of the king. Their bad dream about Herod's true intention enabled them to outwit his wickedness. In biblical times people often thought of bad dreams as warnings from God. Perhaps we should think of them that way too – warnings that we are overdoing things, or letting our anxieties get on top of us and our imagination run riot. The best thing to do then is to do as the wise men did and take steps to remedy the situation and discover new ways around our problems.

For many vulnerable children in our world today, who still live under the sway of tyrants, real life can be worse than any nightmare. Their sufferings often haunt our dreams. We need to offer what gifts we can to help remedy their situation too, in the name of the One who himself was once a refugee child, fleeing into Africa to escape the might of armed force.

✻ *Lord Jesus Christ, may we offer to you*
through our gifts to your children,
the gold of our wealth,
the frankincense of our prayers
and the myrrh of our dedication
to the way of self-giving love
in a world still swayed by the madness of hate. Amen

To cleanse the Temple

Jesus as a child must often have heard these words from the prophet Isaiah read in the synagogue. They came immediately into his mind when, as a grown man, he visited the Temple and saw how the rich were robbing the poor and how foreigners were being cheated in its outer courts. It is one of the rare occasions when we are shown how angry Jesus could become at this kind of exploitation, and he quotes directly from this passage, 'My house shall be called a house of prayer for all nations.'

One of the lessons churches are having to learn today is how to become far more inclusive in their worship and the welcome they give to those who come from beyond their own immediate community. Not only do churches have to become, for example, more physically accessible to people with disabilities, but they need also to ensure through the language of their liturgy, as well as in the activities of their congregation, that people of all races, of both genders, of various sexual orientation, of different abilities and of every age feel equally at home in their Father's house.

✳ *To ponder:* **Think particularly today of members of your congregation who are different from you in any of the ways mentioned above and ask God to show you how you can be more welcoming to them in the coming year.**

To open the mystery

Many prophecies relating to the coming of the Messiah had sounded like riddles. He would be both victorious king and suffering servant; 'the glory of the people Israel' and 'a light to lighten the nations'; 'Son of man' and 'Son of God'. Now in the coming of Jesus the riddle had been solved. People recognized in him One who spoke with authority but acted in humility; he had called himself a Son of man, but others had acknowledged him as the Son of God; and among the first to call him the King of the Jews had been Gentiles. Just as on earth he had insisted that the Temple should be a house of prayer for all nations, now he has opened the Kingdom of heaven to all believers.

So in a letter circulated among the early churches, the writer pleads that they must open their communities to all people, whatever their race or nationality. They have been made one in Christ.

* *Lord, help us to welcome into our communities*
  all who with us are fellow heirs of the Kingdom of God.

Tuesday December 31   *1 Peter 2.1-10*

Building God's house

This passage is so full of references to the prophecies that it is worth looking up the various texts referred to in the footnotes, particularly Exodus 19.5-6 and Hosea 2.23. In the building of God's household (in Greek *oikos*, from which is derived the word *oikoumene* – 'ecumenical') there is no hierarchy of status. Every stone is essential, and all are 'living stones', the *laos* – 'the people of God' (from which is derived our word 'laity'). They all share the royal priesthood in which both priest and king are responsible for the spiritual well-being of the whole household. The only special stone is the cornerstone, which holds the whole structure together. Rejecting or neglecting that stone would cause the whole edifice to collapse. It is Christ alone who is our cornerstone, yesterday, today and forever.

* *A prayer for New Year's Eve:*
  Lord, help us to renovate your Church
  by strengthening its foundations,
  enlarging its rooms,
  cleaning its windows,
  opening its doors
  and restoring its cornerstone to its proper pre-eminence,
  through him who holds the whole household together,
  Christ Jesus our Lord. Amen.

For personal reflection or group discussion

How far is a sense of continuity important to you in your faith? How do you strengthen your links with people of faith in all ages and in all lands? Which words do you associate most with the coming of Jesus: power or weakness; majesty or service; simplicity or mystery? Which do you think are the most important attributes to stress?

ACTION

Resolve in this new year to take some action that will widen your own community: e.g. ensuring that your own church is more easily accessible to people with disabilities or people who are of a different race or social background from those who usually come; or join with others in a cause working for the values of the Kingdom, such as the Campaign against the Arms Trade or the World Development Movement.

Acknowledgements and abbreviations

We are grateful for permission to quote from the following versions of the Bible:

GNB Good News Bible (The Bible Societies/Collins Publishers) – Old Testament © American Bible Society 1976; New Testament © American Bible Society 1966, 1971, 1976

NEB The New English Bible (Oxford and Cambridge University Presses) © 1970

NIV The Holy Bible, New International Version (Hodder & Stoughton) © 1973, 1978, 1984 by International Bible Society, Anglicisation © 1979, 1984, 1989

REB The Revised English Bible (Oxford and Cambridge Univeristy Presses) © 1989

RSV The Holy Bible, Revised Standard Version © 1973, Division of Christian Education of the National Council of Churches of Christ in the United States of America.

NRSV New Revised Standard Version Bible © 1989, Division of Christian Education of the National Council of the Churches of Christ in the United States of America.

The editor and publisher express thanks for permission to use copyright items. Every effort has been made to trace copyright owners, but if any rights have been inadvertently overlooked, the necessary amendments will be made in subsequent editions.

BCE Before the Common Era

CE Common Era

BCE and CE are often used today in place of BC and AD. In a world of many faiths and cultures we are exploring the use of more inclusive language.

* Readings from the Joint Liturgical Lectionary (JLG2)

For the Scheme of Readings for 1997, please see page 214

For the Scheme of Readings for 1997, please see page 214